THE ASTROLOGY OF FILM

THE ASTROLOGY OF FILM

◆

THE INTERFACE OF MOVIES, MYTH, AND ARCHETYPE

edited by Jeffrey Kishner and Bill Streett

iUniverse, Inc.
New York Lincoln Shanghai

THE ASTROLOGY OF FILM
THE INTERFACE OF MOVIES, MYTH, AND ARCHETYPE

iUniverse, Inc.

For information address:
iUniverse, Inc.
2021 Pine Lake Road, Suite 100
Lincoln, NE 68512
www.iuniverse.com

ISBN: 0-595-32099-6

Printed in the United States of America

Contents

Part III   Individual Films

Introduction

Cinema, like life, is only worth living when it is in the service of something beyond the explicit and the mundane.

—James Broughton[1]

Archetypes

The young George Lucas, while revising his early drafts for *Star Wars*, revisited his college texts for creative inspiration, looking for anything that would help give his fledgling film idea some added depth and dimension. The most fundamental volume that Lucas rediscovered was Joseph Campbell's *The Hero With a Thousand Faces*, a revolutionary book of comparative mythology that suggested a deep structure lies beneath the diversity of hero myths from different cultures and different times. With Campbell's work, Lucas was able to form, adapt, and shape the bits of creative inspiration from early visions of *Star Wars* into a compelling whole. Lucas's first drafts of his science fiction epic held moments of brilliance but lacked a gripping narrative structure. Through the aid of Campbell, Lucas would have a map to which he could bind his imagination and vision.

Underlying the figures and critical moments in *Star Wars*—and as outlined in Campbell's *The Hero With a Thousand Faces*—are the building blocks that make great stories and myths. Carl Jung called these building blocks *archetypes*, a term that inspired Campbell. After reading *The Hero With a Thousand Faces*, Lucas understood that the utilization and manipulation of these archetypes were necessary to really grab hold of the public imagination. However, archetypes without content are merely empty vessels that hold little power and persuasion. Creative genius, it might be said, is the result of concentrated insight and originality wedded to that which is eternal, timeless, and universal. Lucas now knew the territory of any great hero's story but that did little to ensure that *Star Wars* was to be great or successful. Nevertheless, Lucas was lucky, innovative, and inspired enough to make these timeless motifs as outlined by Campbell come strikingly alive for generations. The subtle nuances, futuristic details, and original touches he imbued in his characters were poured into these timeless molds, or archetypes, and Lucas would be universally hailed a genius for it.

In contemporary parlance, that which is *archetypal* is a textbook example of an entire category because it holds or manifests some quality *in its essence.* With his black cloak, impersonal, faceless mask, and James Earl Jones's deep and sinister intonations, Darth Vader is *archetypal* of evil and has become the essence of evil, or more accurately, darkness, for generations. So synonymous is Darth Vader with evil, that if one simply chooses to imitate the stylized, mechanical inhalations and exhalations that made the character famous, nearly everyone would understand the reference because of the deep impact and resonance it has on our culture; Vader is archetypal. Interestingly, the prevalence of the term archetype is due, in part, to the current resurgence of artists like Lucas who popularized the work of Carl Jung and Joseph Campbell. However, to gain a better appreciation of what *archetype* means, it is important to explore the relationship and curious similarities between modern psychology and ancient wisdom.

The development of Western psychology, fueled by faculties of reason and rational thought, has been, in part, a formalized study of what many ancient cultures knew intuitively. The assertion by pioneering psychologists that the human mind and behavior are influenced by a dynamic unconscious is paralleled by the ancient belief that humans participate with something larger and far greater than themselves. This dynamic unconscious that psychologists refer to was to have a more poetic, imaginally rich antecedent in ancient cultures—the "dance of the gods." From the clinical perspective of a psychologist, the ego stands in relationship to the unconscious, sometimes nourished by its influence and other times overwhelmed and at odds with its power and persuasion. From the point of view of bards, poets, healers, and shamans, gods and goddesses were the powers that determined fate, sometimes acting on behalf of heroes and cultures, at other times creating strife and conflict.

The correspondence between the findings of many branches of modern psychology and the beliefs of ancient cultures goes even further. The psychologist Carl Jung, who delved deeply into the terrain of the dynamic unconscious, came to believe that this realm was comprised of multiple, discrete forces, not just one uniform energy. Jung speculated that our personalities act in relationship to several identifiable and distinct patterns. Similarly, ancient cultures from Greece to India intuited that we do not participate with just one god but with a rich and varied pantheon of gods and goddesses, each with his or her own individual temperament, strengths and vices, and idiosyncrasies.

Jung revived the term *archetype* to describe these fields of psychological potential, these gods and goddesses of the psyche. Although Jung would be the thinker who best articulated the idea of archetypes, he acknowledged his debt to ancient philosophers and esoteric thinkers who first originated the concept. [2] To Plato and St. Augustine, these organizing principles were responsible for creating the earthly plane, a world that is a tainted and faint copy of these original archetypes. Jung paid homage to these speculations but adapted these ideas to fit his own psychological practice. For the majority of his career, Jung made no assumptions about whether these archetypes said anything about the nature of reality. Nevertheless, from exploring the contents of his own consciousness and his patients' inner life, Jung did assert that archetypes spoke volumes about human psychology. However, towards the end of his life, Jung believed that archetypes were not merely energies locked up in our own heads. Archetypes, rather, would become for Jung patterns of existence that informed our own subjectivity as well as the world outside of us. That is, archetypes, in Jung's final estimation, saturated and molded our lived experience in the world and were not simply responsible for sculpting the contents of our own minds.

In essence, Jung was drawing closer to the original belief of archetypes and the ancient cultures out of which these great speculations arose. Jung's final assumption about archetypes and the ideas from which Jung drew inspiration share in common the conviction that these archetypes cannot be seen, quantified, or measured but can be known only through how they influence our world—the visible world of time, space, and matter. In other words, we need certain intermediaries to know the archetypes, as we cannot know them in and of themselves. In our current context, we need images, art, and ideas to explain and amplify archetypes in the same vein that the Greeks needed their pantheon of gods and goddesses to help explain their influence in antiquity. Equally important, the recurrent belief in archetypes suggests that these fields are not by-products of our imaginations but have some sort of independent status, and that archetypes cause (or at least partially influence) our reality. Archetypes are not just helpful explanatory devices that make sense and order out of that which is inherently meaningless and random. On the contrary, archetypes are guiding principles that construct and inform the passage of time and the experience of life. Hence, archetypes live through us, and we experience their potentials through our lives; we do not dream and imagine these archetypes, rather, they dream us.

Film and Archetype

One thing becomes apparent when studying archetypes. Like the great mediators who play out their dramas—humans—archetypes are rather fickle and do not enjoy stagnation. Archetypes are particularly impulsive when it comes to their wardrobe; they demand new and novel ways to be dressed up and represented to us. However, their insistence on new styles is not entirely capricious. Rather, archetypes search for more potent, more beautiful, and above all, more accurate means for their representation in the visible world. If it is true, as Plato suggested, that the world of the senses is but a mere facsimile of the world of ideal forms, then it could be argued that archetypes are constantly in search of better and more accurate means for their representation.

From the first cave paintings in Lascaux, through writing, to photography, and now film, cultures have created media to express archetypes. Film is the greatest medium yet developed to capture the workings of archetypes in the manifest world. In the short time that the moving picture has been around, tremendous developments in technology—notably the advent of computer animation—have allowed directors to create whole new worlds that bear little resemblance to the ones we inhabit, or to add depth and insight into the world that is our own. It is the richness, depth, and aliveness of movies that allows one to enter into the archetypal realm in an experiential way that could never be achieved beforehand.

Psychologists and film historians note that all films—from horror movies to heroic epics, love stories to comedies—package and re-package timeless, or archetypal, themes and narratives that have their roots in cultures before our own. With or without conscious intent on the part of their creators, movies can never stray far from universal themes and eternal motifs. Underneath the window dressing of the latest special effects and computer graphics, movies employ a deep structure of narrative that have their origins in tales, fables, and legends molded by previous generations. Strip down and deconstruct the latest box-office smash and find, at core, that the scaffolding of the story is not only similar to blockbusters of our own time but to nineteenth century novels, Elizabethan drama, songs of the Troubadours of France, and oral traditions of early civilizations. However archaic or cutting-edge one's mouthpiece or medium, there remain enduring themes and patterns that transcend culture and time.

Movies—more than any other cultural phenomenon—are the entry point that allows a society or culture to tap into something transcendent. It is not uncommon for moviegoers to report that, next to falling in love and the birth of one's child, movies are the one thing that creates something like a "peak experience," an awe-filling state of awareness that is marked by intense ecstasy and joy. Even the most prosaic and ephemeral film is connotative of "something more" and can transport viewers beyond the confines of a poorly written script and a flawed production value. The intense states of emotion that film elicits stem from film's ability to translate and mediate archetypes in such a way that we come closer to the core of the archetypes themselves.

Although from one perspective popular film indulges an escapist tendency to take us *out* of our lives, from an archetypal perspective, film engages us to enter more fully *into* our lives. Film's popularity may be superficially assigned to its entertainment value, the "effortlessness" needed to appreciate its value relative to other diversions and art forms, and its unparalleled ability to allow us to "kill time," escape our problems, and to transcend our predicaments. However, film's durable and increasing popularity is more due to its ability to translate the gods and goddesses of our psychology in a fascinating, captivating, and novel manner.

Archetypal psychologist James Hillman called image-making the royal road to soul-making. [3] Thus, through film, we psychologize our world. We create larger-than-life movie stars and fantastic plots to safely contain, deepen, and stimulate our own experience. Film acts not only as a vehicle to hook or capture the psychological energy of the archetypes at work in our lives, but they more importantly add meaning and deepen our experience. Ironically, in an age of reductionism that has "de-souled" the world, the forces of science and technology have created the greatest vehicle—film—to amplify and enliven the timeless, archetypal themes of life.

Astrology and Archetype

Whereas film acts to amplify and deepen our experience of archetypes, astrology is the conscious study of the archetypes as they influence and permeate our lived experience. Astrology is one of the earliest attempts made by cultures to unearth the hidden meaning and order behind the seemingly chaotic nature of this world. By studying astrology or visiting an astrologer, we may illuminate how, when, and to what degree a particular force, god, or archetype is operative in our lives.

Planets under astrology's arrangement are primarily symbolic. Just as a metaphorically-inclined mind might turn a tree into a symbol representing the phases of life, the astrologer sees the planets beyond the objective stare of the scientist as symbols, with each planet connoting a wealth of interconnected ideas, images, experiences, and myths. However, unlike the poet, the astrologer retains some of the precision of the scientist in that the symbolism associated with each planet is not the result of whimsical, free fantasy, but the consequence of careful observation of planetary cycles in relation to collective and individual experience. Thus, the symbolism associated with planets is best seen as psychological fact rather than scientific fact, truth of the soul's condition rather than mere objective certainty.

At the core of the symbolism associated with each planet lies an archetype, and just as Jung and Plato believed that their first principles, or archetypes, could not be witnessed directly, the effects of the astrological archetypes can be felt, seen, and experienced but not observed firsthand. Archetypes within astrology are much closer to the transcendent universals that Jung was arguably approximating in his later life. Not merely confined to one's subjectivity, the archetypes associated with planets are principles which bridge, connect, and ultimately transcend lived experience within an objectively measurable reality. It is within this vision of the cosmos that humans are intimately coupled and participate within a creative intelligence.

The pantheon of astrological archetypes, then, divides something the equivalent of the collective unconscious into different categories and dimensions of lived experience. The archetypes of astrology express the full anatomy of the psyche. Moreover, astrological archetypes appear to affect and inform all levels of reality, from the subtlest shifts in conscious attention and the most sublime works of art to the grossest forms of matter. The movement of the planets, miraculously as it might be, appears to consistently correlate with archetypal energies that are active both personally and collectively. In this astrologically-informed version of the universe, the solar system seems to be a clock that tells, for lack of a better expression, "what archetypal time it is." Planets in this system do not *cause* anything, rather they act as a mediating and neutral third force between inner experience and worldly reality. In other words, if we truly are living within something the equivalent of global mind, planets are merely the bridge connecting our inner world *as we experience it* with an external one *as we observe it.*

Film and Astrology

A synthesis between film—the great medium that amplifies archetypal truth—and astrology—the great systematic study of archetypal reality—was inevitable. However logical and obvious a marriage between film and astrology may appear on the surface, we have needed to wait over a century since film's birth for their union. The delay in matrimony proves to be advantageous. Since the invention of cinema, astrology has matured as a field of study, moving from a deterministic form of prediction to a psychologically sophisticated study enhancing personal growth and insight. During astrology's rebirth as a refined model of human potentials, the film world has created a veritable archive that contains the most extensive map yet of the human imagination.

Films—from super 8 creations of aspiring Spielbergs to triumphant Academy Award ® winning epics—are the text of the mythic, invisible realm, and like any text that is to be meaningful and valuable, there must be a grammar and deep structure to this text. The essays in this volume suggest that there is a logic and a timing to these archetypal themes found in film. Beneath the apparent chaos of film history, if one looks deep enough and if one retracts one's perspective far enough, a multi-faceted pattern crystallizes, and one is amazed to find that there is a hidden order to the apparently random output and diversity of movies produced and distributed season after season, year after year.

Just as scientists who developed chaos theory in the 1960s were able to illuminate a hidden order in the ever-changing flux of the natural world, astrology sheds light on the oscillation of the world of the imagination. Astrology suggests that the ebb and flow of symbols and visions that pervade our inner imagination and populate images in media and film are not arbitrary but ordered and follow a deep logic. In the same way that a thoughtful Jungian analyst can help a client see that there is indeed a pattern and structuring to his or her dream life, the authors of this volume attempt to show through the aid of astrology that there is likewise a patterning beneath the seemingly random evolution of film history. More specifically, through looking at planetary cycles and their archetypal meanings, a rich mandala emerges out of the happenstance of film's rich past.

It is not the intent of this collection of essays to expound upon film solely as a mythic medium. However, how this volume distinguishes itself is to wed *mythos* with *logos*, to synthesize the archetypal themes of film history with patterns and cycles as seen in astrology. It is our hope that after one reads this volume, one sees film history in a radically new way: as the endless ticker tape of the collective unconscious—a celluloid snake that has recorded the vicissitudes of a world soul meandering purposefully, but to an unknown destination.

◆   ◆   ◆

1.   Christopher Hauke and Ian Alister, eds, *Jung & Film: Post Jungian Takes on the Moving Image* (New York: Brunner/Mazel, 2001) 30.

2. Jung acknowledges that thinkers such as Philo Judeas, Irenaeus, and Diony-
    sius the Areopagite employed the term in their writings. In his essay, "Arche-
    types of the Collective Unconscious," Jung also suggests that his use of
    "archetype" had its predecessor in Plato's notion of ideal forms. It is often
    the equivalency between Jung's "archetype" and Plato's *eidos* that receives the
    greatest attention from writers and thinkers who attempt to explain the ori-
    gins of Jung's meaning of the term.

3. James Hillman, *Re-visioning Psychology* (New York: Harper Perennial, 1975)
    23.

How to Use This Book

How Does Astrology Work?

Astrology is based on the premise that the movement of the planets relates to inner psychological changes and observable, external experiences on Earth. This relation is not causal; that is, it is not the case that the planets exert some force that causes changes in human beings. Rather, in some astonishing and still unexplained fashion, psychological and environmental experiences are synchronous with the movements of the planets: "As above, so below." Moreover, this connection is not metaphor, it is not a naïve psychological projection or mass hallucination based on a common need for connection and unity with the universe. Astrology is not an "as if" wish but a deep and sophisticated discipline that suggests that inner and outer, subject and object, consciousness and matter are two sides of the same coin.

Astrology's truth does not mean that we human beings have lost all control of our free will. Each planet symbolizes an *archetype*, a universal principle or ideal form that structures and exerts influences on individual and collective experience. For example, Mars psychologically symbolizes our need to assert ourselves, to *act*. On a physical level, Mars corresponds with fire, sexuality, competition, war, and sports. The Mars archetype encompasses all of these manifestations. The placement of your Mars within a particular sign of the zodiac, a particular house (area of experience) and in angular relationship with other planets will suggest how this archetype will play out in your life. Its expression will change over the course of your lifetime as you integrate this planet, that is, when its function is harmonious with the totality of your psychology as expressed in your natal, or birth, chart. The planets as they are aligned in your birth chart may play themselves out in your life in many different ways.

How does free will come into play? When you are *conscious* of the expression of the planets in your natal chart, then you have more power to choose *how* you will express these archetypes. An unconscious Mars may manifest as attacks of rage over which you feel you have no control. A conscious Mars may manifest as an intentional use of your passion to effect changes in your life, for example, to assert your will to accomplish goals.

Transits are life cycles that correspond with the movement of planets in relation to the position of the planets at birth. For example, the *Saturn Return*, which occurs between ages 28 and 30, happens when Saturn is in the same position in the sky that it was at your birth. It takes approximately 29.5 years for Saturn to revolve around the Sun. Transits of the outer five planets (Jupiter, Saturn, Uranus, Neptune, Pluto) signify major changes in our lifetimes. Once again, a transiting planet does not *cause* change, but it *signifies*, or correlates with, a transformative period in one's life. Crises, or periods of upheaval, that transits signify are not totally under our control. As planets symbolize facets of the collective unconscious, we can never be completely certain of what is in store for us when an outer planet transits our birth chart. However, with consciousness, we can move with the current of life rather than against it. A resistance to change will only result in a change from without rather than from within. This is when it feels like events happen *to* us.

Introduction to the Archetypes

In astrology, there are ten "planets." These include the eight planets other than earth in the solar system, plus the Moon and Sun. These ten planets are the celestial bodies that most significantly revolve around the earth. Although we know that all but the Moon travel around the Sun, from a human perspective (and we *are* the centers of our universes) these bodies travel around our home planet. Until the eighteenth century, the only recognized planets were those able to be seen by the human eye: Mercury, Venus, Mars, Jupiter, and Saturn. These planets are named after the Roman gods. The wise astronomers who studied the movements of these planets found that their movements correlated with changes in human experience. Each planet was named appropriately, for the relations of these planets to human experience related to the personality and mythology of the Roman gods after which they were named. Even after the Scientific Revolution, when scientists gave no credence to astrology, two of the three outermost planets were appropriately named. That is, the archetypes of both Neptune and Pluto relate to the personalities and mythologies of these gods. The only planet that seems to have been inappropriately named is Uranus, which seems to actually act more like Prometheus, the semi-divine creature who stole fire from the gods. [1]

A short introduction to each of the planets will give the reader a sense of what each archetype means. Please note that each planet is so rich in meaning that books have been devoted to individual planets. So each description is necessarily brief, with only the attempt to outline the basic meanings of each planet.

The *Sun* is the center of one's personality, one's ego, one's identity. Our urge to creatively express ourselves. The masculine principle of creation.

The *Moon* is our emotional self. It indicates how we go about feeling secure, obtaining a sense of belonging. The Moon is the mother, the child, the home. The feminine principle of relating.

Mercury concerns communication and short-distance travel. Language, words, speech.

Venus is love, beauty, art, aesthetics, value, fairness, socializing, relationships. The maiden.

Mars represents how we assert ourselves in the world. The warrior archetype. Anger, sexuality, war, sports.

Jupiter is the planet of expansion. International travel. Faith, belief, the religious impulse. Higher education. Law, philosophy, ethics.

Saturn is the planet of restriction. Boundaries, tests, limitations. Manifestation. Hard work, responsibility.

Uranus is the planet of disruption, liberation, sudden changes. Revolution. Technology.

Neptune is the planet of transcendence. Illusion, delusion, image, spirituality, mysticism.

Pluto is the planet of death and rebirth. The underworld. Taboos. Eroticism and Shadow. Healing and regeneration.

The archetypes of the outer planets operate on both individual and collective levels, whereas the inner planets relate specifically to individual concerns. An individual with a birth chart that emphasizes the outer planets may mediate these profound energies for the collective. These are often the reformers, geniuses, prophets, poets, artists, rebels, saints, visionaries, and outsiders who transform societies in a significant way.

Aspects

When two planets make angles (typically divisible by thirty degrees) to each other, then the two archetypes combine to yield a conflict or inherent gift, depending on the planets involved and the angle they make to each other. Planets are said to *aspect* each other in this situation. For example, Saturn is opposite Pluto when, from our perspective on Earth, these planets are approximately 180 degrees away from each other. The word *approximately* is used, because two planets do not have to be exactly 180 degrees apart to be *in orb*, that is, in effect. An *orb* is a number of degrees from exact that two planets can differ, while still being archetypally potent. Different astrologers use different orbs, based on experience and the astrological literature. If an astrologer uses an orb of 10 degrees for oppositions, then, say, if Saturn were at 10 Gemini and Pluto were at 18 Sagittarius (these two zodiac signs are opposite each other), then these planets are still in orb, even though they are eight degrees from exact opposition.

The main aspects are the conjunction (zero degrees), sextile (60), square (90), trine (120), and opposition (180). To simplify matters, *hard* aspects (square and opposition and sometimes conjunction) result in a conflict surrounding the integration of the aspecting planets; the individual who has this aspect is required to exert energy and find creative solutions to resolve this conflict. *Soft* aspects (sextile, trine) result in an easy integration of the aspecting planets, such that the individual experiences this combination as a gift, or takes it for granted.

Transiting planets aspect natal planets. For example, transiting Pluto at 15 Sagittarius squares one's natal Sun at 15 Pisces because the position of Pluto as it is moving through the sky is ninety degrees from where one's Sun was at the moment of birth. Each planet has a specific function when it transits a natal planet; Uranus disrupts or excites, Neptune dissolves or sensitizes, and Pluto transforms or intensifies.

Signs and Houses

Although the focus of most of the essays in this volume will only require a basic understanding of planets and aspects, some will discuss signs and houses. We will not define the meaning of each sign and house; each writer will define the meanings of each as needed. *Signs* are the twelve equal divisions of the zodiac into thirty-degree segments. Signs are *ruled* by particular planets, which typically means that a sign will have a meaning similar to that of its ruler. For example, impulsive and impatient Aries is ruled by Mars, the planet of assertion of one's will. When a planet is placed in a sign, the planet will express itself through the filter of that sign's style. For example, if at the moment of one's birth the Sun is placed within the thirty degree section of the zodiac called Aries, then one will express one's self (Sun) in an impulsive, action-oriented manner (Aries). For each of the twelve signs, the Sun will 'shine' in a distinctly different manner depending on its placement. Likewise, each of the ten planets can be placed within any of the twelve signs, yielding many different combinations of how these archetypes express themselves.

Houses are the areas of experience in which planets express themselves. The natal chart is divided into twelve houses; however, these sections are not usually divided equally into 30 degrees. There are many different *house systems*; it is beyond the scope of this book to explain how they differ. Suffice it to say that the most important way of determining the placement of the houses is through knowing where the *Ascendant* and *Midheaven* are. The Ascendant is the exact degree of the zodiac sign on the eastern horizon at the moment of one's birth. The latitude and longitude of the location of one's birth is necessary to determine the Ascendant. The Midheaven is the exact degree of the zodiac sign at the highest point in the sky at the moment of one's birth. The Ascendant is the horizontal line in one's natal chart, dividing the top and bottom equally. The Midheaven is often not exactly perpendicular (90 degrees) to the Ascendant. In a natal chart, it is often a bold line dividing the left side of the chart from the right, but not into equal pieces. The opposite side of the Ascendant is called the Descendant (the right side of the chart). The opposite side of the Midheaven is called the IC or Nadir (the bottom of the chart). These four points are called the *angles*.

Each house is associated with a sign and planet. For example, the 7th house (right above the Descendant) is the area of experience governing relationships, marriage and contracts. This house relates to Venus, the goddess of relationships, and the sign Libra, which concerns fairness and mediation. If the Sun is placed in the 7th house, then one may express oneself creatively (Sun) in the area of marriage (7th house).

Archetype and Film

With the integration of archetypal psychology and astrology, astrologers are now able to view how the astrological gods are present in film. The god that pervades all aspects of cinema is its ruler, Neptune. Neptune is the image, transcending mundane reality. Neptune rules that which cannot be adequately described through words alone. The state of being which cannot be categorized by conceptual thinking is better expressed through visual image, poetry, music and dance. Neptune is fantasy, the ideal that great films portray. Films like *Bladerunner* and *A Clockwork Orange* create whole new believable worlds that transport viewers into a new reality. Neptune is also illusion and delusion. Film fools the viewer into buying into a vision that does not exist in mundane reality.

People go to the movies to escape, to be transported. In this way, Neptune symbolizes a psychological need. Weighed down by life on life's terms, a trip to the movies leaves one feeling renewed, invigorated, ready to go on. In *Hannah and her Sisters*, Woody Allen's character, after a failed suicide attempt, sees a Marx Brothers film, leaving with a sense of meaning that he hadn't had before. In fact, film allows all the planetary archetypal needs to be fulfilled:

> *Sun:* to leave the theater feeling brighter, happier
> *Moon:* to leave the theater feeling emotionally nourished
> *Mercury:* to leave the theater intellectually stimulated, curious
> *Venus:* to leave the theater feeling romantically and aesthetically satisfied
> *Mars:* to leave the theater having vicariously expressed ones aggressive, action-oriented urges
> *Jupiter:* to leave the theater with a sense of meaning
> *Saturn:* to leave the theater with a regained willingness to take on the responsibilities of life and hence to mature; to meet life on life's terms
> *Uranus:* to leave the theater with a new vision of reality
> *Neptune:* to leave the theater having ones imaginative capacities fulfilled, one's spiritual yearnings satisfied
> *Pluto:* to leave the theater transformed/changed

A good movie will fulfill one of these archetypal needs. Much typical Hollywood fare—the romantic comedy (Venus), action movie (Mars), sentimental tear-jerker (Moon)—meets these basic needs. A great movie is one that meets one of the collective needs, as symbolized by the outer planets: meaning, transformation, wisdom, vision. Great films will often correspond with archetypal experiences of the collective, giving viewers a new way of understanding and experiencing the underlying patterns affecting nature and society. For example, Peter Jackson's *Lord of the Rings: The Fellowship of the Ring* was released in late 2001, when Saturn and Pluto were approximately 180 degrees from each other in the sky. This aspect corresponded with the horrible events of September 11th, as well as the economic recession and conflicts in the Middle East and India and Pakistan. This film mirrored the struggle between good and evil, which was a potent theme at the time, and offered a vision of what it would be like to take responsibility for the burdensome task of banishing evil from the world. The ring forced its holders to confront the evil in their own hearts. Thus, the film corresponded with and captured the spirit of the times in an entertaining and enriching fashion.

From an astrological perspective, the age-old question, "Does life imitate art or does art imitate life?" is misinformed; the split is an artificial one. Rather, in astrology's eyes, both real-world events and art are observable manifestations of archetypal forces that are dominant at any given time. Thus, using the example above, *Lord of the Rings* was not made in reaction to the events of September 11th, nor was the release of *Lord of the Rings* an eerie but arbitrary coincidence paralleling the events and zeitgeist of the day. More correctly, as astrology suggests, both events emerged as the result of something that we can allude to and connote rather than pinpoint with absolute clarity: forces, archetypes, gods, energy, resonance. Planets of the solar system are merely the timekeepers that show when and roughly how long these forces, or archetypes, remain operative in the collective. To reiterate, the planets do not cause events to happen but merely correlate in a predictable and uncanny fashion with the events and experiences of the spirit of any particular time.

A Note on Convention

The names of the planets used throughout this anthology refer directly to the astrological archetypes, not simply the physical planet in isolation. Thus, when encountering the name of any planet in this volume, unless otherwise noted, the name refers to the meanings, themes, and archetypal expression of that particular planet. This convention is utilized for stylistic purposes, as the need to isolate the archetype and symbol of a planet's name apart from the physical planet would become quite tedious and ponderous for the reader.

1. In his book *Prometheus the Awakener,* author Richard Tarnas was the first to suggest that Uranus's archetype is more fundamentally similar in character to the Greek Titan Prometheus than the sky god Uranus. The act of stealing fire from the gods and giving its power to humanity is the mythological theme that is at the core of the archetype. Prometheus's act of rebellion that emancipated and liberated humanity is repeated over and over in different guises when Uranus makes significant aspects to other celestial bodies.

PART I
Archetypes and Film

As the medium of film grew in popularity in the twentieth century, it became necessary for audiences, critics, and creators to categorize films into different genres. Passionate film buffs to casual moviegoers are familiar with these standard divisions: romance, horror, comedy, drama, science fiction, and so forth. From an astrological standpoint, categorization of films can be achieved through cataloging films with astrological symbols. That is, certain movies exemplify or express archetypal motifs powerfully. The authors have chosen films that most potently and most accurately capture the essence of the archetype at hand. For instance, author Natori Moore uses *Chariots of Fire* as a film exemplary of the many facets of the astrological Jupiter. Bill Streett chooses *Pleasantville, Easy Rider*, and *Waking Life* among films to deeply appreciate the archetype of Uranus. In the final essay of this section, Ray Grasse illustrates how popular films demonstrate the striking shift from the Age of Pisces to the emerging Age of Aquarius. In this fashion, film aficionados can quickly appreciate the astrological pantheon of archetypes while the beginning student and the advanced practitioner of astrology can profoundly deepen their knowledge of astrological symbols.

The Liberator: Jupiter as Archetype in Chariots of Fire

Natori Moore, C.A. NCGR

There's nothing like a funeral to draw human attention to spiritual matters. The death of someone significant to us inspires us to think about our philosophy of life in a way few other events can. What happens after death? What will become of our loved one? Who will protect, guide or give us solace, and how will we gather strength to go on? What comfort can our religious traditions give us in a time of transition and grief? What is the nature of God? What is the meaning of life?

Opening our minds to these types of broad soul-searching questions is one aspect of what a great film with a strong Jupiter theme can do. The award-winning film *Chariots of Fire* begins and ends with scenes at a funeral—the 1978 funeral of British Olympian Harold Abrahams. In his youth, Abrahams was a student and star athlete at England's Cambridge University who, along with Scottish runner Eric Liddell and other members of the British Olympic team, delighted the world with medal wins at the 1924 Paris Olympic Games. As a Jewish man, Harold Abrahams finds his determination to excel at running in response to the prejudice he encounters in predominantly Christian England. Eric Liddell, a devout Christian, runs for the glory of God and postpones the missionary work his family expects of him in order to train for the Olympic games. Abrahams and Liddell are each put to the test when their athletic ambitions are blocked by short-sighted Cambridge University and Olympic authorities. Olympic teammates who come to Abrahams's and Liddell's aid include Harold Abrahams's best friend and confidante Aubrey Montague (played by Nicholas Farrell) and the exuberant and wealthy Lord Andrew Lindsay (Nigel Havers). *Chariots of Fire* is the glorious study—based on a true story—of the ambitions and motivations of all these runners.

We might find it odd that a movie about athletics, aspiration, and the pursuit of excellence starts off on a bleak funereal note. Yet the funeral scenes at both the start and end of this film are an effective framing device and a type of relief against which the achievements and pleasures we find in the movie's central portion appear more grand. As a young man, Harold Abrahams epitomizes ambition and relishes his success. One of the most exciting scenes in *Chariots of Fire* occurs early in the film when Abrahams challenges the record for the Caius College dash, racing around the perimeter of a staid old university building at top speed, collapsing in the arms of his classmates after breaking the record, drinking champagne and being lifted high on their shoulders in celebration. Grandness and celebration as themes relate astrologically to the planet Jupiter. In fact, there are a variety of ways in which elements of *Chariots of Fire* reflect the essence of Jupiter. It will help to take a closer look at this planetary symbol.

The Nature of Jupiter

Jupiter is the largest known planet in our solar system. Its diameter at the equator is 88,680 miles (compared to Mercury's 3030 miles at its equator) and its volume is more than a thousand times greater than Earth's. It's a large gaseous entity, with sixteen known moons or satellites, more than any other planet.[1] Like the largeness of the planet Jupiter itself, the number of items, concepts and themes that fall under Jupiter's astrological rulership is vast. Jupiter-ruled entities run the gamut from abstract thinking and advanced degrees to visions, voyages, and world assemblies. Jupiter also rules items as diverse as birds in flight, lavish expenditures, and courts of law. Yet to make things more manageable, we might group the primary themes related to Jupiter into six major categories:

1.   travel, international relations, foreign countries, and cultures

2.   sports and athletics

3.   higher education, particularly university level and beyond

4.   ethics, faith, philosophy and religion, especially orthodox religion

5.   anything large, expansive, growing, abundant

6.   aspiration to expand outside one's current sphere of life

The common principle among these themes is broadening horizons—physically through travel and athletics, mentally through study and learning, or spiritually through church membership and spiritual exploration. As astrologer

Anthony Louis puts it, Jupiter rules broadmindedness, adventure, and willingness to gather experience along life's journey.[2]

The Jupiter impulse can express itself in numerous ways. One can go to college, travel, participate in sports, or pursue the entrepreneurial aspects of business. In previous eras, and sometimes still today, these kinds of opportunities were only available to those with means. Therefore, Jupiter came to rule the upper classes as well. In Roman mythology, Jupiter was considered the Lawgiver (though he didn't always obey the laws himself); thus Jupiter as an astrological symbol has come to rule legal issues and concerns. In *Chariots of Fire*, Harold Abrahams's friend and fellow runner Aubrey Montague notes that Abrahams is studying law at Cambridge. Eventually, Abrahams becomes a barrister.

Spiritual aspirants who built cathedrals and made pilgrimages to holy sites in the Middle Ages were inspired by the Jupiter urge. We find this urge today in those who surmount considerable obstacles of time, money, or distance to pursue outdoor adventures or cultural exploration in foreign lands. In part, the Jupiter impulse is the healthy desire for broad experience and education, which can give an abundance of meaning, a willingness to share knowledge, and a basis for wise decision-making. When it sours, the Jupiter urge can become social snobbery, the attempt to know it all, and the urge to dominate or proselytize others with narrow-minded legal, philosophical, or religious understanding. There's such a thing as reaching too far with Jupiter as well. People who travel internationally with great frequency in a restless search for belonging might find what they're seeking if they stayed closer to home. Jupiter-influenced people can sometimes live too far in the future, too, believing the grass is always greener someplace else. They may need to learn to appreciate the value of present time and associations.

Mythic Origins

Jupiter's power as an archetype in *Chariots of Fire* becomes clear when we further examine his mythological ancestry. Whether called Jupiter (Roman mythology) or Zeus (Greek mythology), this god of the Sky was known to descend from a difficult parental lineage. In the Greek telling of the story, when Zeus' grandfather Ouranos joined with his grandmother Gaea to create and populate the earth, their children threatened Ouranos' power to such a degree that he began to swallow them as they were born. Gaea appealed to one of their sons, Cronus, for help, and he overcame Ouranos by castrating him. A similar scenario developed in the following generation, when Cronus got jealous of his own children and began to swallow them as well. Cronus' wife, Rhea, helped their son, Zeus, escape this fate by giving Cronus a stone to swallow in Zeus' place. Cronus fell for this trick and Zeus was exiled to Crete to grow up unharmed. Eventually, Zeus returned and persuaded Cronus to regurgitate Zeus' brothers and sisters, thus giving them life again. Zeus also fathered many Olympian sons and daughters, among which are some of the best-known names in mythology: Athena, the twins Apollo and Artemis, Hermes, Dionysus, Aphrodite and Perseus. Zeus also is considered to have fathered the Fates, the Seasons, the Graces, and the nine Muses.

Author Jean Shinoda Bolen states that Zeus was a pivotal figure in the evolution of the character of the Sky God, present in both Greco-Roman and Judeo-Christian thought, from a hostile to a more parental figure.[3] He was the first to grant freedom and encouragement to his children. To be fair, Zeus didn't offer this to all his children. He was known to be cruel to some (Hephaestos, Persephone) and cold to others (Ares), but he was leagues beyond his own father, Cronus, and grandfather, Ouranos, in his ability to set his children free to fulfill their true natures. Consider as examples Athena and Apollo, guardians and protectors of culture and the city-state, who were allowed not only to share in Zeus' power, but to develop their own to a great degree.

Interestingly, Zeus did not seem to have evolved to the point where he could grant the same freedom and encouragement he gave his children to his wives, consorts or other goddesses and women. This is reflected in the limited ability of the Jupiter archetype to appreciate women's needs or concerns. *Chariots of Fire* has limited women's roles or exploration of female-specific themes. It's a very masculine story—there are eight men's names in the cast list before a woman's name appears, and only two women are listed in the top 20 cast members. It is left to other films to expand upon the nature of women's unique athletic journeys and spiritual realizations. But within the masculine arena characteristic of Jupiter, *Chariots of Fire* represents a fine piece of filmmaking and a story of inspiration for all who seek to unfold their greater potential.

In another link to the mythology of Zeus, *Chariots of Fire* makes multiple references to feet and wings. At the beginning of the film, Lord Lindsay speaks at Harold Abrahams's funeral, reminiscing that in the past the runners had been "…Young men, with hope in our hearts, and wings on our heels." One of the spectators at the college dash challenge says to Abrahams, "I say, Abrahams, what've you got on your feet—rockets?" to which the crowd lets out a laugh. Later in the film, Sybil Gordon, Harold Abrahams's girlfriend, remarks to Abrahams in an attempt to encourage him after a loss, "You ran like a god." These allusions to fleet feet and the film's title hint at the winged chariot of Zeus, said to be no mere chariot but a powerful vehicle fitted with large and thunderous horses to make a highly focused equipage. The Greeks contrasted Zeus' sleek and powerful racing chariot with the "Irrational Vehicle of Human Souls," a dense and awkward carriage akin to a mule cart, representing the lower aspects of human nature.[4] Thus the implication that Zeus' chariot can stun and inspire with the ferocity of its divine energy.

Characteristic of the mythological creature that rules Jupiter's astrological sign, Sagittarius—the half-man, half-horse centaur—*Chariots of Fire* does a good job of showing us the part human, part divine aspects of our nature. Some say that runner Eric Liddell, with his strong focus on Christian belief and inspiration, represents the divine potential we all possess, and that Harold Abrahams, with his strong will and work ethic, as well as his belief in the need for personal action to achieve success, represents the more human part of our beings. Yet the more earth-bound Abrahams states that he thinks Liddell "runs like a wild animal." In the end, the divine and human distinctions between these characters may not be broken down so simply, because both men possessed great capabilities as well as frailties. The film is about how they both harnessed extraordinary forces, of faith and of will, to achieve great ends.

A Vedic Note

In Hindu astrology or Jyotish, Jupiter is not considered an enemy to any other planet.[5] (Mercury and Venus are considered enemies of Jupiter, due in part to their basic nature as planets of more temporal rather than philosophical concern, but Jupiter itself is not an enemy to any other planet.) This points to the benefic nature of Jupiter, who wishes no harm upon others, and in fact gives an increase of good fortune. With Jupiter's pure essence, there are no cagey calculations or strategies, but generosity, trust, faith and grasp of truth. In the words of Vedic astrologer Chakrapani Ullal, "Jupiter, the greatest benevolent planet, reminds us of Divine Grace. Jupiter is called the planet of expansion, growth, progress, prosperity and spirituality. It is the only planet that promotes both material and spiritual aspects of the native equally."[6] Vedic astrologer Ernst Wilhem goes on to note that esoterically, Jupiter is the vehicle of the body, used for the spiritual journey.[7] This combination of corporeal and spiritual aspects within the essence of Jupiter makes the relationship of Jupiter to a film called *Chariots of Fire* particularly apt.

The exaltation or best placement of Jupiter is in the Moon's sign, Cancer. The Moon is the only other entity in Hindu astrology that gets special treatment—it has no planetary enemies, and thus when Jupiter is placed in Cancer, purity of wisdom and fertility of mind can flow. The heat of Jupiter does well in the moist environment of the Moon, and growth is encouraged. This is where we derive Jupiter's rulership of expansive and growing entities.

Modern Connotations

Those with astrological experience will wonder why, if Jupiter is not the planet farthest away from Earth, it represents such far-reaching and expansive experiences. A key is that Jupiter represents far-away places and ideals, but not so far outside cultural boundaries as the outer planets. Uranus, Neptune and Pluto symbolically pierce the veil to see the inner workings of life, whether electronics, metaphysics, psychology or sexuality. Jupiter represents reaching beyond the common mind (Mercury-Gemini) but largely within cultural limits. It usually represents people who express their educational urge within accepted or accredited institutions, and people who express their spiritual urge through alignment with a mainstream church or religious community. In the West, this has historically been through a Christian church or a Jewish synagogue, whereas in Eastern cultures it might be through Buddhist, Hindu or Muslim creeds. *Chariots of Fire* provides a study in the aspirations and beliefs of Olympic teammates, but within a cultural context. Part of the movie's appeal is that the central characters have found a way to express themselves fully and achieve inspiring goals within cultural limits. Those with any tendency to "buck the system" based on a strong Uranus placement at birth might sometimes long for the optimistic, dedicated faith of Eric Liddell and these inspiring runners, who could feel themselves as winners and mavericks within cultural bounds.

Jupiter Themes in Chariots of Fire

Amid worldwide critical recognition and a host of awards, *Chariots of Fire* received seven Academy Award® nominations and four wins—Best Picture, Best Screenplay (Colin Welland), Best Original Score (Vangelis Papathanassiou), and Best Costume Design (Milena Canonero).[8] Eight out of twelve items on the list of keywords for *Chariots of Fire* at The Internet Movie Database are Jupiter-related: ethics, based on a true story, epic, historical, Olympics, religion, running, sport. (The other listed words are 1920, biographical, famous score, racing.) The movie conveys the exuberance of athletic aspiration and team pride as well as frequently displaying the Jupiterian flags and banners of nations. The athletes show a fervor for both their university and their country. There's also a cross-cultural focus—the real-life Eric Liddell was from a family of Scottish missionaries and was born in China. Harold Abrahams was a Jewish man who valued his heritage yet sought acceptance in British culture.

Other Jupiter themes touched on in *Chariots of Fire* include: aspiration to achieve excellence, university education, athletic competition, international relations, truths that cross boundaries, the human spirit, beliefs, religion, faith, social hierarchies, running, enthusiasm, class distinctions, amateur versus professional, celebration, conscience, pageantry, parades, big adventures, and team spirit. Camera angles used in the film often reflect the Jupiterian need for expansiveness as they capture the lofty spaces of cathedrals and university buildings or the wide expanses of the outdoors. The film's cast itself mirrors the runners' aspirations as it consists of a crop of young hopefuls of the British film industry aiming for long and successful careers like that of their co-actor, Sir John Gielgud.

Running and Athletics

The famous opening credits sequence of *Chariots of Fire* shows the British Olympic athletes in training, running on a beach. All parts of the body have an astrological ruler, and it's interesting to note that Jupiter rules the hips and thighs. Symbolically this is because the hips and thighs are the parts of our body that stride toward the future. A group of young men striding confidently toward their future is the epitome of Jupiter energy. Though the Mars impulse is also significant in physical activity, the willingness to engage in sport and athletics, especially at the university and Olympic levels, is symbolized by Jupiter. The runners aim high, work hard, and in time, hit their target of winning Olympic medals (the bow and arrow being another symbol of Jupiter).

Conscience and Ethics

A central conflict of *Chariots of Fire* involves Eric Liddell's belief that he must not run in the 100 meter heat scheduled on a Sunday, considered to Christians the Sabbath or Lord's day, a day of rest. Liddell's appearance before the Olympic committee in an effort to resolve this matter provides some of the most sophisticated dialogue of the film. In taking his controversial stand, Liddell goes up against the head of the British Olympic Committee, the Prince of Wales, and other high-ranking British officials. A few of the officials encourage Eric to change his mind based on what is expedient for them. Yet we understand by the end of the dialogue that Liddell means to put God before country, whatever it should cost him. In doing so, Liddell shows the unified face of Jupiter, strong in belief and brooking no opposition.

Luckily, in the midst of the conflict, Liddell's teammate Lord Lindsay arrives like a breath of fresh air to propose a solution. "Another day, another race," Lindsay says, and after mild protest from Liddell that Lindsay would wish to make this sacrifice, all agree that Liddell will not run in the 100 meter heat but take Lindsay's place in the 400 meter race instead. This outcome exemplifies another aspect of Jupiter at its best—the "11th hour success" or lucky break that comes just when we think we've exhausted all our options. As an added note, the 400 meter race in which Liddell does participate turns out to be held on a Thursday, the day of the week ruled by Jupiter.

University Education and Ideals

A strong focus on Cambridge University and the lives of educated men runs throughout *Chariots of Fire*. In addition to Jupiter's astrological association with academic pursuits, the all-male extracurricular societies available to Cambridge students of the era epitomize Jupiterian fraternity. Harold Abrahams and his friend Aubrey Montague belong to the Gilbert and Sullivan Society, a popular group at English colleges, whose members perform Gilbert and Sullivan operettas. Though Abrahams enjoys his participation in this and other campus activities, he understands that the university upholds a cohesive philosophy of "the good life" and has distinct opinions about who is entitled to enjoy it.

In one pivotal scene, Abrahams finds himself confronted by two university authorities about the fact that he has hired a professional coach (Sam Mussabini, played by Ian Holm) to advance his running career. The authorities present their view that university athletics are to be a strictly amateur pursuit, and that hiring a coach is beyond the proper limit for the upper classes. As John Gielgud, playing the Master of Trinity College, says to Abrahams, "Your approach has been a little too plebeian. You are the elite, and expected to act as such." Abrahams retorts that the university upholds archaic values, and wants success only if it's "achieved with the apparent effortlessness of gods." Abrahams retains his right to secure professional assistance, and the university officials don't seem to stop him. The sting of their disapproval only seems to fuel his determination to win.

Runner Eric Liddell does not attend Cambridge, but rather grows up in China and on the highlands of Scotland. His gift for running is not cultivated by a university athletics team, but honed through practice, good coaching and his native faith. There's something refreshing about Liddell's playfulness and lack of pretense, demonstrated when he admonishes yet at the same time encourages a local Scottish boy who is playing ball on the Sabbath because he "doesn't want him to grow up thinking God's a spoil sport." Unique gifts and qualities of character like Eric Liddell's may or may not be developed through a strictly academic path. Liddell didn't need to attend Cambridge to develop himself fully. He found success in athletics and missionary work, two Jupiterian pursuits.

Class Distinctions and Other Jupiter Problems

Since Zeus only liberated some of his children, we find that the largesse of Jupiter often applies to only some in society. While many benefits may be conferred on the educated and professional classes that pursue careers in medicine, law, engineering or education (today, for example, they may receive discounts on auto insurance since they are statistically believed to be less accident-prone), these classes can also become smug in their perceived superiority. Jupiter as a symbolic representative of the elite has always frowned upon the merchant class. Like their mythological namesake, Jupiterian people may presume they are a law unto themselves, and can get away with anything. Often, luck does sustain them for a while. However, a strong Saturn or Pluto transit will cause the luck to run out. This occurred for actor Hugh Grant, whose Jupiter in Sagittarius was aspected by Saturn when he was found with prostitute Divine Brown in Los Angeles and his reputation took a blow. Jupiter can protect or give license for a time, but not forever.

In essence, especially when positioned in fire signs such as Sagittarius, there is more entitlement than compassion in the nature of Jupiter. When Harold Abrahams and Aubrey Montague first arrive as students at the train station for their taxi ride to Cambridge, physically disfigured caddies help Abrahams and Montague load their baggage into the cab. Abrahams and Montague are not unkind to these men, but consider it their due to be pursuing such privileges. The caddies seem to have more awareness of class distinctions when one of them says to the other, "That's what we fought the bleedin' war for, to give shifts like these [Abrahams and Montague] a decent education."

Fathers as Stiflers (Saturn) or Liberators (Jupiter)

In the story of Zeus' parentage, we learned how his father Cronus (Saturn) and grandfather Ouranos (Uranus/Chaos) couldn't fathom their children's need to exist as separate beings. Many fathers swallow progeny by their selfishness. Movies that demonstrate this tendency for the sins of the father to be visited on the children include *Affliction* and *The Royal Tenenbaums.* As Marilyn Waram says in *The Book of Jupiter:* "How many modern fathers live...out [this tendency] as the father either ignores his children—and thereby imprisons a significant part of their psyches—or uses them as targets for the anger and fear he generates in himself during the day at work—thereby symbolically swallowing them? Fathers are responsible for giving their children a sense of their own power; many fathers instead use their power against their children, to put down and overcontrol rather than to model effective use of it."[9]

This is what makes *Chariots of Fire* a rare treat and a joy to behold. Like Zeus freeing his children, this film presents father figures that liberate the central characters. This liberation is important in and of itself, but liberation for practical achievement is the distinct goal of these fathers. Sam Mussabini, when he agrees to sign on as coach to Harold Abrahams, says: "Mr. Abrahams, I can find you another two yards." He believes in Abrahams and helps liberate him for further athletic success. He writes him a note in a fatherly tone just before Abrahams's big race in the 100 meters, and gives him a lucky charm that belonged to his own father. Mussabini also exhorts Eric Liddell's brother-in-law and coach after Eric takes a fall during a race to "Take good care of this lad of yours, because if you don't, you'll never find another one like him." The transmission of wisdom and protection, two Jupiter virtues, becomes important to Mussabini.

Eric Liddell has his heart set on following his father in missionary work, but when his father learns of the extent of Eric's athletic gifts, he encourages him to run. Eric Liddell believes as well in the power of Jesus, son of a heavenly Father, to liberate. Liddell's faith in God, his strong human father and his brother-in-law coach are presented as benign but firm forces in keeping him on a productive path. The runners also free each other in important and sometimes unwitting ways, as when Lord Lindsay gives up his spot in the 400 meters so that Liddell can run, and when Liddell bows out of the 100 meter race, giving Abrahams an unexpected chance to win it. In the end, as is often the case with benevolent and ever-abundant Jupiter, Liddell, Lindsay, and Abrahams all become medal winners.

Even Cambridge University itself, despite its flaws, is presented as a liberating force in preparing these men for leadership in the world. We learn via a speech by the Master of Caius College at the Freshman Dinner that the new arrivals are receiving an opportunity for education that many who fought and died in World War I will not. The students are taught to appreciate history and their place in the flow of time. At the funeral of Harold Abrahams, Lord Lindsay says, "Let us praise famous men and our fathers that begat us. All these men were honored in their generations and were glory in their days." While it is made clear in *Chariots of Fire* that there is no advancement without cost, there is beautifully expressed appreciation for those who use their lives to advance, rather than swallow, the future.

Jupiter's Quest for Truth: Art Reflects Life

Chariots of Fire is based on a true story. Eric Liddell and Harold Abrahams were actual persons who competed in the 1924 Paris Olympic Games. Though feature films rarely present characters based on real persons completely accurately, fascinating links sometimes exist between the charts of movie subjects and the actors who play them. The real-life Harold Abrahams and the actor Ben Cross, who portrayed him in *Chariots of Fire*, were both born under the sign of Sagittarius, ruled by Jupiter. In fact, they were born within a day of each other in different years (Abrahams born 15 December 1899, Cross born 16 December 1947). [10] Thus their natal chart Suns fall at the same degree of 23 Sagittarius. They each embodied the aspirations and ideals of Jupiter, including being great runners. When *Chariots of Fire* was released in 1981, Neptune, the planet that rules film and film images, was transiting between 23 and 25 degrees Sagittarius, conjunct these men's natal Suns. This points up the fact that both men came into the spotlight through this film.

The real-life Eric Liddell was born with the Sun and Jupiter conjunct in the sign of Capricorn. Those with Sun conjunct Jupiter are considered "honorary Sagittarians," due to Jupiter's rulership of Sagittarius. They will often display the qualities of optimism, faith, and enterprise characteristic of Jupiter-influenced Sagittarians. Though Jupiter in Capricorn can present challenges and indicate that most victories are hard-won, it also suggests a person who is disciplined and delivers on a promise. Jupiter positioned in Capricorn can paradoxically represent the hard life of missionary work as well as the privileged life and social status of Lord Lindsay.

A fascinating link in Jupiter placement exists between the real-life Eric Liddell and three actors involved in *Chariots of Fire*. Eric Liddell was born 16 January 1902 in Tientsin (Tianjin), North China. [11] He has the Sun conjunct Jupiter in Capricorn at 25 degrees. Actor Ian Charleson, who portrayed Eric Liddell in *Chariots of Fire*, was born 11 August 1949 in Edinburgh, Scotland. Charleson has Jupiter at 24 degrees Capricorn. Nigel Havers, who portrayed Lord Andrew Lindsay, was born 6 November 1949 in London, England. He has Jupiter at 25 degrees Capricorn. Brad Davis, who portrayed American runner Jackson Scholz, was born 6 November 1949 in Tallahassee, Florida. His natal Jupiter falls at 26 Capricorn.

These three *Chariots of Fire* actors were born roughly 48 years or four twelve-year Jupiter cycles later than Eric Liddell. All of them have Jupiter in Capricorn within one degree of real-life Eric Liddell's Jupiter and Sun. This suggests via astrological symbolism that, even through playing movie roles, these men have had a beneficial effect on Eric Liddell's life and helped him gain recognition. These three actors were, in fact, probably the most beneficial to the real-life Eric Liddell in terms of the *Chariots of Fire* story. Ian Charleson did a superb job portraying Liddell, reportedly even reading the Bible from beginning to end to prepare for the role.[12] Nigel Havers exuberantly portrays Lord Lindsay, who generously sacrifices his own participation in the 400 meter race so that Liddell may follow his conscience and race on a day other than Sunday. Brad Davis, portraying American runner Jackson Scholz, gives Eric Liddell an encouraging note that reinforces Eric's stand of conscience just before Liddell's climactic 400-meter race.

Many of the cast and production crew on *Chariots of Fire*, as well as the real-life Harold Abrahams and Eric Liddell, and the actors Ben Cross and Ian Charleson, have the dynamic fire signs Aries, Leo or Sagittarius emphasized in their astrological charts. Certainly a film with this conflagration of astrological heat among the participants is aptly entitled *Chariots of Fire*. Director Hugh Hudson has Jupiter and most likely the Moon in Sagittarius. Colin Welland, the Oscar-winning screenwriter, has Moon in Aries. The real-life Eric Liddell has Moon in Aries as well. Ben Cross has the Sun, Mercury and Jupiter all in Sagittarius. Ian Charleson has Sun in Leo. John Gielgud, that most classical of actors, has Sun, Jupiter, Moon and Venus all in Aries. Lindsay Anderson, who played the Master of Caius College and compatriot to Gielgud's Master of Trinity College at Cambridge University has Sun in Aries. Dennis Christopher, who played American Olympian Charles Paddock, has Sun and Mercury in Sagittarius. Greek electronic music composer Vangelis, who created the well-known music for the film, has the Sun in Aries. David Watkin, the British cinematographer who captured the style of the 1920s with fluidity and grace, has the Sun and Mercury in Aries (lots of Pisces too). And although we have no birth data for Costume Designer Milena Canonero, according to the Internet Movie Database, she is "known for the large budgets and extravagant measures she needs to realize her beautiful designs." She uses many capes, kilts and draped pieces of fabric for her costuming in this film, yet another indication of the grandness and excess that may be associated with the Jupiter-Sagittarius theme.

As the Planets Turn

In 1981, when *Chariots of Fire* was released, there were several aspects or angles between Jupiter and outer planets [Jupiter sextile Neptune (60 degree angle), Jupiter conjunct Pluto in Libra, Jupiter semi-square Uranus (45 degree angle)]. These aspects included Jupiter conjunct Saturn in Libra, demonstrating a time that the public might seek aesthetic representations of aspiration (Jupiter) based on balance, beauty, and proportionality (Libra). Certainly *Chariots of Fire* qualifies as one such representation. Also, world conditions in the early 1980s mirrored those in the early 1920s, the time period portrayed in the film. Both periods were characterized by relative world prosperity in developed world economies. Audiences in these cultures would be receptive at this time to a movie about privileged (Jupiterian) sorts of people.

From roughly 1970 through 1984, including the year 1981 when *Chariots of Fire* was released, the planet Neptune was in Sagittarius. Ecstatic celebrations such as weddings, art openings, film premieres and spiritual illuminations are characteristic events that might take place under a Neptune transit. At its best, Neptune is a planet of spirituality, divine "highs," inspiration and ecstasy. With Neptune in Sagittarius—the natural home of the planet Jupiter—during this period, these kinds of "highs" might be achieved through film and visual arts, sports, religion, epic stories, adventure, travel, interactions between nations, and quests for greater meaning. *Chariots of Fire* represents this kind of Neptune in Sagittarius high point.

The current (1995 through 2008) transit of Pluto through Jupiter's sign—Sagittarius—has brought to light many excesses in Jupiterian institutions (the Church, professional sports, universities, corporations). Whether via profligate professional athletes or priests who molest children, we have seen the way the elite or advantaged of society can use their positions as license for excess. This reveals the dark side of Jupiter, the lawgiver who won't obey his own laws, the disregard for others' needs, the pursuit of pure abandon. It will be interesting to see what happens when Pluto reaches the later degrees of Sagittarius (23–25 degrees in 2005–2006), which will conjoin Harold Abrahams's and Ben Cross's natal Suns and conjoin Neptune at the time of the film's release. Perhaps there will be renewed recognition for the film or an emergence of information about it of which we are not yet aware.

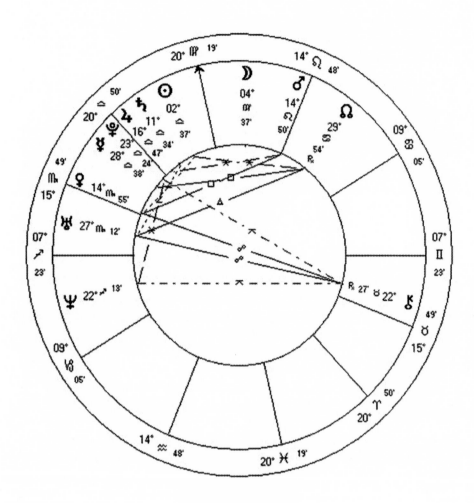

Release for *Chariots of Fire*
September 25, 1981
Los Angeles, California
12:00 PM

The Great Father (Jupiter) and the Great Mother (exaltation in Cancer)

As noted earlier in the section on the Vedic Jupiter perspective, the planet Jupiter, which via its protective and benevolent qualities can be considered the Great Father, performs optimally in the sign of Cancer, the Great Mother. Whenever we see the male and female principles unite in astrological symbolism, we know we are headed for a satisfying experience of wholeness. The Moon and Jupiter complement each other perfectly. The Moon can soothe and nurture Jupiter enough so that Jupiter can take risks and create; Jupiter can inspire the Moon to expand its sphere of nurturing care to wider realms. Without the Moon's influence, Jupiter can be hotheaded, arrogant and narrow-minded. Without Jupiter's influence, the Moon can be frightened, damp and needy. Together, the Moon and Jupiter may offer a full experience of both the interior and exterior worlds.

The screenwriter of *Chariots of Fire*, Colin Welland, born under the sign of Cancer, provides the ideal script container for the Jupiter-related ideas of this film to flourish. Positioning the Jupiter energy of the central section of this film between the more contemplative opening and closing sequences at Harold Abrahams's funeral puts the events of the film in historical and emotional context. Welland also includes a Moon-themed or lunar element by including scenes in which Aubrey Montague, an intermittent narrator and arguably the soul of the film, writes to his mother (mothers are symbolized by the sign Cancer) about the exciting Jupiterian events unfolding for the athletes.

Opening and closing *Chariots of Fire* with funeral scenes also reminds us that great achievements live on past our earthly lives. Since the film's debut, several of its principal participants have died, including Ian Charleson, Lindsay Anderson, Sir John Gielgud, and one of the film's executive producers, Dodi Fayed, who was killed in the 1997 automobile accident that also killed Diana, Princess of Wales. We have the memory of their achievements in this film to inspire us on our own journey.

The Joy of Jupiter

The great Western astrologer Robert Hand says that in medieval astrological thought, the sign of Sagittarius is called the "joy" of Jupiter, meaning that's where Jupiter is the happiest and functions best.[13] (Mr. Hand is a Jupiter-ruled Sagittarian himself.) Certainly Sagittarius is where Jupiter is at its purest, unadulterated by other benign (such as the Moon exaltation we looked at above) or not-so-benign influences. Jupiter usually brings pleasure, good fortune and a better-than-average experience—as long as we don't overdo it. Yet despite its reputation for abundance, some say that Jupiter represents a circumscribed type of pleasure. Jupiter's approach to joy is certainly not the romantic and youthful sensuality represented by Venus, as in Franco Zeffirelli's version of *Romeo and Juliet*. It's not the aggressive, animal pleasure of Mars demonstrated in *Braveheart*, nor the exciting multi-dimensionality of Uranus displayed in the unique production values of *Moulin Rouge!*. Nor is Jupiter's pleasure the satisfaction of probing psychological depths in the manner of a Pluto-themed film like *The Piano* or *The Godfather* series.

Rather, *Chariots of Fire* is a classic and exquisite display of Jupiterian pleasure—the highest and noblest achievements of athletics, education, religion, international and intercultural relations, optimism, faith, and doing what's right by one's own conscience. Amid all the darker forces of nature, it can be wonderful to bask in the outward-facing, upward-rising light of Jupiter. As Eric Liddell joyfully puts it in one of *Chariots of Fire's* finest moments: "I believe God made me for a purpose. But He also made me fast. And when I run, I feel His pleasure."

All actor chart data and movie specifications, unless cited otherwise, are from www.imdb.com, The Internet Movie Database.

1. Pamela Forey and Cecilia Fitzsimons, *An Instant Guide to Stars & Planets* (New York: Bonanza Books, 1988), 103–107.

2. Anthony Louis, *Horary Astrology* (St. Paul, Minnesota: Llewellyn Publications, 1991), 496.

3. Jean Shinoda Bolen, M.D., *Gods in Everyman* (San Francisco: Harper & Row, 1989) 22, 32, and 49.

4. I.W. Cleve, "The Chariot of Zeus," *The Meadow: A Journal of Philosophy, Religion, Mysticism and Allied Arts*. Somerset, England: The Prometheus Trust, Issue 1, Spring 2001.

5. Hart de Fouw and Robert Svoboda, *Light on Relationships: The Synastry of Indian Astrology* (York Beach, Maine: Samuel Weiser, 2000) 43–44.

6. Chakrapani Ullal, from a lecture entitled "Jupiter: The Divine Guru" given at the 8th International Symposium on Vedic Astrology, Sedona, Arizona, November 11, 2001.

7. Ernst Wilhelm, *Vault of the Heavens: Treatise on Vedic Astrology* (Occult Publishers, www.vedic-astrology.net, 2001) 156.

8. www.filmsite.org.

9. Marilyn Waram, *The Book of Jupiter* (San Diego: ACS Publications, 1993), 32–33.

10. Harold Abrahams's birth data from "Abrahams, Harold" in Encyclopædia Britannica (www.britannica.com/eb/article?eu=2589).

11. Chart data from www.eric-liddell.org.

12. www.imdb.com.

13. Robert Hand, "Dealing with Difficult Chart Combinations," audiotape of a workshop given for the San Diego Astrological Society and the San Diego

chapter of the National Council for Geocosmic Research, San Diego, California, March 16, 2002.

BIBLIOGRAPHY

Bolen, Jean Shinoda M.D., *Gods in Everyman*. San Francisco: Harper & Row, 1989.

de Fouw, Hart and Robert Svoboda, *Light on Relationships: The Synastry of Indian Astrology*. York Beach, Maine: Samuel Weiser, 2000.

Epstein, Joseph, *Snobbery: The American Version*. Wilmington, Massachusetts: Houghton Mifflin, 2002.

Forey, Pamela and Cecilia Fitzsimons, *An Instant Guide to Stars & Planets*. New York: Bonanza Books, 1988.

Giamario, Daniel, "A Shamanic View of Astrology," in *The Mountain Astrologer*, August/September 2002.

Lee, Linda, *Success Without College*. New York: Doubleday/Random House, 2000.

Louis, Anthony, *Horary Astrology*. St. Paul, Minnesota: Llewellyn Publications, 1991.

Sullivan, Erin, *The Astrology of Family Dynamics*. York Beach, Maine: Samuel Weiser, 2001.

Waram, Marilyn, *The Book of Jupiter*. San Diego: ACS Publications, 1993.

Wilhelm, Ernst. *Vault of the Heavens: Treatise on Vedic Astrology*. Occult Publishers, www.vedic-astrology.net, 2001.

The Outer Planets and Film: Uranus, Neptune, and Pluto

Bill Streett, M.A.

The Uranus Film

In the mid-nineteenth century, Charles Darwin proposed that biological evolution was due, in part, to the constant variation in life forms over time, an assumption that was held long before Darwin but substantiated by his observations. Although it would take Gregor Mendel to identify the precise mechanism of this variation, Darwin noted that life is inclined to produce novelty and to vary over generations. Nature, in a sense, is inclined to experiment, to find new and better ways of adapting to environments; nature gropes. Scientists and theorists have also convincingly hypothesized that this variation and mutation of form is not something confined to the strictly biological but is also a function in societies, individuals, groups, and systems more complex in organization than biological forms. Societies are constantly mutating, changing customs, and challenging conventions, even when it is not adaptive to do so. On an individual level, we can feel the pull for chance experimentation and creativity creep into our lives, and it often takes great resistance to push down on these experimentations. In astrological terms, this fumbling for new forms and the innate proclivity to experiment is the force of the archetype of Uranus. As astrologer Robert Hand states, "Uranus represents that random element of mutation that is necessary for creative innovation." [1]

To draw further upon biology, a strong but vocal minority of scientists currently believe that evolution is not simply the result of random, arbitrary forces but the result of *intelligent design*: the complexity of life forms is best explained by an intelligence that directs the forces of creation. Mathematical probability suggests that in-built intelligence is more likely to account for evolution and creation than contingency and randomness. This hypothesis of an engineering intelligence in the universe is another face of the archetype of Uranus. When Uranus's flash of

21

creative inspiration is unleashed, the informing deep structures of mind, the universe, and creation are unveiled. Uranus was conspicuously highlighted in astrological alignments at the times when the laws of physics, the scientific revolution, the theory of evolution, and the discovery of the unconscious were ushered into collective awareness. Thus, like a lightning storm at night that illuminates the environment around us, when Uranus is highly active in our lives we are able to see the normally veiled and hidden intelligent structure that is operative in the world.

In order to understand the archetypal Uranus more fully, it is important to understand the meaning and origin of the terms "genie," "magic," and "avant-garde." Genie is a hybrid of the Muslim "jinn" and the Latin "genius." The jinn were supernatural, shape-shifting beings that were created by Allah from divine fire. The jinn were more powerful than humans but seated below angels in the spiritual hierarchies. They were spirits found within all humans that could be capable of both good and evil. The second etymological source for "genie," the Latin "genius," literally means to procreate and to beget. Taken together, the genie, then, is a creative, generative spirit of fiery origins. The genie in modern form, as seen in a Tale of One Thousand Nights, is a creative figure, that, when summoned, is able to grant supernatural powers to humans often at great cost or with unforeseen consequences. Similarly, the archetypal Uranus is the creative, inspirational force that lies dormant within us until "summoned."

Uranus is affiliated with what the late astrologer Richard Idemon called "superyang" energy—a hypertrophied, masculine creative force. The creative powers affiliated with Uranus are not the mother of invention dictated by necessity but the father of originality and innovation. When the creative fire of Uranus is ignited societally, cultures take a gigantic advance in novelty, breaking new ground in sciences, the arts, mores, and freedoms. However, even though the creativity of the genie may be summoned with benign intent, the unstable and mutable creative fire of the genie—and thus of Uranus—may turn against culture but can never be "put back into the lamp." Genetic manipulation, splitting the atom, and many advances in chemistry—all originally created with benign or good intentions—have their destructive sides and have come at high cost to humanity.

"Magic" has its historical origins in Persia and is the art that is used to control or forecast natural events, effects, or forces by invoking the supernatural. Although thought to be a primitive practice that has found its expiration date in modern consciousness, using this broad definition we can see that applied science and related methodologies are indeed forms of magic. Objects all around us are supernatural: televisions, airplanes, computers, and appliances that we take for granted. Although these common objects are not supernatural in the common usage of the term, with its mystical and mysterious connotations, the information age is a supernatural one in the most literal sense. The global monoculture is increasingly becoming a world that is beyond, or transcendent, of nature and loosely speaking, we have used rituals of magic to come to this current state of affairs.

The archetype of Uranus is an impulse very much aligned to the art of magic. When the archetype of Uranus is active on an individual or collective level, the urge for liberating ourselves from our more natural, "herd-like" impulses—the need for going beyond security, roots, and the shelter of conformity, for example—becomes intensified. We may act out upon this Uranian impulse by simply rebelling against our status quo conditions, or we may channel these energies into effective, strategic means—magic. Hence, magic may be thought of as applied or useful channeling of the psychological force associated with the archetype of Uranus. The Industrial Revolution—at its peak of activity during the discovery of the planet Uranus—had its basis in helping humanity detach and transcend its dependence on economic means based on unpredictable, natural cycles. Similarly, the motivation for the creation of the birth control pill (implemented during the highly Uranian, revolutionary time of the 1960s) was to allow women to have greater sexual freedom through transcending natural cycles of fertility. Arguably, we are on the precipice of the most purely magical, Uranian time in history with the applied technology of genetics becoming a very real social, ethical, and economic reality.

The expression *avant-garde* originated from the French term used to designate the frontlines of an army that clears unknown territory for the safety of the larger ranks. Currently, the term is more applicable to the cultural pioneers who proceed boldly and courageously into new and novel forms of artistic and social expression. The *avant-garde* of any age is comprised of the bohemians, the rebels, the experimenters, and risk-takers who challenge our assumptions, disrupt status quo thinking and relating, and dissent against tired, worn, and conservative structures. More often than not, the majority of us who prefer the security of the mainstream and stand on the sidelines of life chastise, criticize, and mock those who are willing to challenge convention and push the creative envelope. However, privately we esteem the inventors, boundary-pushers, and geniuses who take the plunge into the creative unknown and liberate us into new worlds and universes. The truly Uranian individual is the hero who lives the impulse of liberation, creation, and vitality for the collective, and, although these heroes rarely get public validation, they have the inner satisfaction of knowing that they followed the impulse of their own creative spirit, their own genie.

A truly Uranian individual is a magician, a genie, a societal mutation, a member of the *avant-garde*, and one who is intuitively in touch with the supreme intelligence and design of the universe. These free spirits and independent minds are the source of re-invigorating culture and are responsible for opening new vistas and landscapes in civilization. There is often a charismatic spark around Uranian individuals that is infectious—a fiery and electric magnetism that implies danger, wisdom, and change. To an ordered, structured, and sheltered lifestyle, a Uranian individual is akin to the serpent who shocked Adam and Eve out of their innocence and naïveté and ushered them into wisdom, awareness, and consciousness. The urge to recapitulate the original "biting of the apple" and to increase knowledge and true wisdom is not only a necessary motivation and drive, but, as astrology teaches us, is cyclical, for culturally it is imperative that we renew our civilizations through breaking boundaries and comfortable habits from time to time for the sake of growth and transcendence.

When Uranus is operative in our culture and in our personal lives, we mutate, create, and understand. The tensions between traditions and new frontiers heightens; the need for learning new and invigorating ways of being impresses itself from the outer environment; the need to shake up, discover, and agitate the world around us increases; underdeveloped creativity emerges; and deep and penetrating insight into the structure of our own lives and the world around us grows exponentially. Just as variation is necessary for biological evolution and species vitality, the variation that occurs in our lives when Uranus is active is necessary for our personal growth and vivacity.

"Uranian times" can be as unnerving and jarring as they are creative and rejuvenating. The shocks or disturbances of Uranus often wake us up to a new perspective or level of insight that was unconscious beforehand. In personal life, Uranus's archetypal presence is often felt as a shattering of beliefs or life structures that, in retrospect, make sense. The inner dialogue in the wake of a peak Uranus time in one's life might be: "If I were truly honest with myself, I could see the job loss, the divorce, or other tragedy coming because I felt a growing discomfort and unease—an 'inner itch'—with the status quo and how things were." Like an innate intelligent design that exists on a universal scale, we see a queer logic to the journey and story of our life in the aftermath of a Uranus detonation.

However, there are problems and difficulties in the personality that is overly identified with the archetype of Uranus. Often people with too much Uranus suffer from what might be called "transcend-itis"—an inflammation of the need to transcend structure, security, rootedness, and instinct. People with this partic-ular affliction have existential, philosophical problems but not legitimate difficul-ties grounded in everyday experience. Rather, their concerns are too macroscopic and visionary to be rooted in "right here, right now" terms, and their need for mental conceptualizing without concrete action can be truly crippling. Secondly, there is often too much emphasis upon needing new, unconventional, or cutting edge experience; the immature side of Uranus is the drive for new opportunity without pain, conflict, follow through, or challenge. The exhilaration and excite-ment of making personal breakthroughs and making new discoveries can be something like an addiction, and the freedom that one searches for becomes a trap and jail rather than enduring liberation. Finally, there can be a "truth at all costs" fanaticism and obstinacy in the individual merged with the Uranus arche-type. Often the individual will detach from situations that reek of superficialities, conventions, and shallowness in the desperate search for something higher and nobler. What results is a wandering highlighted by aloofness, irritability, and loneliness.

◆   ◆   ◆

Rarely does a Uranus film come to you without effort. These are not Holly-wood studio films but rather films shown in art houses or likely to be found in the cult or independent section of a video store. These are films that break new ground, that experiment, challenge, and grope. The Uranus film is made for the seeker, the curious, the detached social critic, the inventive mind, and those bored with the formulaic.

Perhaps the common denominator of all Uranus films is *difference*, and, risk-ing difference, they fall either significantly above or significantly below the usual criteria for evaluating films. Many films typifying the Uranus archetype are too experimental, too self-indulgent of a director's fantasies, or simply too bizarre and nonsensical to be considered memorable or even worth viewing. Some Uranus films, however, vibrate with life and vitality and are successful in their experimen-tal nature and in pushing new creative edges. Still fewer films that typify Uranus are revolutionary and truly groundbreaking. These are the rare works of genius that irrevocably alter the course of film history and assume an iconographic status in society. Upon an initial viewing of a truly revolutionary film, we may not understand what we are seeing—we may in fact be slightly disturbed by what we are seeing—however, there is an uncanny and instantaneous recognition that the radical innovations and level of creativity have changed something forever—have "let the genie out of the lamp."

The following films, ranging from the truly bizarre to the truly groundbreaking, show different faces and functions of the Uranus archetype. Although some of the films are not typically "Uranian"—they remain within conventional boundaries of storytelling and technique—they do revolve around typically Uranian themes: rebellion, individuation, deviation, and awakening.

To Awaken, To Liberate:

Pleasantville (Ross, 1998)

> "What's outside of Pleasantville?"
>
> —Reese Witherspoon as Mary Sue

A small minority of critics noted that for all of its messages and allegorical lessons on the necessity for cultural awakening through rebellion, *Pleasantville* is a rather safe film. This would have been a radical and groundbreaking film forty years ago, made in the time that it was addressing. *Pleasantville* is no longer a social critique that makes us nervous, anxious, or squeamish, but it serves as a "feel good" movie that makes us proud of the progress that has been made in the last fifty years.

The film itself is not extraordinarily fitting of the Uranus archetype; it is a benign, comfortable look at the revolution of the 1960s that is neither horribly provocative or at all edgy. It is more of a family movie in the vein of *Back to the Future*. *Rebel Without a Cause* or *Blackboard Jungle*, made when the first rumblings of a societal earthquake were felt, were much more edgy and confrontational—and thus, Uranian. However, the creative solution that *Pleasantville* offers is to look at the sexual, cultural, and political revolution of the 1960s in reverse, through traveling back in time.

Protagonist teenagers Tobey Maguire and Reese Witherspoon inadvertently enter into the pre-1960s universe of Pleasantville, a perfectly ordered, innocent television town that is held up by artifice and nauseatingly polite discourse *a la Leave it to Beaver* and *Father Knows Best*. Over time, Maguire and Witherspoon become liberators and social emancipators for the town, shattering the ordered conventions through ushering in creativity and eroticism, and awakening impulses for freedom and independence. Pleasantville stirs from its dogmatic black-and-white slumbers and literally wakes up to a world of color. The structured, polite, dull, and limited world of the town is exchanged for one of vitality, sexuality, awareness, and unpredictability.

Gary Ross, writer and director of the film, was experiencing the generational transit of Uranus opposing his natal Uranus during the filming and release of the film. The generational Uranus opposition occurs in everyone's life around the ages of 38 to 42 and acts as a rejuvenating impulse, urging one to redefine one's self and to shake loose from confining structures. At the same time, transiting Uranus was squaring Ross's natal Sun and Moon. As the Sun and Moon are the constituents of the natal chart comprising one's core identity, the filming of *Pleasantville*, it can be assumed, must have been a time in which Ross was fully identifying with the creative and liberating impulses of the Uranus archetype.

Given the emphasis of Uranus in this time of his life, it follows that Ross was attracted to creating a film about the decade of liberation, awakening, and rebellion of the last century, the 1960s. Ross recreates the countercultural rumblings of the era with an enthusiasm and freshness that evokes nostalgia for those who experienced that time, and stimulates curiosity for those too young to have undergone that particular cultural awakening. However, for Ross, everything that is liberated from the collective unconscious in this movie is "good." Uranus's urging for societal change is not always as "pleasant" as the one that took place in *Pleasantville*. The 1960s was as confusing, tense, riotous as it was colorful, creative, and liberating. Similarly, the ideals of liberty, fraternity, and equality of the French Revolution—our first truly modern Uranian revolution—were immediately followed by the Reign of Terror. The revolutions and awakenings that Uranus is notorious for are two-sided: the liberation presents us with more existential choice and anxiety; the creative impulse is accompanied by fear, risk, rejection, and knowledge; and increasing consciousness assumes more responsibility and pain.

Waking Life (Linklater, 2001)

> "*The angry human spirit that refuses to submit.*"
>
> —Alex Jones III as "Angry Rebel"

Waking Life performs exactly the opposite function that most movies are supposed to carry out. Instead of being light entertainment that allows us to escape from our questions, concerns, and problems about life, *Waking Life* amplifies these nagging questions and concerns, making them the very subject matter of this innovative animated feature. *Waking Life* is a movie that bristles with energy, disquiets through a penetrating look into questions of ultimate concern, and reminds us that underneath our societal conventions lies quiet desperation, insubordination, and, most of all, awareness.

The constant cerebral conversation that carries the film takes quite an adjustment for the viewer; only *My Dinner with Andre* and *Mindwalk* dare to be more longwinded. From one vantage point the film is didactic, overly preachy, and pretentious, but from another viewpoint the film is brilliant and interesting, proving that philosophical discourse—its probing, provocations, and prying—serve a function in life. As the title suggests, *Waking Life* shocks us into a condition that Plato called *anamnesis*, literally *against amnesia*, an illumined condition in which the soul remembers its true self and its immortal essence.

The Uranian stamp is all over the film. The entire stream-of-consciousness monologue that drives the film seems to be coming straight from the center of the archetype itself: "Don't box me in," "Where there is fire we will carry gasoline," "Creation seems to come out of a striving or imperfection." All characters represent the various faces of Uranus: angry rebels; questioning amateur and professional philosophers; the disenfranchised; idealistic youth; idiosyncratic eccentrics; fanatical politicians; wanderers; the worldly wise. Even the interpolated rotoscoping used to create the film—an experimental advance in animation—represents the trademark "groundbreaking development" that is Uranus's signature.

Even though the overall tone is celebratory of the expression of Uranus, Linklater does not shy away from the shadow side of the archetype. Uranus can represent a life of glorious potential, awakenings, and insight, but as one character in the film resigns, this is a life of "all theory without action." An overly-developed Uranus function can come through in the fire starter, the rabble rouser, the hairsplitting theoretician, and the navel gazer, all of whom lack groundedness or staying power to realize their revolutions in concrete, useable terms. Secondly, in what might be the great aphorism in the film, one wise elderly man mourns, "There are two kinds of sufferers in the world: those who suffer from a lack of life, and those who suffer from an overabundance of life." Uranus, being chaotic, dynamic, and highly unstable, is a force of vitality; it can lead to an overabundance of life. The cure is not to cut off the impulses of life that Uranus can bring, but, as astrologer Caroline Casey suggests, to create "disciplined wildness" in one's life. [2]

Like Ross's *Pleasantville*, Linklater created and released *Waking Life* when Uranus opposed his natal Uranus. The new, more digestible phrase "middlescence" has now entered the common vernacular to describe the period once (and still) called the "midlife crisis" years. Interestingly, as Linklater entered his middlescence, not only did he choose to explore Uranian themes of awakening, rebellion, and liberation in *Waking Life*, but he chose to re-visit the time of late adolescence through his protagonist, portrayed by Wiley Wiggins. In astrological terms, this confusing but liberating time is when Uranus forms a ninety degree square to the natal position of the planet, occurring roughly between ages 18 through 22. Much like Wiley's experience, during this time period we usually make the first attempts at leaving our family of origin; are confronted by strange, bizarre, and challenging beliefs and behaviors; and learn that Mom, Dad, and high school didn't necessarily teach us all that there is to know about the world around us. Not only does *Waking Life* succeed in making a philosophical movie work, but it succeeds in capturing the turbulent, exciting, and somewhat frightening period of growth in both adolescence and midlife.

To deviate, to "perversify," to make bizarre:

The Rocky Horror Picture Show (Sharman, 1976)

> *"That spark that is the breath of life."*
>
> —Tim Curry as Dr. Frank-n-Furter

The Rocky Horror Picture Show is the king of all freakshows, and, although the record for all-time grossing movie seems to be surpassed every other year, *The Rocky Horror Picture Show* will likely remain safe in its claim of being the highest grossing cult classic for a long time to come.

The film has Brad (played by Barry Bostwick) and Janet (portrayed by Susan Sarandon) as a naïve and conservative couple who wind up entering an ominous and foreboding castle for help one fateful evening and, by doing so, have their worlds shattered and their lives completely changed forever. The threshold for the new universe that Brad and Janet are about to enter is introduced by one of the most successful musical numbers of the film, "The Time Warp." It is during this song that the castle inhabitants suggest to Brad and Janet that the conventional world—the world of time, stasis, and control (and all features of the Saturn archetype)—will be warped, bent, and twisted—all fundamental actions of Uranus. As Brad and Janet continue to enter their new world, they are confronted by polymorphous perversity, are assaulted by eccentric and peculiar behavior, and are initiated into a fuller awareness of themselves and their potentials. Hence, Brad and Janet go beyond their secure and conventional world and are "tricked" (a favorite Uranian hobby) into a new, more colorful, more dazzling universe.

The Rocky Horror Picture Show is undoubtedly one of first truly postmodern films. Its level of irony and sophistication often escapes viewers who assume that they are merely watching a B-movie with a high production value and rollickingly good soundtrack. However, *The Rocky Horror Picture Show* is an "anything goes" pastiche where American kitsch and conventions are scrambled, jumbled, and reassembled into a very peculiar experience, indeed. This tongue-in-cheek culture jamming is highly indicative of the Uranus archetype, as it is the function of Uranus to be playfully creative, taking disparate elements that have no good reason for being together but result in a startling new synthesis.

It is hard to exactly say why *The Rocky Horror Picture Show* has been so successful. Perhaps, as one critic suggested, it is the unabashed celebration of difference that makes the film so unforgettable and unique. Certainly the movie has provided an outlet for otherwise marginalized subcultures and subgroups to return to over and over (and over) again. Arguably the movie's appeal is due to the infectious soundtrack by Richard O'Brien, the wonderful castle interiors, and the vamp aesthetic. Undoubtedly, however, any credit for the film's success has to include Tim Curry's one-of-a-kind performance as Dr. Frank-n-Furter, the gender bending, alien scientist and leader of the Transylvanians.

Curry experienced a once-in-a-lifetime Jupiter-Uranus transit landing on his natal Sun during the release of *The Rocky Horror Picture Show*.[3] Jupiter's influence combined with Uranus makes for an expansion and successful celebration of the creative, wild, and electric energies of Uranus. In every way, Curry's Frank-n-Furter is a shameless embodiment of the archetype of Uranus, a Promethean creature by all means unbound. Frank-n-Furter's obsessional need to make the perfect, eerily Aryan human shows the headstrong tendency of Uranus to create without any eye toward future consequence. Secondly, Frank-n-Furter shows the often willful and narcissistic obstinacy associated with Uranus that can be truly ruthless if its visions and plans for the future are thwarted and blocked. Finally, Frank-n-Furter's personification of a perverse creature is often the trademark of Uranus's influence. There is often a need to bend—often in a playful and strange way—the conventional when Uranus is strongly indicated.

Schizopolis (Soderbergh, 1996)

> *"Come Early! Come Often!"*
>
> —Promotional Tagline

Schizopolis sticks out like a three-dollar bill in Steven Soderbergh's increasingly impressive oeuvre. Although Soderbergh could be called eclectic, his list of work doesn't warrant the label eccentric. However, *Schizopolis* is certainly an oddity compared to his acclaimed *Traffic* and *Erin Brockovich*.

In the tradition of Woody Allen's *Bananas* and Tim Robbins's *Bob Roberts*, *Schizopolis* is an unusual satire that deviates from almost every conventional narrative device in filmmaking. Plot is seemingly inconsequential in this farce that has Soderbergh playing a speechwriter and dentist in parallel universes that intersect. Although storylines merge, crash, and deconstruct at every turn, *Schizopolis* has an uncanny way of keeping the viewer interested through its shocking and effective word play, parody, and general zaniness.

The comedy shows Uranus's irrationality at work in our lives. Sometimes the general crazy-making of a Uranus transit cannot be made sense of rationally. Rather, we must enter into the bizarre and peculiar territory with what the Buddhists call "Beginner's Mind"—a non-evaluative stance of awareness and acceptance. When Uranus makes a significant transit to our natal chart, such as the Uranus square or opposition to its own position, we must abandon the conventional, linear, and straightforward and dive into a new game with new rules, behaviors, and outcomes. Soderbergh's *Schizopolis* might be called a "quantum comedy" because its rules, logic, and structure is more akin to the quantum world of nonlocality and observer dependence than the Newtonian-Cartesian world that we normally function within.

Critics and fans attribute *Schizopolis*'s genesis and reason for being to Soderbergh's dissatisfaction with his recent Hollywood projects, pressure from his hectic schedule, and his lack of having a hit since *Sex, Lies, and Videotape*. All factors being valid, Soderbergh was experiencing a transit from Uranus to his natal Sun in Capricorn at the time of the film's completion and release. When asked why he wanted to make *Schizopolis*, Soderbergh offered, "Just the ideological freedom…*Schizopolis* was an effort to get back to the kinds of films I made when I made short films, which were much funnier, more energetic and much more playful than any of the features I've made."[4] When we receive a significant Uranus transit to our natal chart, freedom, creativity, and energy—all ingredients that Soderbergh mentions were responsible for *Schizopolis*—come to the fore as primary psychological needs and motivations. Often when we feel stuck in drab, dead-end, and dreary jobs and relationships, a Uranus transit rejuvenates us; we wake up, heed an inner call, and experiment and play with the electric juices of creativity.

Schizopolis may not be Soderbergh's finest film, but it will go down as his most daring and unconventional, and, although *Schizopolis* doesn't always succeed in what it attempts, Soderbergh illustrates that it's okay to go off the deep-end and be a bit crazy with things once in a while—and what better timing than with his Uranus transit to his natal Sun. Moreover, *Schizopolis* shows that Uranus has a sense of humor. Evolution created the platypus, did it not?

To create brilliance, to create works of genius:

Persona (Bergman, 1966)

> *"The hopeless dream of being—not seeming, but being"*
> —Margaretha Krook as the Doctor

Persona is a film about cracking, cracking the medium of film and cracking the human personality. Although Bergman established his reputation with earlier films like *The Seventh Seal* and *Wild Strawberries*, *Persona* is his most revolutionary film, challenging the conventions of storytelling and the nature of human behavior. Although prior to *Persona* there had been more experimental films, more wildly radical movies, *Persona* is monumental because the edges that Bergman pushed work on multiple levels and carry profound significance to the nature of film as a narrative medium.

Critic John Simon compared *Persona* to James Joyce's *Ulysses*.[5] Both works forever changed the grammar and vocabularies of their respective mediums, and, like all works of genius, all subsequent films and novels had to contend with the revolutions that their authors initiated. In the first eight minutes of shockingly bizarre but effective montage, Bergman deconstructs the narrative structure of film to make the medium transparent to the viewer. What elevates these random images beyond mere shock effect and to the level of genius is that so many layers of meaning are implicated; the images evoke timeless and eternal paradoxes and struggles of the human condition, foreshadow the drama of the film, demonstrate the relationship between consciousness and unconsciousness, and question the relationship between viewer and image. Although *Persona* settles into a conventional narrative, the complexity of the film and the multiple levels of meaning are sustained. Bergman provokes us to question whether we, as viewers of the film, are watching two autonomous women going through identity crises or whether we are watching more of a dream where two figures metaphorically symbolize two aspects of the same psyche battling for supremacy of consciousness.

Not only are *Persona*'s levels of genius inspired on multiple tiers of meanings, it also captures Uranus at work on multiple planes of meaning as well. The jarring dissonance from radical juxtapositions of images, the narrative breakdown, and the confrontational clash between the two female figures of the film captures the experiential tone and crisis-like atmosphere of the mid-1960s in microcosm. As Uranus was conjoined by Pluto and opposed by Saturn in the middle of the 1960s, many of the narratives, scripts, and structures that held nations and groups together were being broken down. Sex and sexual relations, political ideologies, identity issues, and racial barriers were being deconstructed and re-scripted. Likewise, every art form at the time was going through major re-visioning and reformulation. *Persona* was among a handful of films that aesthetically captured the harsh discord and deconstruction of the time. Moreover, the emergence of the true self and the discarding of the false identity—a subject that Bergman explores with harrowing realism in *Persona*—is often the result of a significant Uranus transit. One may feel psychologically fragmented, and one's public masks and presentations may shatter as an authentic self begins to emerge.

Finally, Bergman himself was experiencing an important Uranus transit to his natal Venus and Sun during the filming and subsequent release of *Persona*. Of the film, Bergman himself said, "I went as far as I could go."[6] Pushing boundaries was certainly "in the air" at that point in time and Bergman himself was feeling the pull of Uranus. *Persona* is one of the very few films we have whose complexity and ability to disturb arises from a depth of genius and not idle pretension.

Raging Bull (Scorsese, 1980)

"If you win, you win. If you lose, you still win!"

—Joe Pesci as Joey LaMotta

On rare occasion, editing, cinematography, performance, script, direction, and technical brilliance come together to create a movie greater than the sum of its parts. *Citizen Kane* is one of those movies; *Raging Bull* is another. Like *Citizen Kane*, *Raging Bull* is an unapologetic and unflinching glance at the nature of obsession and the irredeemable aspects of human nature. Ironically, *Raging Bull* is a psychological passion play of high art that uses the most primal and instinctual sport, boxing, as its subject. In thematic content, the jealousy, brutality, tragedy, and gritty underworld elements of the film speak more to the archetypes of Pluto and Scorpio; however, the sheer and searing brilliance of the film—the editing, storyboarding, and the performances—could only emanate from Uranus.

The brilliance of the film is derived from its unforgettable portrayals, flawless execution, and technical achievements. Scorsese, an obsessive student of film, borrowed techniques liberally from every conceivable influence and added his own unique innovations to create a truly magnificent vision. With *Raging Bull*,

Scorsese consistently deviated from traditional film conventions to create nothing less than poetry on screen. The boxing sequences—built from differing film speeds, impeccable editing and storyboarding, stylized choreography, uncharacteristic sound effects, and extreme camera angles—are unmatched masterpieces. However, the seamless and extraordinarily intuitive stylistic and technical aspects that hold the film do not overpower the performances. *Raging Bull* is one of the few films that contains tour de force acting from a number of performers to match the equally stunning and impressive stylistic elements.

Working on their fourth project together, Scorsese and De Niro experienced significant Uranus transits to their natal charts during the creation of *Raging Bull*. The visual brilliance of the film is not something born from a lifetime of study but must be dependent upon other intervening factors. The uncanny and flawless execution of the direction and visual elements of the film suggest a person in the throes of a tremendous influx of inspired perception and imagination. As reviewer Michael Thomas comments, *Raging Bull* is a film "with imagination and life, revealing the thunder, sensitivity, and artistry of a director on a continuous creative high."[7] Indeed, as the natal chart suggests, Martin Scorsese was experiencing a once-in-a-lifetime Uranus transit conjoining his natal Sun. Recovering from drug addiction and very close to ending his career as a filmmaker, Scorsese made the comeback that Jake Lamotta, *Raging Bull's* subject, failed to make. Scorsese has made pictures that have been equally as powerful and as emotionally gripping as *Raging Bull*; however, nothing he has touched has equaled its artistic perfection.

De Niro turned in arguably the greatest performance of a long and remarkable career with his portrayal of Jake LaMotta. As Scorsese was receiving the powerful conjunction from Uranus to his Sun, De Niro was receiving a 90 degree square transit from Uranus to his natal Sun. The performance earned De Niro an Oscar and cemented his reputation as one of the greatest actors of his generation. The complexity, subtlety, and searing intensity that De Niro brings to the role of LaMotta was truly a once-in-a-lifetime performance, mirrored by his Uranus square Sun transit.

To disrupt, to rebel:

Easy Rider (Hopper, 1969)

"*What the hell's wrong with freedom? I mean, that's what it's all about.*"

—Dennis Hopper as Billy

Easy Rider, difficult for the generation that grew up with its significance to acknowledge, is a period piece. To the generations born after the 1960s, the loose talk of self-determination, the hippie aesthetic and lexicon, the psychedelic interludes, and the freedom rock soundtrack of the film are now the stuff of satire that simply doesn't compute or resonate. To the youth that came of age with *Easy Rider*, a re-witnessing of the film in one's full maturity would evoke many disturbing and perplexing—possibly even painful—responses. Laughter, shame, puzzlement, and betrayal may all emerge from seeing a film that was the definitive artistic statement for the generation that was to change the world.

Peter Fonda, playing a detached and laconic "Captain America," opens the film with the definitive anti-establishment gesture. By throwing his wristwatch to the ground, Fonda defines the *modus operandi* of the entire film: to liberate one's self from the artifice and constraints of a society that is unjust, hypocritical, and pungent from the odor of rotting standards. Fonda, and fellow travel companions played by Dennis Hopper and Jack Nicholson, set out on the open road in search of freedom. However, they soon find that the absolute liberty and free will they choose to exercise is so dangerous and threatening to the establishment that they die as a result.

Easy Rider was released during the tumultuous and riotous summer of 1969 under a Pluto, Jupiter, Uranus triple conjunction. This once in roughly one-hundred twenty year alignment correlated with some of the most remarkable and unforgettable events of an already distinguished decade: the Moon landing, Woodstock, the beginning infrastructure of the internet, the continuing proliferation of student rebellions on either side of the Atlantic, the irrefutable general tenor of insurrection and freedom. With the archetypes of Pluto and Jupiter dilating, uplifting, empowering, and intensifying the innate potentials of Uranus, this was truly a unique and special time. Creativity, technological innovation, rebellion, and the need for freedom—all facets of the Uranus archetype—soared to new and unprecedented heights during this brief cultural renaissance.

Fonda, Nicholson, and Hopper were carriers of the Uranus archetype for their generation. The freedom of expression (as evident in their clothes and speech), the freedom from governmental restraints, freedom from economic accountability, and freedom from societal ties and responsibility showed the extreme psychological thirst for independence and self-determination that was in the air at the time. Fonda, Hopper, and Nicholson were also nomads, searchers, and seekers, expressing Uranus's fundamental need to wander and to explore uncharted lands and alien territories.

Easy Rider was the rallying cry of the countercultural ethos that is all but buried now. However, the universe seems to operate on a strange logic. Just when the principles that fueled the film seem dead—ideals such as freedom, independence, experimentation, and rebellion—it is often a sure indication that times are rife for the rekindling of such desires.

Roger and Me (Michael Moore, 1989)

"I was born here in Flint, but I don't know anything about it."

—Bob Eubanks

Never mind that Michael Moore owns a 1.9 million dollar home in the Hamptons, he did it the American way, by making an institution of exposing the corruption and injustice of a U.S. mega-corporation. Although not the first documentary to take on the subject of corporate greed and disloyalty, *Roger and Me* became the benchmark of a new kind of documentary, where entertainment and consciousness-raising were no longer mutually exclusive propositions.

Released just months before the fall of the Berlin Wall, *Roger and Me* and the destruction of the Wall were both symbols of velvet revolutions of sorts, signaling swift and major changes in their respective empires. The landscape of corporate America changed radically in the 1990s, with the introduction of horizontal structures, increased employee benefits, and casual Fridays. Was *Roger and Me* the "shot heard 'round the world" that signaled the coming changes? Probably not. However, like the fall of the Berlin Wall, *Roger and Me* was not the product of one angry and aware citizen but the result of many complex and subtle forces, mirrored by a very important and rare triple conjunction of Uranus, Neptune, and Saturn in Capricorn.

With his natal Uranus square to Mercury, Moore demonstrates that the most successful weapon of subversion is a caustic wit and dry irony. This film's exposé would have fallen completely flat had Moore gone into the General Motors fray with a valiant, self-righteous determination. Instead, and like all good David versus Goliath fights, Moore allows General Motors and the Reagan Era logic to defeat itself; Moore is simply there to be a conscientious, witty, albeit highly biased, reporter.

Though the weapon used in the film is primarily humor, the creation of the film must have taken an incredible degree of courage, guts, and—as critic Hal Hinson points out—"rage."[8] Moore saw a tremendous opportunity to create awareness around the growing discrepancy between the power elite and the common man in America occurring around him. At the time of the premiere,

Michael Moore was experiencing both a Uranus transit to his natal Mars (a conjunction) and to his natal Sun (a trine). Any significant Uranus transit to natal Mars can be a time when we take our rallying cries for freedom and truth into action, a time when we become rebels for a cause. Moore's Mars—his point of action, determination, and self-assertion—became both ignited and catalyzed through a significant transit by Uranus. To walk into a shareholder's meeting of one of the most powerful corporations in the world and to stand firm (as Moore does) epitomizes the audacity, brazenness, creativity and freedom-loving capacity of Uranus as it also symbolizes the daring and boldness of a fully-functioning Mars. Like Moore, we can become transformed into champions for the underdog and become freedom fighters during significant Uranus-Mars transits.

To perfect what is left unfinished:

Zardoz (John Boorman, 1974)

> *"Here Man and the sum of his knowledge will never die but go forward to perfection."*

> —Elder Scientist

Astrologer Liz Greene rightfully points out in her book *The Art of Stealing Fire* that this film is "reeking of Uranus."[9] It's not because of *Zardoz's* idiosyncrasies or sci-fi campiness that makes this such a brilliantly "Uranian" movie. It's not the psychedelic visuals and startling originality and uniqueness that makes this film such a wonderful candidate for carrying the archetype of Uranus. This film is so importantly "Uranian" because the main message of the film is such an important caveat against the unbounded creativity of Uranus's magic—that to perfect nature, to transcend instincts, and to defy mortality comes with unforeseen and dangerous consequences.

Zardoz focuses on a futuristic society not unlike a hybrid of societies found in Huxley's *Brave New World* and Plato's *Republic*. The citizen's within *Zardoz* are a master race—the "eternals"—who have harnessed and display Uranus's wizardry in all its potent manifestations: psychism, utopian democratic procedures, immortality, scientific detachment and curiosity, and androgyny. On paper, the society of eternals is perfect and unblemished; however, the faultlessness and flawlessness that has been established is more of a trap and prison than the hoped-for paradise. The more conscious and outspoken of this perfect race acknowledge the tremendous pain and suffering that this "perfect" condition has brought. Perfection, androgyny, and immortality brings with it an existential malaise and ennui that is incurable, a pain that cannot be heard in the pristine silence of this technocratic Eden.

It takes a mortal, bestial, and instinctual man—a "brutal" played by Sean Connery—to break the spell of perfection that has been cast onto the eternals. Connery's presence is a disruption thought to be easily controlled and mastered by the more powerfully developed and conscious members of the utopia. However, his gifts of eroticism, mortality, and "humanness" (qualities more associated with the astrological Pluto, Mars, and Saturn) prove to be too seductive and alluring for the eternals to resist.

John Boorman scripted and filmed *Zardoz* when transiting Uranus was squaring his natal Sun. In astrological terms, *Zardoz* is a story of a Uranian society done in by something Uranian—an unpredictable, unforeseeable perturbation that disrupts and changes the society forever. John Boorman says of the film, "If there is a moral in all this it's one for the futurologists themselves. Too often, it seems to me, they ignore the power of evolution itself to upset the equation. Some new mutation, something we encounter on the way, some unimagined factor can change the course ahead."[10] According to Boorman's wisdom, a society built entirely upon defeating nature—a society that is overly Uranian—cannot be sustainable. The filmmaker states, "We live these very comfortable kinds of lives where we're cut off from nature to a large extent. I think it's the cause of neurosis if you're not in touch with nature. There's a danger that you become disassociated, and I believe it causes a lot of our problems."[11]

It's hard to believe that a movie that begins with a cheap effect of a floating, detached head is actually so potent, powerful, and complex in its main theme and message. However, if one is able to dismiss some of the anachronistic special effects and costuming, *Zardoz* holds a moral that is too quickly forgotten in our society: that the attempt to transcend nature can never happen if it is out of balance with nature itself.

Stepford Wives (Forbes, 1975)

"Something Strange is Happening in the Town of Stepford."

—Promotional Tagline

Stepford Wives. The term has entered our vocabulary to allude to the rampant social disease of complete shallowness and social vacuity, and what makes this movie truly disturbing is that the prevalence of the condition appears to be growing. The *Stepford Wives* is a movie that resists easy categorization. It is too over-the-top and tongue-in-cheek to be considered a horror film and yet serious and legitimately scary enough to be thought of only as a black comedy. The movie somehow straddles many genres simultaneously without lapsing into one comfortably and this may account for its staying power.

The movie follows a young couple from Manhattan who decide to move to the slower-paced suburb Stepford, Connecticut. Joanna, played by Katherine Ross, becomes increasingly dissatisfied and disturbed with the homogenous, vacant, and superficial housewives that populate the town of Stepford. One by one, Joanna's female friends in the town transform from interesting, creative, and spirited individuals into drone-like housewives who thrive off of cleaning the house and pleasing their husbands. Frightened by the rapid metamorphoses, Joanna plays detective only to find that the members of the Stepford Men's Club, a secret and elite men's society in the town, have been discarding their real wives in favor of robotic versions, programmed to please their husband's desires.

This movie beautifully portrays two sides of the Uranus archetype: one heroic, the other depraved. Joanna is an example of a Uranian individual among a faceless, colorless crowd. Creative, imaginative, and vital, Joanna prizes her hard-won individuality even when the pressure to conform in Stepford is significant. Joanna displays the remarkably tenacious and praiseworthy capability of people to follow their own internal rhythms and guides when external pressures negate these internal voices at every turn. Moreover, Joanna trusts her intuition—a faculty of Uranus—which states that something is amiss in her new suburb even when the town is colluding against her. It is the wonderful ability to be guided by inner faculties and principles that is often the greatest gift of the Uranus archetype, and Ross's Joanna relies on it first for her own vitality and then for her very life.

However, *Stepford Wives* shows a very dark and shadowy side of Uranus as well. The Stepford Men's Club displays the Uranian capacity to take a distorted and misinformed idea of a perfect or idealized society and to implement it into reality. Through technology, the men of Stepford destroy their real wives and replace them with robotic wives that will fulfill their desires, ignore their shortcomings, who will be totally compliant and obedient, and physically perfect. This is Uranus at its most fanatical, mad, and unbalanced. As much as Uranus has been correlated with ideas and visions that have truly benefited humanity—democracy, equal rights, desegregation, and women's suffrage, to name a few—there are also examples in history of zealous individuals who became completely consumed with their own particular, warped vision of an idealized and perfected human nature. Hitler, Wagner, Charles Manson, and Joseph McCarthy are examples of individuals with prominent Uranus's in their birth chart, who, each in their own individual way, became all-consumed with implementing their vision of human perfection.

◆   ◆   ◆

"It has been a rough time for dreamers" says a rogue bohemian from *Waking Life*. Indeed, the current cultural climate is one not noted for voicing new freedoms, encouraging civil disobedience, promoting creative experimentation, or celebrating difference. This is a time where Uranus and everything that it symbolizes in us collectively is very much asleep. However, when the genies, Prometheuses, and Pandoras are released, awakened, and unbound again, may we use the creative fires of Uranus wisely and treat the visionary impulses and revolutionary ideas with care. Perhaps we will walk open-mindedly and curiously into a new universe like Wiley Wiggins in *Walking Life*. Perhaps we will have the audacity to have our freak flags fly and true colors on full display like Tim Curry in *Rocky Horror Picture Show*. Perhaps we will create something of earth-shattering genius like Scorsese's *Raging Bull* or Bergman's *Persona*. Perhaps we will have the courage of our convictions like Michael Moore. Or Perhaps we will be guided by intuition and insight like Katherine Ross's Joanna in the *Stepford Wives*. Whatever the case may be, when treated with respect and when in harmony and balance, the archetype of Uranus is a necessary ingredient for a full and rich life—it is the very divine spark of life.

All birth times from the Internet Movie Database or www.thenewage.com

Gary Ross: November 3rd, 1956, Los Angeles, California.
Richard Linklater: July 30th, 1960, Houston, Texas.
Tim Curry: April 19th, 1946, Grappnhall, Chesire, UK.
Steven Soderbergh: January 14th, 1963, Atlanta, Georgia.
Ingmar Bergman: July 14th, 1918, Uppsala, Sweden.
Martin Scorsese: November 17th, 1942, Queens, New York.
Robert De Niro: August 17th, 1943, New York, New York.
Michael Moore: April 23rd, 1954, Flint, Michigan.
John Boorman: January 18th, 1933, London, UK.

1. Robert Hand, *Horoscope Symbols* (Atglen, PA: Schiffer Publishing, 1981) 22.

2. Casey, Caroline, *Making the Gods Work For You* (New York: Three Rivers Press, 1999) 138.

3. Peter Frampton was also an individual who experienced the Jupiter-Uranus opposition of 1975–1976 on his natal Sun. Both Curry and Frampton burst onto the popular scene in a highly dynamic, unpredictable and unprecedented fashion. Frampton's "Frampton Comes Alive" also plays homage to the Promethean-Creator myth in the same vein of Curry's Frank-n-Furter.

4. http://www.soderbergh.net/articles/1996/roughcut.htm

5. http://www.openix.com/~danb/persona.htm

6. Ingmar Bergman, *The Magic Lantern* (New York: Viking, 1988) 133.

7. http://www.bbc.co.uk/films/2000/11/15/raging_bull_2000_review.shtml

8. http://www.washingtonpost.com/wp-srv/style/longterm/movies/videos/rogermerhinson_a0a906.htm

9. Liz Greene, *The Art of Stealing Fire* (London: Centre for Psychological Astrology Press, 1996) 33

10. http://othyrworld.com/zardoz/

11. http://www.salon.com/people/conv/2001/04/02/boorman/index2.html

The Neptune Film

The archetypal Neptune is the symbol concerning symbols. The capacity to understand symbols and symbolism relies upon the part of our intelligence that grasps patterns, sees relationships, and connects things holistically, for symbols are not literal but connotative. Neptune, then, is closely associated with faculties that can understand symbolism: the imagination, intuition, and other faculties that synthesize (as opposed to analyze and dissect) information. However, to understand Neptune in this fashion is itself rather dry and analytical. To understand and revere Neptune is to honor the poetic, mystical, metaphorical, and spiritual. If Uranus is the lightning bolt of the 'a-ha experience,' Neptune is the creative stirrings of inspiration and feeling. Neptune imbues all with a sense of mystery, enchantment, the cosmic, and the aesthetic.

Within physics and alchemy, "sublimation" is the practice of turning that which is solid into something gaseous and vaporous. However, meant more psychologically, sublimation is the art of rendering something sublime—to raise to a higher ideal, to spiritualize, or to refine. The archetypal Neptune is the agent in astrology that sublimates, inflecting everything that it influences with a sense of a nobler, higher enhancement. Without Neptune, art lacks inspiration and imagination and is reduced to craftsmanship. Without Neptune, one cannot "fall into" love and there is no true desire to meld one's heart with another. Without Neptune, the world is dry, lacks mystery, and our daily existence has no relevance outside itself.

In today's patriarchal, work-obsessed, materialistic, and technological culture, the values and expressions of the archetype of Neptune are often ignored, disregarded, or explained away. Amazingly, within a period of four hundred years, the orientation of the Western world has moved from a focus on transcendent salvation to a secularized, disenchanted materialism. Within the cultural milieu of medieval Europe, the values and expressions of Neptune were given predominance and priority. Although there have always existed a panoply of competing drives and forces within the collective psyche, the search for spiritual sanctification and the reverence and piety toward some wholly transcendent Other—values associated with Neptune—were front and center in the stage of Europe for more than one thousand years. The search for transcendence and the drive for wholeness will always remain a powerful force within the individual and the collective; however, in today's climate, these values are not well integrated into the cultural commons.

The mythic imagination, feelings of inspiration, the religious search, and the urge for personal dissolution—which are arguably the core expressions of Neptune—are indeed on the fringes of the current Western landscape. Immature versions of these Neptunian drives exist but mature recognition of these values is often sought in private, outside of culturally acceptable rituals. Since the dawn of modernity, however, there have been brief epochs when the culture is swept up by the waves of Neptune, often when Neptune forms an angular relationship with one of its outer planet neighbors, Pluto and Uranus. The height of early Romanticism, with the timeless poetry of Keats, Shelley, Byron, and Coleridge and Beethoven's epic and vaulting Ninth Symphony, coincided with a conjunction between Uranus and Neptune. Even more potent in its expression, the conjunction between Neptune and Pluto at the end of the nineteenth century witnessed a total cultural immersion into Neptunian themes: the arrival of Eastern religions into the West, the rise and predominance of metaphysical societies, the academic study of the religious impulse and the nature of altered states of consciousness (as in William James's *The Varieties of Religious Experience*), the peak of opiate addiction throughout Europe and America, the transformation of the artistic image through the Post-Impressionists, the first glimmerings of the phenomenon known as cinema, and the birth of psychology as a distinct discipline.

Modern psychology has had a turbulent relationship with archetypal Neptune and all that it symbolizes. Because of its ambiguous and elusive character, the realm of Neptune—suggesting subjectivity, interiors, and moods—was completely explained away by psychological schools such as behaviorism. Freud himself, who turned psychology's focus on unconscious processes such as dreams and hysteria, would have believed that the impulses associated with Neptune were regressive and were simply the manifestations of preoccupations unresolved in childhood. Signs of the healthy adult could be measured almost entirely by his or her success in relationships and daily affairs. Any other concerns or drives would be a sure signal of neurosis. The religious impulse in particular was deemed by Freud to be juvenile escapism, the "opiate of the masses."

Although both Freud and Jung were influenced by the philosophical and religious matrix of their time, it is accurate to suggest that Jung gleaned more from the Romantic strain of his heritage and Freud from the Enlightenment. Instead of seeing the unconscious as a mechanistic repository of repressed sexual and aggressive instincts, Jung believed the unconscious to hold both lower, instinctual possibilities and higher potentials as well. Dreams, symbols, and images were the way the psyche left "footprints" of its own evolution, its own desire to individuate. Like Jung, archetypal and transpersonal psychologies held the myth-making, image-creating capacity of the psyche as inherently healthy and non-pathological. For Jung and the transpersonal offshoots, the urge for higher realms of consciousness and the religious impulse is expressive of the deep and irreducible desire for the psyche to sublimate itself, that is, to transmute that which is earthly, mundane, and base into something of higher value.

Transpersonal theorist Ken Wilber, with his genius of hindsight, believed that both Freud and Jung (and their respective adherents) were guilty of misunderstanding and misevaluating the religious impulse and spiritual states of consciousness. Freud, Wilber esteemed, was guilty of reducing and packaging any and all spirituality into a regressive infantilism—that any and all religious drives were simply defensive or escapist postures relative to the imposing and daunting monolith that is the "reality principle." On the other hand, postulated Wilber, Jung and his followers were guilty of the opposite error in judgment. Jung was to be charged with inflating or elevating any and all nonrational states of consciousness as signals of health, individuation, and personal growth. The transpersonal and archetypal schools, claimed Wilber, are guilty of an uncritical romanticism toward nonrational states of consciousness, a quasi reverence of any altered state of consciousness simply for the sake of it being nonrational.

Although many astrologers are quick to state that Neptune is synonymous with spirituality, its potentials and archetypal matrix is a much vaster ocean of potential. If Neptune is to symbolize Wilber's nonrational states of consciousness, then the archetype encompasses the most primitive and regressive states of oblivion to the most heightened and perceptive mystical or unitive states of consciousness. Neptune is neutral; it is our response to it that creates distress or, alternatively, deep well-being and peace. As astrologer Stephen Arroyo states, "The most useful way of describing Neptune's essential meaning is to say that it represents the urge to lose one's self in another state of consciousness (whether 'higher' or 'lower' consciousness)....A Neptunian person may be evasive or escapist, or he can be very perceptive of subtleties and extremely compassionate (or a mixture of both!)."[1]

Thus, some responses to nonordinary states of consciousness are highly self destructive and regressive while others are profoundly evolved and mature. The incapacitated drunk in the bowels of the city and the modern day spiritual master, in essence, are compelled by the same drive that Neptune represents, namely the ability to transcend the suffering caused by the desires and limitations of the ego. The difference between the mystic and alcoholic transient, then, is related to the level of personal integration and the ability to master and accept everyday life of this world. Mature spirituality teaches one to "be in this world, but not of it," or more fittingly to "tie one's camel." Most religions suggest the necessity of creating a firm foundation in reality before reaching for the spiritual heights. The inebriated alcoholic longs for the same transcendence of the ego as a spiritual teacher, only the alcoholic has failed to fully accept the responsibilities, obligations, and effort of everyday life.

The difference in mature or regressive responses to Neptune has much to do with the relationship between Neptune and Saturn. Rare is it to find an explanation of the astrological Neptune without a discussion of Saturn. For of all of the polarities and dissimilarities in the astrological pantheon—Venus and Mars, Jupiter and Saturn, Uranus and Saturn—the most fundamental dichotomy lies between Saturn and Neptune. Although shades of difference existence between all the astrological archetypes—and thus their ability to capture the full complexity of the human psyche—Saturn and Neptune are, by definition, *foundationally* different. Almost like a strict algebra, whatever quality Neptune possesses, Saturn must be in strict opposition to, and vice versa. If Saturn is symbolic of the limitations and frailty of human life and its mortality and aging, Neptune expresses the higher order truth of the timelessness and eternal nature of the human spirit. If Saturn is symbolic of the literal, frustrating, and mundane details of everyday life, Neptune articulates the limitless and infinite possibility inherent in the inspiring, soaring visions of ecstasy and imagination. Saturn's energy separates, negates, and hardens while Neptune's influence fuses, softens, and moistens.

It is only through the relationship of Saturn to Neptune that we can understand how Neptune is both symbolic of Maya, the veils of illusion, while also expressing the ultimate source of reality, a samadhi type consciousness. In Hinduism, Maya is the deceptive fog and illusion that entices and ensnares one further into the world. The ego grasps and grabs for the enchantment produced by Maya but either fails in its grasping, or once the object is attained, it loses its appeal, luster, and enticement. Only through time do we become disillusioned with the appeal of the world as it becomes increasingly apparent that the shimmering veils are not what we seek. This disillusioning process, this eroding of the veils of fantasy that coat the phenomenal world, is very much concerned with the relationship of Saturn to Neptune. Saturn deflates the illusory nature of the imagination and its enticements, forcing us to withdraw our projections onto that which was once so captivating.

It is through the gradual process of constant disillusionment that a refinement of consciousness occurs. The gratification that one seeks is not so much oriented to the various pleasures in the real world that hold only false promises, but to a higher world that lays inside. It is only through this reciprocal relationship between Saturn and Neptune that an authentic spiritual quest can begin in earnest. For the illusion-busting influence of Saturn assists one to refine and constantly redefine one's search for something that is sustainably gratifying. Although the archetypes of Saturn and Neptune *are* diametrically opposed in their essential expressions, as a team they work together to produce spiritual growth and spur on the evolution of consciousness.

All outer planets symbolize transpersonal forces, drives which are collective in nature but which also manifest themselves in the individual (and often individuals can become possessed by the archetype, sacrificing their personal potentials). It is unfair in this context to simply equate "transpersonal" as being simply synonymous with "collective" or "generational," for individually the outer three planets can be as significant a personality factor as the inner, personal planets. Rather, transpersonal in this context may be better defined as archetypal energy that is cosmological in reach, is of a larger and vaster scope than conventional experiences, is life-altering or life shaping, and is of a greater magnitude than ordinary consensus consciousness.

If Uranus is symbolic of transpersonal conceptual faculties and Pluto is expressive of transpersonal will and life force, then Neptune is most easily equated with the transpersonal *feeling* life—Neptune is the emotional sensitivity of higher (and lower) states of consciousness. Given this definition of transpersonal, feelings associated with Neptune have a profundity and enormity to them that simply cannot be addressed in conversational vernacular. The bliss or ecstasy of a religious experience—an experience typically associated with the archetype of Neptune—can be of such an overwhelming scope as to cause a conversion experience and to cause the native to completely overhaul her life. More commonly, we are in the grip of the archetypal Neptune when we are deeply inspired, moved, or touched. Art, healing, lovers in union, and deep relational bonds have the power to bring emotional sensitivity and exquisiteness that moves one to tears, touches one deeply in the heart, or rouses an inspired compassion or empathic motivation.

A film that has the same capacity to move one deeply is one that is acutely attuned to the archetypal Neptune. Rare is the film that has the power to deeply touch and move us to states of ecstatic inspiration or a state of cleansing grace. Although we may think of Neptunian films as being solely otherworldly, Neptunian themes can be expressed through the most mundane of themes: relationships of fathers to sons, a redeeming friendship, or a portrait of life in simpler times. It is often through these commonplace themes that the Neptunian force of profound emotion is at its most powerful, demonstrating that the spiritual and transcendent is to be found in the living of life and not necessarily in something ethereal and unearthly.

Although all of film is innately Neptunian—as our collective's increasing desire for moving images indulges the Neptunian drive for altering conventional consciousness—the following films display the range and depth of this infinitely deep archetype to its greatest potential. Of all the archetypes, Neptune is the most resistant to concrete definition and analytical divisions. However, for the sake of simplicity, the following themes display the capacity and range of the Neptunian archetype: the spiritual quest, image and the imaginal, love and union, illusions and realities.

The Spiritual Quest:

The Fisher King (Gilliam, 1991)

> *"A Modern Day Tale About The Search For Love, Sanity, Ethel Merman And the Holy Grail."*
>
> —Promotional Tagline

If astrology is anything, it is the study of the paradox of human nature through symbolism. The deeper one enters into the mystery of astrology, the more one is awestruck by the paradox inherent in each symbol. Such is the case with Neptune. Upon entering the symbol superficially, one is left with the impression that Neptune is the "lightweight" of the astrological pantheon. Impressions, subtlety, inspiration, and invisibles are its signature. Alone, it does not lead to anything truly concrete nor does it manifest in signs of overt power. However, in the quieter moments of self-reflection and even buried underneath the chaos and rumblings of the day-to-day, Neptune's presence is felt. The persistent heartbeat of the archetypal Neptune calls out to you to suggest, "You will never be satisfied, complete, or fulfilled until you return to the source of spirit and the font of life." This quiet stirring, the gnawing divine discontent that stems from being divorced from one's true essence, is the work of Neptune, which makes the symbol the ultimate driving force and arguably the most dominant astrological archetype.

This profound desire to search for salvation, redemption, and wholeness that is affiliated with Neptune is the source of many of the most powerful myths. The myth of the quest for the Holy Grail is one of the most enduring in Western culture, and its imparting of a pursuit of a mystical power that redeems and grants immortality has inspired much of the greatest art in civilization. Terry Gilliam's *Monty Python and the Holy Grail* is not an example of a great art enthused by the Grail myth. His later *The Fisher King* comes closer.

The Fisher King is a story that concentrates on the quest for redemption through the vehicle of a fallen celebrity and his unlikely association with a wise fool. Jeff Bridges plays Jack Lucas, a hip, sarcastic shock jock who finds himself accountable for a killer's shooting spree. Lucas's scornful prodding of a psychologically disturbed individual ultimately ends in disaster—the listener follows Lucas's advice and goes on a shooting spree in a New York restaurant. Due to the untimely circumstances, Lucas is stripped of fame, fortune, and money but left with the pessimism and cynicism that fueled his original popularity. Through a twist of fate, Jack Lucas ends up befriending a street person, "Parry," portrayed by Robin Williams, who was also touched by the tragedy of the shooting spree.

Lucas finds out that Parry is on the quest for the Holy Grail, which in this story is located off Madison Avenue. Parry enlists the cunning of Lucas to track down the object of his desire. Superficially, it appears that Parry is the one needing help and assistance, as the post-traumatic stress induced by tragedies in his life have rendered him mentally ill. However, Lucas too needs Parry to serve as a conduit to his own hope and idealism, buried underneath years of worldliness and skepticism.

As in most renderings of the Grail, in *The Fisher King* it is not the desired object itself that leads to redemption and sanctification, but it is the process and journey toward the Grail which ultimately gives the hoped-for transformation. Through the assistance of Lucas, Parry is able to face inner demons and slay his dragons and return to a state of relatively healthy living. Likewise, through Parry, Lucas is also redeemed, given a sense of purpose, a restored renewal of optimism, and faith in the process of life. In their journey, wounds are healed, a platonic love is cultivated; giving, rather than receiving, is the key that unlocks the spiritual doors they both desired.

Kundun (Scorsese, 1997)

> *"Just like a dream experience, whatever things I enjoy will become a memory. Whatever is past will not be seen again."*
>
> —Tenzin Thuthob Tsarong as Kundun

Although *Kundun* and *The Last Temptation of Christ* have a superficial relationship in that they are departure films for Martin Scorsese, there the similarity
ends. Turning his camera away from the American crime world and the profane
proving grounds of New York City, Scorsese chose to tackle controversial religious topics at the height of his career. However, while both films are overtly religious, Willem Dafoe's Christ has more in common with De Niro's Jake LaMotta
and Travis Bickle than his Eastern Buddhist counterpart of the Dalai Lama in
Kundun. Critics rightly claim that *Kundun* falls short as a film because the characters and themes are portrayed too simplistically. The Dalai Lama's one dimen-
sional piety and wisdom are juxtaposed next to the cartoon-like, fiendish
depiction of Chairman Mao. While Jesus of *The Last Temptation of Christ* writhes
with existential torment and wrestles with his inner and outer demons, the Dalai
Lama of *Kundun* lacks complexity and shadow. The lack of dimension in *Kundun*
may have been equally due to Scorsese's initial reverence for the material and the
fact that film was made in cooperation with the Dalai Lama himself. Nonetheless,
although the film may have disappointed Scorsese's more jaded and angst-ridden
fan base, the lack of Scorsese's more familiar purgatorial intensity allows for an
elegance and simplicity to shine through this film.

One of the simple themes that pervades the movie is the timeless truth that
"things change." More than just an observation of the nature of reality, this
notion suggests that the desire nature of the ego is an inevitable loser, dwarfed by
nature's authority to shift events at will. This truth of impermanence is a centerpiece of Buddhist teaching, informing the cornerstone of the religion, the Four
Noble Truths and the Eightfold Path. In the film, we see the Dalai Lama as a
small child learning the truth of impermanence through war games. In a particular vignette, we see the little Dalai Lama challenge his teacher and sparring partner, attacking his opponent with increasingly stronger toy armies. After an
exchange of power, the teacher admonishes, "Today you lose, Kundun. Tomor-
row you may win. Things change, Kundun." As little children in the West are
taught implicitly and explicitly to strengthen their budding egos, the Dalai Lama
was taught to observe and temper his nascent ego. Through cultivation and practice, the mature Kundun adheres to this truth of impermanence, detached in sur-
veying the enormous changes that his country endures as the Chinese occupy
Tibet.

That things change—this law of impermanence—is not only a central facet of
Buddhism but also one of the signature qualities of the astrological Neptune.
Neptune transits often signify loss, particularly loss where the ego has gained
security or has overly identified itself, excluding other possibilities and potentials.

When one builds a structure in life toward which the ego is overly attached, it is an inevitability that a Neptune transit—sooner or later—will slowly dissolve the attachment. Not only does Neptune's action teach us that "things change," but the necessary letting go and surrendering opens us up to something far greater and vaster than the ego's ambitions and attainments. This greater set of potentials latent within us, known by various names by different religions—Buddha Nature, Atman, Christ Consciousness, Ultimate Reality—offers riches and well-being far greater than the grasping, striving ego.

As much as the Chinese occupation of Tibet brought pain and suffering to the Dalai Lama and his people, Scorsese's portrayal of the Dalai Lama shows him never straying from the Buddhist principles of compassion and nonattachment. Without relinquishing his role of leader and without letting go of his deep desire for freedom from the occupation, the Dalai Lama is able to tap into virtues and kindness for the entire situation, not just his people. By accomplishing this, the Dalai Lama is able to let go of an attachment to outcome without bypassing the deep commitment toward ending the occupation. Through the bloody annexation of Tibet, the Dalai Lama is put to the ultimate spiritual test of his ideals.

Image is Everything:

Days of Heaven (Malick, 1978)

> "Your eyes…Your ears…Your senses…will be overwhelmed."
>
> —Promotional Tagline

This film is not chosen in isolation but represents a class of films whereby evocative imagery and lyrical cinematography are as important as the traditional and foundational elements of narrative films, namely plot and acting. In fact, one could argue that in Days of Heaven and films like it, images submerge more established, linear storytelling so that mood, nuance, and suggestion take precedence. The cinematography of Days of Heaven carries, if not overpowers, the film. In a movie with an epic plot with biblical allusions, it is the imagery—not the storyline—that remains in the viewer's memory.

In many respects, the lavish, lush, and gorgeous cinematography of the film is an ironic counterpoint to the narrative. As beautiful scenes of undulating wheat, heartland sunsets, and prairie campfires flow intermittently throughout the film, a story of deception, betrayal, and revenge unfolds, ultimately ending in the manhunt for the movie's protagonist. The juxtaposition of idyllic scenes of nature set against the destructiveness and wickedness of human folly is director Malick's conscious mediation on the dual aspects of human nature. Throughout the film, characters innocently comment on the angels and devils that possess our nature, but the fullest exploration of this age-old dichotomy is created in the relationship of heavenly imagery versus the sins of the characters.

This jarring contrast between beautiful visual poetics and the horror capable within humanity has been a constant trademark in Malick's tiny but influential output. Realizing just three films over thirty years as director, Malick's "prolific period" in the 1970s saw the filming and release of *Bad Lands* (1973) and *Days of Heaven* (1978). It was during this period when slow moving Neptune transited by conjunction Malick's Sun in Sagittarius. Malick's film debut and sophomore effort displayed the characteristics of one under the influence of a potent transit from Neptune: sublime and inspired imagery, the general theme of a quest for lost innocence, and a sense of timelessness and indefinable presence.

The Neptunian dimension is strong in *Days of Heaven* and in all of Malick's work. Malick's *Bad Lands* and *Days of Heaven* leave impressions—often profoundly beautiful ones—but rarely do those traces of visual beauty lead anywhere definitive. Besides being a compilation of tranquil and surreally beautiful imagery, his films pose fundamental questions about our relationship to nature, purity, and transcendence—all facets of Neptune's archetype. The haphazard and intuitive feel of Malick's filmmaking suggests that, like the viewer, he too is open for answers. Rather than give trite answers to the relationship between transcendence and human failings, Malick allows the evocation of feelings from images employed in his films to not answer, but to deepen the questioning of our own relationship to some wholly transcendent Other.

Baraka (Fricke, 1993)

> *"A World Beyond Words"*
>
> —Promotional Tagline

In his book *Anima Mundi*, Charles Harvey writes, "[An] idea connected with the *anima mundi* is that what we see in all the manyness of creation is a perpetual splitting up or a fragmenting of [the] unified world-soul, so that everything we see in this reality has a tiny piece of the world-soul within it." [2] Philosophers from Plato to Schelling have expounded on this idea and given the *anima mundi* a reality through the insight of their intellectual reflections. Yet, images capture the *anima mundi*'s certainty and give it feeling life. Images speak more directly to the right-brain, the god-side, or mystical, side of the brain. *Baraka* has been one film in a rising genre of non-narrative documentaries that use images to convey their significance, and this film captures, arguably like no other document, the reality of the *anima mundi*, the world soul.

Although the creators of the film did not want to place a fundamental message with the images of the film, one does walk away from the film with a sense of what the title translates into English, "Essence." Images of monks in repose, glittering mosques, burning effigies along the Ganges, and swirling stars somehow distill a fundamental nature of the world, a perennial spirit that pervades everything. By radically going against the convention of Hollywood films, with their emphasis on the latest styles and trends, *Baraka* captures a timeless and eternal beauty that remains untouchable against the backdrop of the ever-changing wheels of culture. Whereas many narrative films allude to something essential through couching perennial spiritual themes in modern day narrative, *Baraka* goes directly to the source, evoking a powerful response in viewers that suggests that there is indeed a spiritual force animating the world.

Baraka is indicative of the contemporary attempt to directly access spiritual experience rather than receive religious dogma or indoctrination in established faiths. The modern spiritual seeker is no less interested in religious sermons than he is in secular pursuits. Rather, the searcher quests to quench his thirst for spiritual replenishment through direct access to the divine or numinous, abandoning the need for intermediaries like churches, preachers, or religious texts. As the creators of the film hoped to bypass intentional messages and defined meanings, their intention was to initiate spiritual exploration and curiosity through evoking a spiritual feeling through images. The lack of narrative and structure was to their advantage, allowing the left-brain to relax and stimulating the right-brain to flex its atrophied muscles.

Baraka was released in 1993, when a powerful conjunction between Uranus and Neptune reached exactitude. The Uranus-Neptune cycle is very much concerned with the spiritual awakening of the world, the illumination of the sacred nature of life. From the ministries of Jesus, to the teaching of Mohammed, to the "Great Awakening," the Uranus-Neptune cycle has always ignited the spiritual flames of the collective. *Baraka* was just one movie in several which reflected to the global community that a religious and spiritual renewal was happening at the time.

Uranus alignments to the outer planets always increase consciousness. When Pluto and Uranus were conjunct in the 1960s, the first images of the earth from space were a stunningly powerful reflection on origins, who we are, what we as a culture are all about. In the same way, *Baraka* was the "Earth" image of the

1990s. The inspiring imagery from the film made us reflect, or more accurately, deeply feel the mysterious unity and sacredness that is inherent in all of life.

The Power of Love:

Life is Beautiful (Begnini, 1997)

> *"An unforgettable fable that proves love, family and imagination conquer all."*

>   —Promotional Tagline

In the late 1930s and 1940s, a promising young Viennese psychiatrist, Viktor Frankl, began to formulate a psychological theory that ran counter to Freud's. Frankl proposed that the fundamental drive of humankind was not based on pleasure, survival, or sex, but on the will toward meaning. In his main work, *Man's Search for Meaning*, Frankl states, "Logotherapy…considers man as a being whose main concern consists in fulfilling a meaning and in actualizing values, rather than in the mere gratification and satisfaction of drives and instincts."[3] Just as Frankl was to release his new theory to the world, Frankl's career was interrupted by the course of World War II, and he was sent to concentration camps for three years. The experience, however, strengthened Frankl's hypothesis. After being released from the camps, Frankl was convinced more than ever that meaning was foundational to life. From his own experience, Frankl saw that those that had the greatest chance at survival in the camps were the ones that held onto hope, faith, and the possibilities of the future. Just two months after the Viennese psychiatrist died, *Life is Beautiful*, the film that is highly evocative of the themes found in Frankl's work, was released in Italy.

In Roberto Begnini's touching film, protagonist Guido is confronted with the horror of the Holocaust. Like Frankl, Guido must place his customary life on indefinite hold as he and his family are sent to a concentration camp. In a fashion that is equally comic and highly inspirational, Begnini's Guido turns the horrific events around him into a game, for the sake of preserving his child's hope and faith in life. What in most contexts would be an extreme form of denial and manipulation, Guido's concentration camp game is undyingly heroic, for, as chances of escape constrict and as even his own son begins to doubt the rules of the game, Guido remains unflappable in his infectious enthusiasm and positivity.

Begnini's movie reaffirms that saviors and saints are everyday people whose spirits are tested by extraordinary circumstances. Begnini's savior is not the martyr; his suffering and sacrifice is a necessary, if not ingenious, way to endure the worst of circumstances. His sacrifice not only preserves his son's life but also preserves the innocence and faith in childhood. The sacrifices that Guido makes and his will for faith seem to come out of a reservoir of unselfish love that is given extraordinarily powerful expression in this movie. Frankl himself witnessed this love in the middle of the suffering of his concentration camp experience:

> "A thought transfixed me: for the first time in my life I saw the truth as it is set into song by so many poets, proclaimed as the final wisdom by so many thinkers. The truth—that love is the ultimate and the highest goal to which man can aspire. Then I grasped the meaning of the greatest secret that human poetry and human thought and belief have to impart: The salvation of man is through love and is love."[4]

A particular facet of Neptune deals with the highest form of love, which may be the most redemptive, affirming force in the universe. Although the movie was criticized for its comedic rendering of the Holocaust, it is nearly impossible to leave this movie without being deeply moved. The archetypal Neptune allows us to tap into that part of us that sacrifices our own life for the redemption of that which is not ours alone—family, a loved one, a community, or the world.

Somewhere in Time (Szwarc, 1980)

"Come back to me."

—Jane Seymour as Elise McKenna

When one usually thinks of cult films, one thinks of offbeat and eccentric movies that are often taboo, exploitive, or otherwise simply too bizarre for mainstream consumption. Historical romance is hardly considered cult material, and yet *Somewhere in Time*, a small production released quietly in 1980, has slowly amassed one of the strongest cult followings over the last twenty years. Resembling more of a Hallmark made-for-TV movie than an epic Hollywood romance, *Somewhere in Time* even has a legendary fan base that makes an annual pilgrimage to a small island in Michigan where the film was shot on location.

What can explain the appeal for such a film, a film that was nearly a critical and commercial flop upon initial release? The acting, though strong, doesn't deserve special mention. The script is somewhat flawed and the science fiction elements demand that one suspend criticality. The direction and cinematography are solid but nothing highly memorable. What then can account for the film's tremendous appeal over time? Although the romance depicted between Christopher Reeve and Jane Seymour is strong and endearing, this film is ultimately homage to the power of love itself. *Somewhere in Time* has gained its cult following because it suggests that the power of love is not only strong enough to bring together star crossed lovers but can ultimately defy the laws of the natural universe. The film suggests that the power of the heart is the most powerful and dominant force of the universe.

In the film, Christopher Reeve portrays a successful playwright disturbed by a bizarre encounter with a woman from his past. In the opening moments of the film he is approached by an elderly woman who says repeatedly in a hypnotic tone, "Come back to me." Some years later but still plagued by the event with the mysterious woman, Reeve takes a respite from his burgeoning playwriting career that quickly transforms into an obsessional pursuit of a beautiful woman who lived many decades before the present. The history, aura, and beauty of this mysterious woman are startlingly compelling to Reeve—as if he had known her previously. As the plot unfolds, Reeve learns that this woman in the past is the same woman who inexplicably uttered the compelling words, "Come back to me" several years earlier.

Through his connections with a college professor, Reeve is convinced to travel back in time to meet this woman who has been haunting him. Without sophisticated technology but through the use of will and self hypnosis, Reeve is successful in his time travel efforts and is transported back in time to finally meet the alluring woman, played by Jane Seymour. Reeve slowly and steadily woos the heart of Seymour, an up-and-coming actress of her time. The two begin to cultivate their romance but as their attraction for each other grows in intensity, Reeve is pulled out of history and back into the time of the present. Grieving his loss and experiencing heartache beyond measure, Reeve ultimately dies from sorrow. However, in the closing moments of the film, we see the fated couple reunited in eternity in a heavenly paradise.

The film smacks of schmaltz, kitsch, and is guilty of overly indulgent sentimentality, and for those who do not have a romantic sensibility whatsoever, this film would be a highly difficult viewing. However, the small film has been embraced by incurable romantics the world over as being one of the greatest love stories on celluloid. As mentioned, the film endures not so much because of the chemistry or romance between Reeve and Seymour (although without a convincing romance the film would flounder) but more because the film breathes truth into the timeless clichés that "love will conquer all" and that "love knows no bounds."

Illusions and Realities:

Solaris (Tarkovsky, 1972)

> *Man was created by Nature in order to explore it. As he approaches Truth*
> *he is fated to Knowledge.*
>
> —Anatoli Solonitsyn as Dr. Sartorious

Until Freud and Jung, belief in an unconscious was rather unsubstantiated and was likened more to a state of being rather than an independent entity—*to be* unconscious rather than *the* unconscious. However, both Freud and Jung, developing on the work of their predecessors, came to discover that the unconscious was a creative, dynamic system that, although mostly inaccessible to consciousness, influenced one's personhood. Dreams, autonomic bodily processes, slips of the tongue, spontaneous recall, and hypnosis all appear to be convincing evidence that consciousness does exist side by side with an unconscious mind. As investigation and interest grows in knowing and defining the unconscious mind, the blind men's hands on the proverbial elephant cover vaster territory, giving more weight to the psychoanalytic belief that we are often puppets to forces greater than the boundary of our own ego.

Like *2001: A Space Odyssey*—considered by many to be the Hollywood equivalent to Tarkovsky's science fiction opus—*Solaris*'s meaning is crucially dependent upon what the viewer chooses to see and bring to the film; the interpretation is up to the mind and heart of the perceiver. However, from a psychologically informed point of view, it is difficult not to view the film as an allegorical discovery and confrontation with the collective unconscious.

In the film, a middle-aged psychologist, Kris Kelvin, is sent on a mission to a space station on the planet Solaris in order to investigate bizarre, unexplained phenomena. Kris knows very little about the current exploration on Solaris; however, he has been informed of a mysterious ocean on the planet. Kelvin learns that many have hypothesized that this ocean is a living, intelligent force that relates and responds to the humans investigating it. Kris, being a scientifically trained psychologist, is highly skeptical of such whimsical and far-flung beliefs. His mission is to apply a rational, logical approach to the strangeness on Solaris that is making otherwise sane people mad. Kris arrives on the space station to find the situation in a far more dire and chaotic state than he anticipated. A respected colleague has committed suicide, surviving scientists appear to be on the fringe of lunacy, and the entire station is in a state of dilapidated disrepair. Disturbed but still adhering to his original mission, Kris is shaken by the events around him but not deterred. However, when Kris's former wife appears before him, his new mission is not to appraise the situation on Solaris but to maintain his sanity. While Kris tries to maintain objectivity over the appearance of his wife, emotional trauma from the past begins to subtly invade his consciousness.

Not knowing whether his wife is real, human, an apparition, or projection from his memories, Kris is determined to destroy her. However, the strategy does not work; after an attempt of disposing of his wife, she returns again to haunt Kris, only this time with greater authenticity and humanness. Kris slowly begins to accept what others on the space station have acknowledged—that the Solaris sea is an intelligence which has the power of manifesting memories and events in one's past in physical form. The sea is studying and manipulating humans more so than the scientists who attempted to study it.

In the character of Kris, we see the human quest to attempt to control, explain, and master the unknown, the mysterious, the irrational, and the unconscious. The film suggests that the ocean on Solaris is infinitely more intelligent than the humans studying it and that its power is vaster than reasoning and enlightened consciousness. *Solaris* attempts to render transparent the folly of our current preoccupation to explain away—rather than revere and honor—the mysteries of the unknown forces in life. *Solaris* serves as a warning; the continued obsessional pursuit in rationalizing the irrational puts our humanity in a vicious *cul de sac*, whereby we only fall back on greater mystery and greater unknowns. Through the hubris of the scientists in *Solaris*, the enigmatic ocean which defies logic and analysis appears to teach the scientists that answers in life come more from a point of openness than supreme rational understanding. It is only in a state of unknowing that we can learn the lessons of faith, trust, love, and dependence.

The Last Wave (Weir, 1979)

> *"Who are you? Who are you?"*
>
> —Nandjiwarra Amagula as Charlie

Before interacting with indigenous people of Australia, the concept of "dreamtime" was a collection of quaint, if not clichéd, explanatory myths to director Peter Weir. Upon encountering the dreamtime folklore, Weir stated, "I didn't like anything I read. They always seemed cute in English, or coy. 'The great great bull was in the sky and he hit the wombat on the head and that's how the sun came.' I just didn't like it."[5] However, it wasn't until engaging aborigines in dialogue that Weir realized that the dreamtime wasn't simply a set of primitive fairytales but an actual way of perceiving the world; the dreamtime was a way of being and inhabiting life. Weir discovered that aborigines were able to access what to Western societies would be an altered state of consciousness, a quasi *participation mystique* that allowed them to see beyond the structures of linear time and discrete events. This perception of dreamtime gripped Weir and led to the genesis of *The Last Wave*, a haunting and eerie exploration of the power of the interior, subjective world.

In *The Last Wave*, we find a young Sydney lawyer (David, played by Richard Chamberlain) embroiled in a murder case involving five aboriginals. Haunted by a series of strikingly prophetic dreams and visions surrounding the case, David is obsessed in uncovering the truth of the murder. Spurred on by a hunt for justice as well as his recurring foresights into the future, David's preoccupation with the murder trial leads him deeper into the mysteries and sacred knowledge of tribal wisdom of the aboriginals. In his quest for truth, David learns that his plaguing visions are the result of contacting the dreamtime, a parallel stream of time that, although not as solid and material as the waking time we inhabit, is actually more real and foundational to reality.

The Last Wave articulates two of Peter Weir's recurrent themes: alienation and the interplay between the mysterious, invisible realm and its relationship with the mundane world. As in *Witness, Green Card,* and *The Truman Show, The Last Wave's* protagonist is a stranger in a strange land. Chamberlain's David is a South American-born man who must adapt to both colonized Australia and Aboriginal Australia—but never being totally integrated into either culture. On a deeper level, David is alien to his own world and the world outside of him. Living in the rational, scientific consciousness of his day, David's immediate environment is secure, easily explainable, routine, and predictable. Although the conventions of his culture give him a sense of mastery and sanctuary, his comfort comes at the expense of a deeper engagement with the world and himself—he becomes alien to the environment around him. As the mysteries of the aboriginal culture and the prophecies enter into David's life, he is equally terrified and energized. His journey is one where he forsakes security and comfort for a greater knowledge of himself and his world.

With a prominent Saturn square Neptune alignment in his chart, it is no surprise that one of Weir's greatest thematic preoccupations has been the interface of the concrete, conventional world—the world that Saturn symbolizes—and the mysterious, religious world of dreams, fantasy, symbols and the imagination—the world of Neptune. This theme gets its most explicit treatment in

Weir's *Picnic at Hanging Rock* and *The Last Wave*, viewed by many critics and fans as a pairing rather than two separate films. However, we see this fixation between these two worlds in all of Weir's films, from the recollection of a superior world in *The Truman Show* to the moody atmospheres and haunting score that carry the very earthly world of military combat in *Master and Commander: The Far Side of the World.*

The Last Wave is one of the great cinematic explorations of what occurs when the collective unconscious (or its corollaries of dreamtime and other ancient descriptions for the invisible world) breaks through into ordinary awareness and disrupts our security and what we know as truth. Films like *Vanilla Sky* and *Don't Look Now* have also explored this territory, but none have succeeded in creating the incredible breakdown between illusion and reality like *The Last Wave.*

Beyond being exceptionally surreal, *The Last Wave* is also an incredible artistic exploration of what occurs during the Neptune square Neptune transit at midlife. The Neptune square Neptune transit is one of a set of midlife transits that occur to change, rejuvenate and breakdown patterns and structures in our lives. As for David, this midlife transition is as confusing as it is exhilarating. For those who value control, efficiency, direction, and security (linear, left brain concepts), this time can be extremely troubling as confusion, ambiguity, and mystery subtly invade our lives. However, for those who cherish inspiration, spirituality, and deeper meaning, this Neptune transit—this breakthrough of the collective unconscious into ordinary awareness—can be extraordinarily cleansing and rejuvenating. *The Last Wave*'s David enters so fully into Neptune's terrain of mystery, symbolism, and sacredness that, depending on your interpretation of the film, his identity becomes completely subsumed by the realm. And such is the power, mystery, and terror of the invisible beyond.

◆   ◆   ◆

Arguably more than any other phenomenon in today's culture, movies help us appreciate and integrate the functions of the astrological Neptune into our lives. Images and symbols have always been used to convey and connote ideas and feelings that are not easily communicated by literal and analytical means. Neptune suggests that the subtler and more refined the expression or feeling, the more nuanced and sensitive need be the medium. As a neutral mode of expression, film is capable of expressing the most depraved, superficial, and base aspects of being human as it is able to articulate the most transcendent and sublime.

The above films capture and convey elements of the archetypal Neptune in an extraordinarily powerful way. Films like *Fisher King* and *Kundun* articulate the surprisingly profound urge toward spiritual redemption that motivates and moves individuals and cultures at particular points in time. The images in films like *Days of Heaven* and *Baraka* connote the exquisite beauty inherent within moving images. The ability of love, grace, and sacrifice to move us to extraordinary ends is explored in films such as *Somewhere in Time* and *Life is Beautiful*. Finally, *Solaris* and *The Last Wave* humble us by urging us to remember that much of the certainty of our lives is constructed over a vast and unknowable mystery.

All birth times from the Internet Movie Database

Terrence Malick: November 30th, 1943, Waco, Texas.
Peter Weir: August 21st, 1944, Sydney, Australia.

1. Stephen Arroyo, *Astrology, Karma, and Transformation* (Sebastapol, CA: CRCS publications, 1978) 43.

2. Charles Harvey, *Anima Mundi: The Astrology of the Individual and the Collective* (London: Centre for Psychological Astrology Press, 2002) 98.

3. Victor Frankl, *Man's Search for Meaning* (Simon and Schuster: New York, 1963) 164.

4. Ibid, 57.

5. http://www.peterweircave.com/articles/articlei.html

The Pluto Film

Like the hero's journey and the trickster figure, the theme of the Underworld is a timeless motif found in myths of many cultures. Although the Underworld may immediately evoke fear and dread, its purpose and associations in myth are beyond simply inducing apprehension and fear. For heroes on their path, the Underworld may be a place that forces them to negotiate and surrender to their vulnerabilities and frailties. For the young maiden, the Underworld is the territory where innocence is torn down and exchanged for experience and maturity. For the Shaman, the Underworld is a trading room, where sacrifices are bartered for knowledge and power.

The Underworld is as much a territory as it is a psychological state of mind. We may only have to venture as far as the intimacies of the bedroom or the psychotherapist's office to enter into the Underworld. Whatever the case may be, at certain points along our journey—just as immortals of myth have done—we must venture into the depths of this murky place. As its name implies, the Underworld is not well illumined. As a place of shadows and darkness, the Underworld may render typical maps and navigational tools useless. Instead, when journeying through this land below, we may have to rely upon tools that are not normally used in the light of day—long dormant feelings, repressed memories, ancient and primitive instincts, and intuition.

In astrology, Pluto symbolizes the Underworld. Pluto in the birth chart may represent an area of obsession, pain, power (and powerlessness), depth, or woundedness. Like the mythological Underworld, the astrological Pluto is complex and shadowy, and thus what Pluto truly signifies for an individual may rest in the dark for quite some time. Arguably the foundation of Pluto for any individual is that it is a symbol of profound transformation. Like for the heroes, maidens, and shamans of myth, a journey into the Underworld—or a voyage into the ramifications of the astrological Pluto—is transformational and life-changing.

Since Pluto defies rational conception and contorts logical analysis, astrologers and astrological researchers have presumably laughed at the prospect of placing Pluto into the standard "cookbook" format dictated by the "metaphysics-to-go" marketing of astrology. Navigating the Pluto landscape through the written word is like taking a standard compass into an M.C. Escher painting. However, the difficulty for an astrological researcher to clearly explicate this archetype pales in comparison to the often painful experience of a difficult Pluto transit. The one common denominator is that there is a degree of powerlessness that forces one to surrender to something greater than one's self.

To begin to illuminate the paradoxical nature of Pluto, a good starting point is to delineate the events that correlate with Pluto's discovery in 1930. Astrologers have noted that the discovery of a planet correlates with events and phenomena that are indicative of the quality of the associated archetype. Pluto is no exception. Around 1930, there were a number of events that broke down and deconstructed firmly entrenched paradigms, structures, and institutions that once gave a certain degree of security and exaltation to human life—by and large the results of the inflation and hubris of enlightenment, rational thinking.

In 1931, the mathematician Kurt Gödel released his famous theorem. Gödel demonstrated that there can always be the creation of statements produced in a logical or mathematical system that cannot be proven true or false, thus a system will always be incomplete in its explanatory and deductive power. Gödel's theorem undermined the hope and assumption that some final system of "everything" could be achieved. More importantly, it can be deduced from Gödel that rational thinking can never penetrate to a final, ultimate truth.

It can also be assumed from Gödel's theorem that reality is akin to a net of interwoven paradoxes, a latticework of opposites. Moreover, we can also ascertain from Gödel that using any system of knowledge to the exclusion of others—using any epistemology in isolation—as a way to discover truth will inevitably collapse upon itself. The laser sharp tool of rational thought was assumed to be the sole apparatus for discovering the truth of things. Gödel proved otherwise. As the parsimonious razor of the scientific method penetrated deeper into the bowels of reality, it treated the waste products of its search as superfluous elements of the system. Analogical thinking, intuition, felt sense, subjective experience, spirit, and soul were all discarded and could not be seen as "babies" being thrown out with the proverbial bathwater.

A similar deconstruction of certainty occurred in quantum mechanics. In 1927 and 1928, just years before Pluto's discovery, the pioneering efforts of the scientists exploring quantum physics reached its zenith (or more appropriately its deepest archeological nadir) with the synthesis of Heisenberg's Uncertainty Principle, Bohr's notion of complementarity, and Schrodinger's wave function, all comprising the Copenhagen Interpretation of quantum mechanics. This same group of eminent scientists stated with assurance that there is no deep reality, that the world of our senses rests on an undefined "something" which is radically divergent from the constitution of the tangible world.

As the world of exterior reality was plumbed to its depths around Pluto's discovery, so too would depth psychologists working at this time excavate the deepest levels of inner space. The psychological idiom that "we are not the master in our own house"—that the ego lay atop a vast unconscious which contained our highest and lowest potentials—was gaining theoretical support by the pioneering efforts of Freud, Jung, and other researchers of early depth psychologies. Equally as important, psychotherapy itself would dramatically rise in popularity in Europe, and, in particular, the United States. The taboo restrictions against this "cure for the Age of Anxiety" would loosen in the more cosmopolitan and intellectual circles of the United States, and the number of analysts and patients rose considerably.

The synchronous events correlating with the discovery of Pluto were not restricted to the musings of affluent *intelligentsias* but had repercussions that affected all levels of society. The U.S. stock market crash of 1929 and the subsequent economic depression were of a severity that could not have been predicted by logical analysis alone; very few economic indicators prior to the crash pointed to an economic catastrophe of this degree. The *laissez-faire* approach to economic theory and policy had been severely challenged by the Great Depression, and classical models that suggested that economies were self-correcting did not correlate with the reality of the situation.

Something was dislodged, decentered, and destabilized around 1930. Like the earth being relegated to a peripheral location within the solar system after the Copernican Revolution, humans would soon be thrown from a safe, secure, and limited universe into a new situation in which the rational mind, financial security, material reality, and the ego's predominance over the psyche were overthrown, threatened, and made subservient to something greater than these products of the Enlightenment. The bottom dropped out, as it were, and the world needed to replenish itself to once again establish the truth of the deep mystery of things that no structure could easily confine.

The archetype of Pluto teaches us that the known world stands in relation to a hidden, unknown world which threatens to destroy our security at any time. What could be used to manipulate, control, repress, and dominate could ultimately turn against us and destroy foundations without much predictability or control. What could be used to inflate the ego's supremacy could ultimately destroy it. The engine used to fuel economic progress could also destroy unimpeded growth without warning. And finally, the noble efforts to find an ultimate truth through a limited epistemology could destroy its own efforts. Another message of the archetype of Pluto is that an opposing force is always contained within—and not merely without—any given thing. Inherent within power and dominance is vulnerability and submission. Inherent within the gift of life is the proposition of death. Pluto is the source of pathology as it is the source of healing. Any act of creation is the destruction of something that existed before it. Inherent within order is chaos.

Pluto is the archetype of the transformative, evolutionary force that governs the conversion of one thing into its opposite. It is the eruptive, volcanic force that unleashes pent up potential energy in the process of nuclear fission, unleashing mass destruction from a tiny subatomic particle. It is the struggle of the embryo, child, or adult that tries to remain comfortable at a point of security and confidence but who is uncontrollably and simultaneously thrown into a new evolutionary situation with new rewards, risks, and challenges. Pluto suggests the existential tragedy and suffering of life but also connotes a life-affirming, unimpeded fecundity. Pluto is the power of rejuvenating life force known variously by the world's religions and sciences as kundalini, shakti, wakonda, and libido. It is the death-rebirth points of the unfathomably long journey of *metempsychosis*: the stages of reincarnation of a soul through many lifetimes. Pluto is the dance of the destroyer god, Kali; the descent and resurrection of Persephone, Jesus Christ, Innana, and Isis; the Apocalyptic visions of the world's religions and belief systems: the Christian Bible's Book of Revelation, Norse Mythology's Ragnarok, the Hopi prophecy of the emergence of the Fifth World, and modern physics' assertion of entropy and heat death of the universe.

The principle of Saturn represents death by acts of negation and finalization in which outworn behaviors, attitudes, and lifestyles are frustrated out of one's life by the reality principle. With Saturn, something ends irrevocably and cycles are culminated and completed. Pluto's energies are a death of different sort. As Saturn represents an external authority or internal disposition that hardens, solidifies, and consolidates against life—a boundarying between self and other—Pluto is the powerful and elemental life force that purges, intensifies, and metamorphosizes a current form into something else. The enormity of power behind this type of energy can feel like a threat or death to the structure in place, particularly during the beginning stages of a Pluto transit. A fully developed fetus being expunged from the safe and secure womb, a moth enveloped by a chrysalis, and a snake molting its skin all capture processes associated with Pluto. Presumably these original forms have no idea what sort of initiation is about to take place as mysterious changes happen in the environment surrounding them.

Pluto is antagonistic to fixation. If we want to remain fixed in a state of arrested development, Pluto will carry us out of our fixed points kicking and screaming. Most importantly, Pluto creates soul. As James Hillman writes, "soul refers to the *deepening* of events into experiences; second, the significance soul makes possible, whether in love or in religious concern, derives from its special *relation with death*"[1] (emphasis his). Survival issues, powerlessness, anger, resentment, and betrayal can all come to the forefront of consciousness, when a fragile ego can't really do anything effective against a very powerful Pluto transit, particularly if something is outworn and ineffective and needs to be annihilated and eliminated. Thus, Pluto is evolutionary, radically so. When Pluto transits an important part of the natal chart, it can feel like a lifetime of experience is compacted into a period of two to three years. The holy fire of purification symbolized by a Pluto transit actually assists in removing blocks toward self-realization. Another paradox of Pluto is that this facilitation of one's evolution is seen as threatening, terrifying, and painful. Only in hindsight are we welcoming of the rejuvenating changes.

As astrology is a knowledge of lived experience, the Pluto phenomenon cannot be known by words, images, or symbols alone, as these are merely connotative of the archetypal qualities of Pluto. Rather, thick in the throes of a powerful Pluto transit, one can feel quite crazy, terrified, enlivened, and exhilarated all at once. For those whom control, precision, and security are number one priorities, the phenomenological burning of a Pluto transit is painful, unjust, and aberrant. For those who desire life's fullest expressions and welcome a time of purification, cleansing, healing, and rebirth, Pluto transits are what life is worth living for.

Film, like no other medium, can instantly transport us into different experiential dimensions. By combining images, sound, action, and narrative all in one art form, film can draw us out of ourselves and place us into a new context, time, and place. More than words or images in isolation, film can capture the significance of an astrological archetype. As Carl Jung stressed, an archetype cannot be known in itself but can only be hinted at or alluded to by words and symbols. However, if any medium has an open conduit into archetypal forces, it is film.

Films that carry Pluto are unmistakable for their powerful and transformative viewing experience. Like the ground of material reality that dropped out for quantum physicists, a "Pluto film" has the effect of dropping everything out of existence except one's complete rapt attention on the images being projected on screen. One's worries fade away, time and space melt away, and major tensions and strains that arise while watching the movie can only fully be expelled during the rolling of the final credits. Like a major Pluto transit itself, a Pluto film has the effect of draining and exhausting the viewer. More than simply a movie, a Pluto film is an experience—a long and winding journey, an encounter with a deep, profound, and often dark terrain that leaves an indelible mark upon one's psyche.

The following films, listed in no particular order, are exemplary for the phenomenological experience of the Pluto archetype. These films do not necessarily deal with explicit Pluto themes *per se*—betrayal, transformation, rage, passion, hidden power struggles, manipulations—however their ability to allow us to access and feel the transformative, powerful, and eruptive force of Pluto are unparalleled. As Pluto is often outside the bounds of convention, these films are far from the typical Hollywood narrative film and cannot be recommended for all viewers. Graphic, frank, explicit, and often violent, these films do not skirt, but often revel, in taboo subject matter that is usually out-of-bounds for most productions.

Last Tango in Paris (Bertolucci, 1972)

"Beauty of mine, sit before me. Let me peruse you and remember you...always like this."

—Marlon Brando as Paul

The shock of this movie had relatively little to do with sex. The barrier for sexuality on screen had been broken several years earlier for feature films after the Hayes Code had been lifted in the 1960s. The upset and controversy over the film concerned more the raw, honest, and utterly realistic portrayal of human sexuality than any merely gratuitous exposure of flesh or exploitative sex scenes. It wasn't so much the nudity that was upsetting and offensive but more the exposure of the vulnerability of the human condition that met with intolerance.

To carry the film, Bertolucci chose Marlon Brando to play a fortysomething American suffering from the anguish and loneliness of the recent suicide of his wife. Brando, an actor with both the Sun and Moon square Pluto at birth, was the actor of his generation to single-handedly break the mold of stilted and affected acting by bringing an authenticity, rawness, and brooding—all Pluto traits—to both stage and screen. With *Last Tango in Paris*, Brando brings these qualities to heights never since surpassed.

Brando's character is a case study of Pluto's extremes and paradoxes. He is at one turn secretive, manipulative, guarded and not forthcoming while simultaneously irrepressibly authentic, honest, and wildly uninhibited. He despises societal convention yet appreciative of its protective veil. He is bruised, wounded and hurt yet finds the strength to abuse, punish, and control others. And finally, he is compulsively ruled by sexuality—the fear of it, the obsessive need to engage in it, the possession of orgiastic release.

And finally, in a monologue addressing the loneliness of the human condition, Brando suggests the key to ultimately overcoming this condition is not withdrawal, repression, or any other defense but simply a courageous entrance into the condition itself. He states: "You are alone until you stare death right in the face"—the key to loneliness and arguably all Pluto problems.

Dead Man (Jarmusch, 1995)

"Some are born to sweet delight; some are born to endless night."

—Gary Farmer as "Nobody"

This metaphysical Western works on so many levels simultaneously to weave what many critics believe to be one of the best independent films of the 1990s. Director Jim Jarmusch, experiencing the generational Pluto square Pluto transit during the creation of *Dead Man*, may have isolated fans of his previous work, but this singular film is certainly his most profound and penetrating portrait to date. *Dead Man* is at one turn a transcendent, allegorical poem concerning the cruel journey we all take toward death while also being a postmodern tome, full of dry irony, unsettling juxtapositions between character and place, and an essentialist myth without the trappings of metanarrative. *Dead Man's* Western frontier is a wasteland where the center cannot hold. However, as odd, idiosyncratic, and acerbic this motion picture is at times, *Dead Man* is able to penetrate to a deep level of understanding that speaks to the human heart.

With the recent death of his parents, Cleveland accountant William Blake, played by Johnny Depp, chooses a new life with opportunity he finds in the Old West. However, as soon as Depp's William Blake enters into a desolate frontier town, he submits to the death of his old self. William Blake is manipulated, cheated, and abused by a web of fated circumstance, at every turn caught in double binds, deceit, and corruption where no solutions work to his advantage.

From the limited perspective of the ego, the liar's paradox and betrayal that Blake finds himself enmeshed within is unjust, cruel, and immoral. However, from the broader perspective of spiritual allegory and mysticism, William Blake's deeper self *is* his experience. He is not just his skin-encapsulated ego. He is both the naïve and unassuming Midwesterner undergoing a transformation of personality, and the cast of characters—from the knowledgeable Native American guide, "Nobody," to the band of journeymen bounty hunters—assisting the metamorphosis. This transformation is cruel from the limited egoic perspective, but, from the perspective of Depp's deeper self, it is merely a falling away, a stripping down, and metabolizing of that which no longer serves a purpose.

It is this transformational journey to authentic selfhood and the final death-rebirth that is a brilliant portrait of the power of Pluto at work. The entire film is a slow journey through purgatory where the definitions between death and life remain ambiguous and where it is hard to discern just when and where Depp's Blake "dies" and where he is "reborn." Death is not presented as a fixed point in time in the narrative but as a process of simultaneous decay and renewal. The film's director, Jim Jarmusch states, "William Blake said himself when he was near death that death was really just getting up and going into another room. So the film as death goes is an extension of life or a part of life—that's the basic idea behind death in the film."[3]

Viewed from the lens of a transformative and powerful Pluto transit, *Dead Man* might be unparalleled in its ability to evoke the "Pluto" experience of the soul's deepening into the processes of life through death to a previous identity. Every character and subtle detail of this film acts like a hospice worker assisting William Blake to his final return to the world of Spirit. Neil Young's raw and piercing guitar motif, Christian Glover's inimitably bizarre psychopomp, Gary Farmer's trickster "Nobody," the amoral ragtag pack of paid-for-hire killers, and, most importantly, the haunting setting of a nameless forest transitioning from fall to winter all guide—sometimes nurturingly, sometimes mercilessly—Depp's Blake through a purgatory of rebirth.

Apocalypse Now (Coppola, 1979)

> "The Horror. The Horror."
>
> —Marlon Brando as Colonel Kurtz

When a powerful archetype is active it tends to act like a black hole. Archetypes have a force that places an inescapable pull on people, events, and places, and a clustering occurs around a similar motif or pattern. In this case, Pluto was the magnet that drew similar themes to the making of *Apocalypse Now*. During the now legendary filming and subsequent release, director Francis Ford Coppola was experiencing a Pluto opposition to his natal Sun. Similarly, the real life experiential material and original serialization of Joseph Conrad's *Heart of Darkness*, the story that provided the inspiration for *Apocalypse Now*, also occurred under a once-in-a-lifetime Pluto opposition of the Sun (and in this case, fittingly, Pluto opposite Mercury as well). Although not the first choice for their roles, Marlon Brando and Martin Sheen, the two male leads for the movie, have not only their natal Sun, but natal Moon in aspect to Pluto. (Martin Sheen with a Moon-Sun-Pluto triple conjunction and Marlon Brando with both the Sun and Moon in square aspect to Pluto.[4] And finally, Jim Morrison, the singer-songwriter of the movie's musical lamentation, "The End"—full of snakes, death, and oedipal fantasy—also had his Sun and Moon in aspect to Pluto.

Like *Dead Man*, *Apocalypse Now* is a journey. Under the pretense of a hero's quest, US Army Captain Willard (Sheen) is called upon to exterminate one Colonel Kurtz (Brando), who, according to military high command, reached and subsequently broke through his own sanity to organize his own splinter army in Cambodia. True to form of Joseph Campbell's conceptualization of the hero's journey, Sheen's Willard is swallowed by the "Belly of the Whale." As Campbell writes, "The hero…is swallowed into the unknown, and would appear to have died."[5]

Willard is uncontrollably consumed by the chaos of the Viet Nam War. The vast majority of the movie is spent as a negotiation of the rational, orderly, and controlled—as represented by a small PT boat cruising the Nung River—in relationship with the taboo, frenzied, irrational, destructive, and rejuvenating elements of nature and mankind, represented by all elements outside of the boat: the hidden snipers, the playboy bunnies, war, the crazed airborne division, Kurtz's army, and the jungle itself. It is outside of the boat where the division between sane and insane, leader and follower, and destruction and replenishment are blurred and ambiguous. Even with the filming itself, the division between entertainment-making and unbridled, threatening chaos became blurred. Of the filming Coppola stated, "There were times when I thought I was going to die, literally, from the inability to move the problems I had. I would go to bed at four in the morning in a cold sweat."[6]

If the jungle is to represent man's own unconscious, then in *Apocalypse Now* it is seen as the ultimate *Mysterium Tremendum*, a force so powerful and destructive that annihilation is seen as the only option available from the point of detached observation. And yet the pull and persuasion remains. Even if rationally—logically—going full into the unconscious is insane, there is a near-compulsive allure of this terrain. Speaking to the most destructive potentials of the human phenomenon—war—the film's screenwriter, John Milius writes, "War is unspeakably attractive. People enjoy intensity. The human animal seems to be drawn to it like a moth to a flame."[7]

Apocalypse Now is a draining, exhausting, intense, and compelling viewing. The film is utterly original and unlike anything that Coppola attempted before or after. There are other war films that equal *Apocalypse Now*'s masterful performances and riveting storyline; however, arguably no war film has been so evocative of the horrors, intensity, and madness of war. Coppola's look into war is unapologetic and without remorse; *Apocalypse Now* simply renders a horrific, but very real part, of the human shadow.

El Topo (Jodorowsky, 1970)

"El Topo is a great film to the viewers who are great."

—filmmaker Alejandro Jodowrosky

Alejandro Jodorowsky, born in the year of Pluto's discovery,[8] stated, "even a flower opening is violent." He is a man who sees the world constantly creating, destroying, regurgitating, and metabolizing itself while others simply see stasis. And because of this, many think that he is legitimately insane.

Pauline Kael called this film "a masterpiece." John Lennon referred to it as "the most powerful film I've ever seen." At the time of its release, the Los Angeles Free Press called it "the greatest film ever made."[9] However, as the millennium turned and many film institutes and critics turned a reflective eye on the past one hundred years, *El Topo* was nowhere to be found—a forgotten curiosity relegated to the psychedelic dustheap of the countercultural peak of the late 1960s. It is difficult to pinpoint a singular origin of the current critical dismissal and unawareness of *El Topo,* but it is rather an interrelationship of the following factors: one, the pendulum dictating the movement of cultural and socio-political zeitgeist has swung so far away from the singular countercultural ethos to render *El Topo's* message and unique film style nonsensical, unevocative, and unintelligible; two, the film is so lopsided in a spontaneous Dionysian and erotic upheaval of the collective Id that critical appraisal had to act as a necessary repressive and authoritarian counterbalance to the film; and, three, the simple inaccessibility of the film.

The film simply cannot be viewed in a traditional sense. Like a Zen teacher whacking its student to achieve a state of satori, the repetition of violence, surrealistic symbolism, and the smorgasbord of religious and occult iconography is meant to subvert waking, conditioned consciousness and speak directly to a seed deeply buried in the collective unconscious that contains the message, "the evolution of spirit in and through the human phenomenon is a painful, eternal recurrence of death and rebirth ultimately leading to redemption." Thus, the film is a brutal, exasperating immolation of the human phenomenon, a Nietzschean-Zarathustrian effigy in which the ubermensch-as-protagonist continually overcomes himself to reach a state of salvation.

El Topo is the hallucinogenic trip of a narcissistic, one-sided anti-hero infused and inflated by the life-affirming energies of the collective unconscious. Through a series of confrontations in which the hubris of his own ego is painfully and ruthlessly exorcised and annihilated from consciousness, Jodorowsky's El Topo evolves from a misogynistic and arrogant outsider to a saintly wise fool, a bodhisattva ensnared in a web of suffering, innocently learning to see himself in others and using his gifts and talents for all.

Besides being incredibly evocative of the "Plutonic imagery," with its carrion birds, carnal suffering, desolate desert beauty, unbridled fecundity, and deep eros, *El Topo*'s allegorical message is essentially about the right use of Plutonic power. Astrologer Robert Couteau has identified the wrong application of Pluto's energies as "the attempt to transform another person against his or her will."[10] Jodorowsky's El Topo evolves from a desirous, lecherous gunslinger dominating others to prove the efficacy of his own will to a humble martyr who helps liberate a group of deformed and downtrodden outsiders. Hence, through a powerful sequence of painful death-rebirths at the beginning of the film, Jodorowsky learns to reapply the power of his will from "power over" to "power with."

The Last Temptation of Christ (Scorsese, 1988)

"What's good for man isn't good for God!"

—Harvey Keitel as Judas

As astrologers have noted, Uranus-Neptune conjunctions (roughly a one hundred and eighty year cycle) are known for the re-awakening of the spiritual impulse, a necessary revolution of the universal thirst for transcendence, and a re-evaluation of the societal structures that help facilitate the mediation between the secular and the sacred. *The Last Temptation of Christ,* created at the beginning of the most recent Uranus-Neptune conjunction, was a controversial and brilliant reappraisal of the Christ myth.

The film was damned by almost every Christian denomination, was protested, picketed, subject to boycotts and bomb threats, and barred from Blockbuster Video.[11] The overt reason for the controversy was said to be over Jesus' fantasy concerning sexual relationship with Mary Magdalene; however, the deeper reality was the threat to Christianity of becoming democratized by this film, with the spiritual struggle of Jesus being presented as the courageous turmoil of everyone's soul. The film presented an alternative to a singular coming of the messiah, and instead laid claim to a more humanized spirituality: Christ Consciousness versus *The* Christ, redemption versus transgression, and, to paraphrase one reviewer's reflection, Christ as All God and all man versus half Man and half Deity.

Scorsese, whose intensity as a personality and director is mirrored by his four planets in Scorpio, directed *The Last Temptation of Christ* while undergoing the generational Pluto square Pluto transit. Known for its seriousness, reflection, and brutally honest self-assessment, the Pluto-square-Pluto transit—the "come to Jesus" transit, in so many ways—led to Scorsese's most personal and meditative film. As reviewer Jaimie N. Christley stated, "*The Last Temptation of Christ* is without a doubt Scorsese's least entertaining film—*Kundun* and *The Age of Innocence* are unmitigated laugh-fests in comparison." [12] Although lacking in entertainment value, the film makes up for it in spiritual depth and will certainly be heralded as one of Scorsese's finest directorial efforts. Transiting Pluto squared musician Peter Gabriel's natal Pluto and Venus during the composition of the film's aptly named, *Passion*. Unlike the progressive rock the Aquarian Gabriel had been known for as solo artist and with Genesis, *Passion*'s world-fusion was thoroughly exotic, seductive, and subterranean—a brilliant juxtaposition to the themes explored in the film.

Christ in this vehicle is paradoxically presented as whole through his fractured being. Unlike the Christian Christ who arrives as almost completely devoid of shadow, wrongdoing, and sexuality, *Last Temptation*'s Christ realizes his divinity through an intense struggle for reconciliation between the opposing forces of his nature. Hence *Last Temptation*'s Christ is more comparable to C.G. Jung's Job than the Christ of the exoteric Gospels. It is the internal struggle of *Last Temptation*'s Christ that is a thoroughly Plutonic one, in which evil, baseness, licentiousness, and manipulation exist as *a priori* dominants of the personality begging for transformation through the living of life.

Belly of an Architect (Greenaway, 1987)

Obsession. Betrayal. Downfall.

—Promotional Tagline

Belly of an Architect is not a great film. Outside of Brian Dennehy's command performance, the acting is sub par and dwarfed by Greenaway's attention to sets and location, the plot is muddled, character development is lacking on the whole, and the narrative is loose-ended and bereft of dramatic tension. However, given this film's failings and flaws, this is *the* case study of the effects of a powerful Pluto transit.

Set in the decadence and decay of present-day Rome, the city acts as an ominous parallel for the fate of one Stourley Kracklite (Dennehy), a powerful architect at the pinnacle of his career whose life is soon to emulate the fall of the ancient city. Dennehy's Kracklite is thoroughly Plutonian. Possessing a ravenous appetite for the sensual pleasures of life, Kracklite appears never to be satiated by enough recognition, success, wine and women. As Pluto also symbolizes the powerful and destructive conversion of opposites, the same devouring lust for life with which Kracklite approaches everything begins to turn on him in midlife.

Mostly unconscious that his hedonistic lifestyle and success are not fulfilling, Kracklite becomes obsessed with the notion that he has stomach cancer. It is arguable that Kracklite somatizes his situation as a defense against looking at the true source of his existential pain. As a Pluto transit demands the highest degree of honest self-assessment and moral courage, Kracklite is unable to face the true source of his hurting, and his world crumbles before him. In the midst of his greatest architectural project, his personal and professional life is deconstructed.

Scared of the vulnerability that emerges within him, Kracklite begins to resort to very human responses to alleviate the anxiety: manipulation, denial, abuse, power plays, and rage. In the end, the disembowelment of his soul and life leaves him with nothing except the necessity and opportunity to rebuild his life more consistent with his real needs and desires.

Greenaway, like many of the directors on this list, was experiencing his generational Pluto square Pluto transit while directing *Belly of an Architect.* Composer Wim Mertens's passionate and relentless minimalism, the film's epicurean feasts, and saturated blood-red sets and costumes suggest the overindulgence, passion, and purgatorial swelling of Pluto. Certainly, this film is a must for all undergoing powerful Pluto transits to personal planets.

Blue Velvet (Lynch, 1986)

> "I'm seeing something that was always hidden. I'm in the middle of a mystery and it's all secret."

> —Kyle Maclachan as Jeffrey Beaumont

When an Aquarian ventures into the realm of Pluto, the results tend to be explosive and strikingly original. There is a degree of comfort with the chthonic, erotic, and serpentine realm that Scorpio and Pluto-Sun directors seem to exhibit. Scorsese's Scorpionic intensity is a natural fit with the jealous, hidden, erotic, and transformative themes of Pluto in films like *Raging Bull, Taxi Driver,* and the aforementioned *The Last Temptation of Christ.* However, asking a usually detached, ironic, and disembodied Aquarian to enter the Pluto landscape can lead to a remarkable and arrestingly unique experience, or a struggle with no interesting synthesis. *Blue Velvet*, created when transiting Pluto vacillated in a t-square between Lynch's Aquarian Sun and natal Pluto, falls in the former category. The Aquarian transcendental blue flame of pure consciousness meeting the intense heat of the Plutonic fire made for one of the most inimitable films of the twentieth century.

The Aquarian stamp is all over the aesthetic choices of *Blue Velvet*: the mocking of American kitsch; ironic, jarring juxtapositions; unsettling behavioral choices given circumstance; disquieting, neurotic characters; postmodern mix-and-match. However, the movie is through and through about the Plutonian realm and the Apollonian spotlight that Lynch throws on the dark world gives tremendous insight into America's underbelly. Although the Plutonic realm of abuse and moral degradation in *Blue Velvet* is so perverted and so rarefied that it loses its human quality—from Dennis Hopper's over-the-top intonations to Dean Stockwell's freakish lip-syncing—it still has a power to transform and compel the viewer.

Lifting the sanitized cover off of a lily-white, homogenized America, Lynch exposes a seething underbelly and the worst potentials of the Plutonic archetype: sadomasochistic abuse, murder, and unredeemable aggression. More importantly, given that there is no proper outlet for the destructive and violent aspects of Pluto in the fictional town of Lumberton, it is secretly passed down vertically generation-to-generation and horizontally between members of the community in the form of abuse.

It is assumed by the viewer that the obsessional craving of Frank Booth—portrayed by Dennis Hopper—for ritualized sadomasochism is a very primitive method of expunging abuse that he incurred as a child. Unfortunately, as Booth fails to transform the rage, grief, and loss he feels, he transfers the unprocessed base feelings onto reluctant victims and martyrs. The process continues as Hopper's victim, Isabella Rossellini, models the behavior she sees as she dominates submissive Kyle Maclachlan. Hence, the Plutonic shadow side of the community is tossed about like a medicine ball between characters of the film, never being fully transformed, only transferred.

American Pop (Bakshi, 1981)

> *The heartache is that you could've been a star.*
>
> —Frank Dekova as "Crisco"

Ralph Bakshi is justifiably called the "anti-Disney." Possessing a natal Sun square Pluto and three personal planets in Scorpio, Disney's world of cuddly, cute creatures and made-for-children enchanted fairy tales is not his. Rather, Bakshi has felt more at home in the urban jungle where the taboo underbelly and harsh and grim realities of life can be exposed for what they are.

American Pop is a sweeping animated epic that, as the title implies, covers evolving musical styles in the United States. Through following four generations of fathers and sons of an emigrated Russo-Jewish family, Bakshi weaves together a vivid, electrifying, and powerful re-creation of the history of popular music of the previous century.

The continual evolution of the spirit of the times is foregrounded in *American Pop*, and character development and plot details are obscured and vague. Assuming that the de-emphasis on character and narrative was purposeful, Bakshi and writer Ronnie Kern infuse the movie with a mythic sensibility and intelligence. In *American Pop*, the evolution of American music becomes not the tale of discrete individuals entirely responsible for their contributions to a particular genre; rather, the sweeping scope, rapid pacing, and surreal nature of the animation brings to light the archetypal quest of any individual's desire to manifest unbounded creativity, genius, and brilliance.

Through this perspective, we see that Bakshi views the creative life as the devil's bargain, a Faustian dilemma. The price for inspired, transcendent creativity—for stealing artistic fire from the heavens—Bakshi implies, is a great one. Inextricably bound in tapping pioneering and inspired genius is decay, self-destruction, and death. Those who storm heaven are banished to hell. This appears to be a fact of life for Bakshi, and, staying true to the lives of many of the creative musical geniuses of the previous century, seems not just the province of fiction or animated films. In astrological terms, we can view this as the tense but fated interrelationship between Uranus and Pluto. The brilliance, stimulation, and excitement over creation and innovation affiliated with the archetype of Uranus are bound to the death-rebirth renewal process correlated with Pluto. In other words, creating awe-inspiring novel forms, in this case in music, demands that natural seasons of death and rebirth must occur.

Bakshi's perspective of the creative life, presumably coming from his own lived experience, is a realistic one. Although the risks are far too great, the sacrifices dire, and the lifestyle—from a rational, clinical perspective—perhaps pathological, the irrational compulsion to pursue one's muse persists, if not dominates, the creative psyche. The brilliance of *American Pop* is that it illuminates the intuition that transpersonal forces dictate the show of life and that humans are somehow subordinate to these gods and goddesses. *American Pop* is a flawed film, but one that reveals timeless truths and illuminates a deeper reality of nature.

◆   ◆   ◆

Besides giving an important phenomenological experience, or "feel," of the Pluto archetype, the above films show a number of different ways to manage and handle Pluto. Scorsese's Christ, Jodoworsky's El Topo, and to a lesser degree *Last Tango's* Brando are transformed and redeemed with the struggle with the archetype. *Dead Man* and *Apocalypse Now* depict courageous individuals who submit to the energy and enter into profound death-rebirth phases of their existence. *Belly of an Architect* explores a man unwilling to let go of control and power, who is painfully broken down by a force greater than himself. *Blue Velvet* investigates a fragmented town that, in its inability to acknowledge its dark side, tosses Pluto pathologies mercilessly between one another. Finally, *American Pop* illumines the larger death and rebirth cycles interwoven within the evolution of human creativity.

The conclusion one can draw from these films is that although Pluto arises in some form in all of these films, there is a large freedom of choice with how to deal with the energy. Equally important, the degrees of freedom seem to be intertwined with the level of consciousness at which the protagonists, antagonists, and communities are operating. The greater awareness that one has to acknowledge that the pain and crisis that arise from Pluto are somehow part of one's self, the greater the ability to let go to the process and be transformed.

Birth times from the Internet Movie Database:

Marlon Brando: April 3rd, 1924, Omaha, Nebraska.
Jim Jarmusch: January 22nd, 1953, Akron, Ohio.
Francis Ford Coppola: April 7th, 1939, Detroit, Michigan.
Martin Sheen: August 3rd, 1940, Dayton, Ohio.
Martin Scorsese: November 17th, 1942, New York, New York.
Peter Gabriel: February 113th, 1950, Woking, Surrey, England.
Peter Greenaway: April 5th, 1942, Newport, Gwent, Wales, United Kingdom.
David Lynch: January 20th, 1946, Missoula, Montana.
Ralph Bakshi: October 29th, 1938, New York, New Yok.

Birth times from Thenewage.com:

Joseph Conrad: December 12th, 1857, Berdichev, Russia.

Jim Morrison: December 8th, 1943, Melbourne, Florida, 11:55 AM

Birth Data from www.hotweird.com/jodorowsky.html:

Alejandro Jodoworsky: 1929, Iquique, Chile

1. James Hillman, *Re-Visioning Psychology* (New York: Perennial, 1975) xvi.

2. http://www.suntimes.com/ebert/ebert_reviews/1995/08/992043.html

3. http://www.fortunecity.com/roswell/rune/90/interwiew.html

4. It is worth noting that the collaboration of Francis Ford Coppola and Mar-
    lon Brando on the films *The Godfather* and *Apocalypse Now* occurred under
    similar transits to points in their birth charts. Both possessing Aries Suns,
    Coppola and Brando underwent the stimulating awakening of a Uranus
    opposition to the Sun during their career pinnacle of *The Godfather*. With
    Apocalypse Now, Coppola and Brando incurred the arguably more problem-
    atic but richer and deeper energies of a Pluto opposition to the natal Sun.

5. Joseph Campbell, *The Hero With A Thousand Faces* (Princeton, NJ: Bol-
    lingen Series, 1972) 90.

6. http://film.tierranet.com/films/a.now/filming.html

7. http://film.tierranet.com/films/a.now/filming.html

8. There is considerable debate concerning the year of Jodorowsky's birth.
    Because of the enigmatic nature of the man, it is not known whether he was
    born in 1930 or 1929.

9. http://www.hotweird.com/jodorowsky/hoberman.html

10. http://www.dominantstar.com/tpluto.htm

11. http://www.firstthings.com/ftissues/ft9602/iannone.html

12. http://www.rottentomatoes.com/click/movie-1011984/
    reviews.php?critic=all&sortby=default&page=1&rid=216515)

Cinema and the Dawning of Aquarius

Ray Grasse

Since its invention during the late 19th century, cinema has enjoyed a popularity that has exceeded even the wildest dreams of its early pioneers. As astrologers, however, we have the added advantage of being able to appreciate the astrological dimensions of movies in ways that shed further light on their meaning and signif- icance for our culture. In earlier articles, I've explored some of the ways movies mirror global planetary trends at the time of their release, along with how they reflect the horoscopes of their directors.[1] In this article we will consider the way films might even reflect broader trends—including the shifting Great Ages. In the paragraphs that follow, I'll present selected material from my book *Signs of the Times*, along with material not included there, to show how the shift from Pisces to Aquarius may already be expressing itself, in both subtle and obvious ways, within the imagery of modern films. First, though, it may be helpful to say a few words about the meaning of these two signs, as a way to help set the stage for the examples that follow.

By element, Pisces is a water sign, and thus is more concerned with emotions, and all devotional forms of expression. Aquarius, as an air sign, is more intellec- tual and mental in its expression. Whereas Pisces is more religious or mystical in temperament, Aquarius is comparatively secular and technological in character. Simply put, if we were to symbolize Pisces with an image of a cathedral, Aquarius might well be symbolized by an image of a computer, or even a rocketship.

Importantly, while both Pisces and Aquarius are group-oriented or even cos- mic in their focus, there is an important distinction: in the case of Pisces, we see an emphasis on larger wholes that tend to dissolve individual distinctions and details; while in the case of democratic Aquarius, we find an emphasis on wholes that simultaneously *preserve* individual distinctions and interests—ideally, at least. A simple analogy to illustrate this difference would be the contrast between a Gregorian choir and a modern jazz band: in the case of the Gregorian choir (a

Piscean Age art form), individual singers come together in a way that sacrifices individual creativity in service of a higher ideal; whereas with the jazz band (an Aquarian Age art form), we see a form of group project in which individuality and personal expression are actually encouraged, without in any way compromising the integrity of the larger system. As we shall see, this subtle difference will prove a critical one toward understanding the mythological transformations currently sweeping our world.

The Wizard of Oz

It is one of the most popular and enduring tales of modern culture, yet who would have guessed that it also holds an important key toward understanding the shift of consciousness we call the Aquarian Age? In L. Frank Baum's story, our four protagonists (Dorothy, the Lion, the Tin Man, and the Scarecrow) set out on a great mission to find the answers to their important life-quests: one is looking for courage, another for brains, another for heart, and another simply for a return to home. Along the way, they meet up with a great and powerful wizard who sends them packing on a series of difficult trials, as prerequisites for attaining their dreams. Yet on completing their tasks, they experience a great disillusionment, for they discover that the "great and powerful" wizard is in fact nothing of the sort; he is simply an ordinary man. Instead, they learn that the things they seek lie somewhere much closer to home. "The answer has always been *within* you," the good witch Glinda tells Dorothy.

In this timeless tale we see a beautiful expression of the seismic shift taking place in the unfolding of our spiritual sensibilities, as we move from a time when the answers were largely seen as residing outside ourselves, in the form of gurus, priests, or God-figures of one sort or another; to a time where the Divine is coming to be seen as being *within* us. "Pay no attention to that man behind the curtain!" the figure yells out, as our protagonists discover their God-like figure was nothing but a sham. In a similar way, we are realizing that the old institutions and God-symbols have lost much of their currency. It echoes an idea expressed by the German philosopher Nietzsche, who declared over a century ago that God was dead, though it was never an idea intended to address God's objective existence so much as our outworn *conceptions* of Him/Her. Likewise, *The Wizard of Oz* isn't suggesting there *isn't* a Divine, merely that we must re-think our approach to this reality, with a spirituality more rooted in personal experience, that looks within for "salvation" rather than without. Said another way, we are not the servants of God, but *co-creators* with Him/Her.

Did Baum himself intend these more esoteric implications with his seeming child's tale? It's fairly safe to say that he did, since Baum (born with Sun conjunct Uranus) was a member of the Theosophical Society since 1892, and even wrote publicly about Theosophical ideas for a South Dakota newspaper, the Aberdeen Saturday Pioneer. Amongst the central tenets of Theosophy is the belief that "Divinity" resides inside of us, rather than in any external forms or intermediaries. As Blavatsky herself once put it, the essence of spiritual Esotericism can be summed up as the idea that "the personal God exists within, nowhere outside, the worshipper."

The Truman Show

Directed by Peter Weir and scripted by Andrew Niccol, the lead character in this ingenious 1998 film is depicted as the star—or is it victim?—of a mass media show he doesn't even know he's part of. As a result, every move he makes is carefully captured by a constellation of TV cameras and broadcast to a worldwide audience who follows his every move like some character in a soap opera. Over the course of the film, he gradually awakens to the nature of his predicament, and struggles to break free of this media-saturated world to forge his own life, free from the domination of the God-like powers manipulating his world.

On one level, this story speaks to the potential dangers we are all facing as our lives become increasingly entwined with cameras and information-gathering systems of every stripe, from credit card companies to security cameras in public places. This could easily be one of the downsides of the information-oriented Aquarian Age, when individual life could be scrutinized by technologies such as these, and personal privacy becomes an increasingly scarce commodity.

But Weir and Niccol's story touches on a much deeper level of resonance for any student of the Great Ages. Notice how its protagonist's struggle to awaken involves an effort to break free from a world bounded by *water* (Pisces) into one of *air* (Aquarius). Specifically, Truman Burbank must overcome a gripping fear of water and each time he attempts to break free from his world, he is lured back by the enticement of alcohol (Pisces, in its negative aspect). In the movie's closing sequence, he overcomes that fear and is shown literally stepping into the sky, ostensibly to begin a new life.

Further underscoring the symbolism is the fact that the God-like "creator" controlling his world goes by the name "Christof"—*of Christ*, one might say—a subtle reference to the Piscean Age religion bearing this figure's name. (And note how, in the movie's script, Christof's boss is named *Mose*—a symbolic reference to one of the luminaries of the *previous* Great Age, Aries.) In short, Truman's efforts to break free of the grip of Christof reflects our own collective struggle these days to break free of the lingering influence of the Piscean Age, and it's comparatively dogmatic mindset, in order to pursue a more independent, self-initiating lifestyle. In that respect, the film offers a message vaguely similar to that found in *Oz*, since Truman must leave behind the external "God" symbols of his world to become a fully authentic person, or *true man*—an Aquarian revelation of the highest order.

Titanic

James Cameron's mega-blockbuster from 1997 centers around the ill-fated maiden voyage of this luxury class oceanliner as it made its way from Europe to a final collision with an iceberg in the north Atlantic. At the emotional core of the story is the tale of an ill-fated love affair between two young passengers on this ship, played by Leonardo DiCaprio and Kate Winslet.

There are obvious Aquarian themes in several elements of this film, including the high-technology represented by the original ship itself, and celebrated in Cameron's film. When first constructed, the Titanic was seen by many as the apotheosis of modern "progress"; the subsequent sinking of the ship on its maiden voyage came to represent, like other modern disasters such as the Chernobyl and Shuttle tragedies, a cautionary tale regarding our blind faith in the possibilities of Aquarian science and technology.

Yet it is ultimately the film's personal side that holds the vital clues we must look to. As various commentators have pointed out, the dominant thread in this story is really Rose's journey of awakening and survival. Over the course of her journey, we see a dramatic shift in her character from the "old world" values of her European background, and their more rigid attitudes towards class structure and women's rights, to the more-freedom-loving values represented by Leo DiCaprio's character and, indeed, America itself. At film's end, we glimpse photographs near Rose's deathbed revealing she has lived a life inspired by ideals of freedom and self-determination; and within that shift we see a shift from the values associated with the Piscean Age to those of the Aquarian Age, where personal freedom will no doubt be the dominant theme shaping our lives. Further underscoring that emphasis is the way Leonardo DiCaprio's character is shown completely bypassing the established norms of where passengers should or shouldn't go on this ship; though booked in lower-class sleeping quarters, he freely moves between decks, even mingling at one point with wealthy passengers in the first class dining room. In so doing, he reflects the more democratic and comparatively classless ideals of both American and Aquarian society.

Chocolat

As anyone with a strongly amplified Pisces/Virgo axis in their chart knows, this zodiacal polarity can be a difficult one in the way it sometimes veers toward a more dutiful and pleasure-denying approach toward life. During the Piscean Age, that emphasis gave rise, among other things, to a world religion championing the virtues of austerity and sacrifice, as embodied in the grim image of a man hanging on a cross. During this Age, it was not uncommon for individuals to believe there was something inherently virtuous in suffering itself, and that pleasure was somehow "unspiritual." In Islam, too, we see a spirit of abstinence regarding such things as sex and alcohol—but qualified with the promise of great pleasures in the afterlife!

In the Aquarius/Leo Age we can expect a vastly different value system to arise, where the pursuit of personal pleasure will not only be acceptable, it could even become an end in itself. That tectonic shifting of archetypal values is nicely portrayed in Lasse Halstrom's 2000 film *Chocolat*. Set in the 1950s, the movie pivots around a conservative Christian town in France, where all forms of personal pleasure and independent thought are strongly discouraged by the local church authorities. That worldview is suddenly challenged when a free-thinking woman comes to town and opens a gourmet chocolate shop, the offerings of which manage to tempt these long-repressed citizens. Adding to the community's anger is her blithe refusal to join the local church, as she instead opts to pursue a more independent lifestyle. The problems reach their climax when she begins fraternizing with a group of long-haired vagabonds, proto-hippies of that time, who arrive by barge down a nearby river, and whose liberal ways are even more threatening to local sensibilities. When the two world views finally clash, tragedy results—though not without the community being transformed in the process, and awakened to a new world of personal pleasure.

The rigidly dogmatic and self-denying values advocated by the local church in the film perfectly embody the negative aspects of the Piscean Age; on the other hand, the woman and her long-haired associates reflect the more life-affirming and liberal sensibilities of the Aquarius/Leo Age coming into play (so to speak). The movie's collision of world views reflects a very real one that has been gaining momentum for several centuries now, as personified in such real-world figures as Lord Byron, Jean Jacques Rousseau, and the latter-day hippies, all of whom point the way to a more pleasurable and life-affirming approach to life. The film shows us the more positive side of this trend; but for the other side of the coin, let us turn now to our next film.

Citizen Kane

At first glance, it may be hard to see what this story of a powerful tycoon has to do with the Aquarian Age. Yet both its cinematic style and thematic content contain a motherlode of clues which the astrologer can mine for insights into the shift we are engaged in.

First of all, note that this movie was released under a truly extraordinary set of planetary energies: the world premiere occurred on May 1, 1941 (with the L.A. premiere occurring one week later), and that very week saw the following patterns reaching exact culmination: Uranus conjuncting Jupiter; Uranus trining Neptune, and Jupiter trining Neptune, with these in turn being framed by a major planetary line-up in Taurus. Clearly, *something* powerful was opening up within the collective psyche that made possible the emergence of some truly unique cultural expressions, and *Kane* was one of those.

In terms of its storyline, the film touches upon some of the potential dangers we might expect during the coming age, including raw materialism and the blind pursuit of pleasure. Whereas *Chocolat* depicts the more life-affirming dimensions of pleasure, *Kane* shows us what can happen when this drive becomes an end in itself. In the film, Charles Foster Kane builds a sprawling "pleasure palace" in Florida called Xanadu (coincidentally not far from where the real-life Disney World would eventually be built!). His entire life is a living testament to the acquisition of hollow pleasures and "things"—sculptures, girlfriends, newspapers, etc. We even find a curious parallel with *The Truman Show*; for just as Truman is shown to be the first human being to be owned by a corporation, in "Kane" the lead character is adopted at a young age by a bank. Perhaps this is a subtle warning as to the potential dangers of *our* being "taken over" by materialist and consumerist values in the times ahead.

The movie touches on yet another concept mentioned in *The Truman Show*, that being the enormous power of media in shaping our lives. Specifically, Kane is owner of a newspaper called the Enquirer, and shamelessly uses his power to ruin lives and manipulate public opinion. ("People will think what I *tell* them to think!" And, "If the headlines are big enough, the *news* is big enough!"). There is no question mass media has contributed much to our lives, in terms of broadening our horizons and allowing us to see the larger world around us; yet films like these point in no uncertain terms to the potential problems they hold, too.

Like *The Truman Show*, *Kane* also underscores the issue of personal privacy, for throughout we are shown scenes where the most intimate details of personal lives are displayed before a hungry public. This even includes a scene reminiscent of the Monica Lewinsky affair, where Kane's private tryst with a younger woman is broadcast to the world via front page headlines. Indeed, the entire movie is structured around an investigative reporter's quest to get at the bottom of Kane's personal life, as he seeks to unravel the meaning of Kane's dying word, "Rosebud." (In a fascinating directorial touch, Welles never once shows the actual face of this reporter—perhaps a reflection of the way media is *always* anonymous and impersonal in its workings.) As we have already been seeing in recent years, the Aquarian downside of the emerging hi-tech world could be that we may *all* become subject to the prying eyes of information-gathering systems of one sort or another.

Stylistically, there is something subtly Aquarian in the film's narrative, with its uniquely decentralized, jigsaw approach to both its story and Kane's character itself. Rather than portray Kane's life from a single perspective, it treats us to a wide *range* of viewpoints on who he is—including ex-wife, past friends, butler, business associates, and so on. (Ten years later, Japanese director Akira Kurosawa would extend this stylistic innovation a critical step further with his pioneering film *Roshomon*, by featuring three *completely* different versions of the same story, with absolutely no indication as to which one was "right.") One of the key metaphoric qualities associated with Aquarius is *decentralization*; whereas Leo brings all things to a center, Aquarius distributes energy to *many* centers and hubs, *a la* democracy or the internet. Similarly, Welles' masterpiece decentralizes the classical narrative into multiple perspectives, in so doing foreshadowing the cinematic styles of other directors like Robert Altman (*Nashville*) and P.J. Anderson (*Magnolia*). That same decentralized quality is also reflected in the movie's pleasure palace, Xanadu, built in a highly postmodern style that juxtaposes motifs from many different cultures and eras; in that respect, one could think of Xanadu as a metaphor for modern civilization itself.

2001: A Space Odyssey

As Joseph Campbell pointed out in his classic book *Hero with a Thousand Faces*, the timeless story of a hero struggling against great odds to obtain some boon or life-changing transformation has existed throughout every culture and era. But while the essential message of these tales remains much the same, the surface details can change from culture to culture. And it's within those subtle variations that we gain important clues into the worldviews of these cultures. So whereas in earlier times the obstacle to be overcome may have been a great dragon or supernatural demon, in Kubrick's self-styled "Space Opera," *2001: A Space Odyssey*, our hero must overcome a powerful *computer*—Hal. (As some have pointed out over the years, note how this name changes when you move each of those letters up a notch in the alphabet!) "Man versus machine"—it's a theme that's been echoed by countless science fiction tales through the years, but it's also one of the great lessons facing us in the Aquarian Age, as we learn to grapple with the challenges not only of technology but of *mechanistic logic,* of perceiving the world through a mindset of pure rationality, devoid of feeling or compassion.

Kubrick's story features an Aquarian message on other levels, including a look at the expanded potentials of human nature. As already mentioned, the coming age will see an emphasis upon the entire *Aquarius/Leo axis,* since each zodiacal sign is inextricably entwined with its opposite sign. On one level, this portends a time when ordinary humans could well be transformed into "mini-gods" of a sort, as average men and women awaken to their own heroic potentials in creative, political, and spiritual ways. With a subtle nod of the hat to Nietzsche's "superman" concept (underscored by Kubrick's use of Strauss's music for *Also Sprach Zarathustra*), we see astronaut Bowman traveling through a hyperdimensional stargate of sorts, to be eventually reborn at movie's end as a mysterious Starchild, shown floating in space above the Earth. In the Age ahead, we, too, could be "lifted up" to levels of higher potentiality that will fundamentally change our conception of what humanity is. Will that be brought about through genetic technologies, expanded educational techniques, or, as Kubrick's movie suggests, contact with non-human intelligences? As they say, stay tuned!

Close Encounters of the Third Kind

The notion of humans being "lifted up" is a motif that also figures prominently in the mythic tale most associated in the Western mind with the constellation of Aquarius: the Greek tale of Ganymede, the water-bearer. Said to have been the most beautiful youth alive, he was watching over his father's sheep one day when he was abducted into the heavens by Zeus, where he became immortalized as a servant to the gods.

As the dominant star-myth associated with the coming Age, it is intriguing that just as we are about to enter an age governed by a tale of heavenly abduction, we are flooded with accounts from around the world of people being abducted into the sky by celestial beings. True, there have been stories of "abductions" throughout history, as for example the fairy legends of Celtic lore or Judaism's tale of Enoch's ascension; yet there can be no question this phenomenon has accelerated in recent decades, starting with the famed Betty and Barney Hill case of 1961. And while the abduction motif figures prominently in many of our science fiction films, it found an especially conspicuous expression in Steven Spielberg's blockbuster film, *Close Encounters of the Third Kind,* which featured a story pivoting around a young boy who was abducted into the sky by non-human beings.

The question is, "Are these abduction tales based on fact, or are they simply an expression of our collective fantasies, a result of overactive imaginations?" Fortunately, for our purposes, it doesn't completely matter, since either way we can explore the *symbolism* of these stories for the insights they hold into the shifting Aquarian zeitgeist. But to do this, we need to explore what the "abduction" truly *means.* Archetypally, abduction refers to a process of becoming caught up in some powerful state of consciousness beyond the control of one's conscious ego, as the psyche is overtaken by mysterious impulses and energies. But there is an important difference between abduction *upward* and abduction *downward;* for instance, the image of Persephone being abducted into the underworld by Pluto suggests a process of getting sucked down into a more emotional, subterranean level of psychic energy. In a sense, whenever we feel overwhelmed by anger, depression, or fear, we've been "abducted" into the "underworld."

However, the myth of Ganymede features someone being abducted *upward* into heavenly realms—a very different connotation indeed! This suggests a shift in consciousness that is predominantly *mental* in character. (Some would see the direction of "up" as having a more spiritual connotation, yet spirituality is more properly related to the balance-point represented by the *horizon,* the proverbial "crack between worlds.") The myth of Ganymede, along with films like Spielberg's *Close Encounters,* may be omens suggesting that humanity will find itself swept up in an increasingly *cerebral* mode of experience during the coming millennia. This seems especially likely when one stops to consider the meaning of "air" associated with Aquarius, and its connotation of intellectuality. At its very best, it could portend a genuine awakening of humanity's higher mind; but practically speaking, it might also point to a more prosaic possibility, as our lives become increasingly dominated by the influence of TV sets and computers.

Star Wars

An overnight sensation when first released in 1977, George Lucas's film treated audiences to sights and sounds unlike anything they had ever seen before. As one friend of mine remarked at the time, it was almost like stepping into an entirely different world with its own inhabitants, atmospheres, even logic. Part of the reason for that enormous appeal, of course, was the skillful way Lucas managed to incorporate the timeless themes of myth and religion into his story, and reframe them in the clothing of space-age technology and values. As such, he crafted a truly Aquarian vision that provided us with a glimpse of humanity's possible future destiny in the stars, perhaps even the prospect of an interplanetary society.

Further clues into this film's significance may lie within Lucas's own horoscope, and its attunement to "futuristic" trends. Astrologically speaking, there are several ways one can detect a person's attunement to Aquarian themes and symbols, but one of the key ones would be the position and quality of Uranus in the horoscope. In George Lucas's case, this planet was positioned at 8 degrees of Gemini when he was born, on May 14, 1944. Why is this important? Because this was the exact same zodiacal point Uranus inhabited when the Declaration of Independence was signed, on July 4th, 1776 (and not far from the zodiacal degree where this planet was positioned when it was discovered several years later, in 1781). In short, George Lucas was born during America's second "Uranus return," a planetary cycle that occurs roughly once every 84 years.

How shall we read this? For starters, this being the planet associated with futuristic and technological interests, Lucas's close connection to this degree in America's horoscope suggests he is plugged directly into the innovative and high tech sensibilities of the American psyche. As just one example of this, Lucas's first major blockbuster, *American Graffiti*, was essentially an homage to America and its technologies, centering almost as much around souped-up automobiles and radios as it did its human characters. He also founded one of America's premiere special-effects houses, Industrial Light and Magic.

But let's take it a step further. As I've argued elsewhere, the American nation could well be a microcosm for the Aquarian Age itself, in the way it reflects the emerging values, politics, and cultural forms that will characterize the coming era. Indeed, if one had to pick a single horoscope to represent the birth chart for the Aquarian Age, one could do far worse than choose the horoscope of America itself. As such, the 84-year Uranus return cycle of America suddenly assumes significance far beyond any national boundaries, in the way it ushers in a new wave of innovation and complexity relating not just to America but the entire coming Age.

As noted, George Lucas was born precisely as Uranus was making its *second* full swing back to this point, at 8 degrees of Gemini. Because of that link between America and Aquarius, one might say Lucas is deeply in touch not only with American tastes, but the emerging currents of the Aquarian Age. With his own Uranus plugged directly into the "home" position it occupied in America's chart, and not far from this planet's discovery point several years later (at 24 degrees of Gemini), Lucas has his finger on the pulse of the emerging consciousness.

And from the start, Lucas's work reveals a recurring interest in futuristic themes and technologies. His first theatrically-released film was titled *THX 1138*, and offered a bleak look at the challenges of technology and individualism in the coming age. Several years later, *Star Wars* finally established his reputation as a artistically-minded futurist—and a technology-minded businessman. Looking back, it's curious the way this movie mirrors the themes and struggles of the Revolutionary War itself, with its group of rag-tag, "frontier"-style rebels going up against a more organized and powerful empire, spearheaded by a great tyrant (in the one case, King George, in the other, Darth Vader). And in both cases, the overriding concern on display is one of *freedom*. Perhaps this correspondence holds an omen or two for our future; if so, America's destiny might well foreshadow that of the Aquarian Age itself. Both Lucas's film and the Revolutionary War will prove to be precursors of coming trends with their mutual emphasis on freedom and attaining independence from depersonalized or oppressive systems in our world, be they governmental, corporate, or technological. [2]

Fantasia

Walt Disney's 1940 film is structured around a series of animated sequences that serve to illustrate key pieces of classical music. Yet arguably the most iconic of the entire batch (and one that has become virtually emblematic of Disney's empire itself) is that of the Sorcerer's Apprentice. Set to Paul Dukas's composition by the same name, this imaginative episode features a number of Aquarian resonances worth pondering.

To my mind, the most interesting of these involves the startling stylistic synchronicity between this musical piece and another work composed several years later by Gustav Holst, namely, his "Uranus" suite from the musical composition *The Planets*. I once heard a musicologist claim there was no clear evidence Holst ever heard Dukas's piece; but even if he had, it wouldn't explain why Holst chose this *particular style* to represent the planetary qualities of Uranus. To my mind, this synchronicity holds an important symbolic clue into the deeper nature of both Uranus itself and its associated age, Aquarius.

In Disney's version of this ancient story we see a character (Mickey Mouse) usurping his teacher's magical powers and tapping into energies far beyond his understanding. In the process, he nearly brings destruction down upon himself, and possibly the entire world. In some ways, this could be a fitting description of the role Uranus has itself played in modern history, in terms of the various energies and technological capacities it has awakened for us over the last few centuries. And notice how this is accomplished in Disney's version by means of a magical cap with *stars and planets* emblazoned on it—a further Aquarian touch hinting at the cosmic/celestial knowledge associated with this archetypal principle. As with some of our other cinematic examples, we again encounter the familiar "man versus technology" motif, as the broom Mickey Mouse orders to perform his chores (as water-bearer, curiously enough) runs amok, and eventually splits, clone-like, into multiple copies of itself. Notice, too, that while Mickey is getting carried away with his fantasizes of controlling the world, it's specifically an *environmental* disaster that he sets into motion. Sound familiar?

In the end, Disney's depiction of The Sorcerer's Apprentice could prove a cautionary tale for the Aquarian Age in the way it describes both the perils and promises of our newly awakened capabilities. This obviously applies to such areas as atomic energy and genetics, but it may even hold relevance to the burgeoning field of "personal empowerment," and the awakening of our psychological potentials. Will we use these energies wisely, or wind up destroying ourselves? Disney's tale makes one point clear: it isn't a child's game anymore.

Free Willy

Yes, I'm serious! The archetypes of change express themselves as much through low art as they do through high, and this 1993 crowd pleaser is no exception. One doesn't need to have seen this film to remember the key image associated with it—an orca whale sailing through the air over the head of a young boy. The symbol of a whale gaining freedom was a conspicuous expression of the Uranus/Neptune conjunction culminating that same year, illustrating the blending of planets ruling liberation and oceanic concerns. But remember, these planets also rule the two Great Ages we are presently straddling: Uranus governs Aquarius and Neptune governs Pisces. In that light, the image of a sea creature escaping confinement and becoming airborne, precisely as these planets were merging, presents us with yet another symbol for the transformation of consciousness from the old era into the new. Incidentally, it was a symbol that would be echoed seven years later in a similar fashion, with the image of airborne whales in Disney's *Fantasia 2000* (released on the first day of the new millennium).

Of course, the transition between eras is not always quite so smooth as this, with the interests of the emerging age sometimes attacking those of the older one rather than tolerating or transforming them. The government's destruction of the David Koresh compound in Texas in 1993 illustrates the potential dangers of what can happen when the secular interests of Aquarian society run roughshod over the religious values of a Piscean one. Still another example would be Herman Melville's oceanic novel, *Moby Dick*. In Melville's story, a man associated with the whaling industry (sometimes called America's first true industry) sets out to kill a great whale, rather than free it. Here, too, we glimpse the passing of the old Piscean order, but in a way that doesn't allow for a creative appropriation of its lessons and blessings.

The Matrix

It's sometimes called the *Star Wars* of a new generation [3], with a wide-ranging influence not only in cinema but such areas as fashion, TV commercials and shows, and video gaming. It's beyond the scope of this article to explore all the Aquarian resonances in this series, but a few of the more important of these might include the following:

* Aquarius rules the concept of networks, grids, and webs of every type; and this film, down to its title, features matrices, networks, and grids as an integral part of its visual landscape, just as its story addresses the potentials and perils of living in a world permeated by them.

* As with *The Truman Show*, the awakening of individuals into freedom is depicted in *The Matrix* as involving a transformation from a water-bound state to an air-breathing one, exemplified by Keanu Reeves's emergence out of the amniotic sac into the open air.

* Its storyline about a computer-generated world offers what is in some ways the quintessential Aquarian mythos; and with its depiction of a future overrun by computers, *The Matrix* echoes the "man vs. machine" motif in other works like *Frankenstein, Terminator*, and *2001*, to name a few. In the Age ahead we will no doubt witness machines and computers of staggering capacity and scope shaping our world in countless ways; the question is, can we remain in control?

* With lead characters who can fly through the air (in the computer-generated world, at least), the movie hints at the anti-gravitational aspects of both Uranus and Aquarius—energies that offer the promise of freedom from the traditional constraints of more earthbound Saturn. And with Uranus trining Saturn throughout most of 2004, it's fitting that the sequels feature innovative approaches in their depiction of both space *and* time.

* With its clever fusion of cross-cultural references, ranging from Eastern martial arts to cyberpunk and postmodern philosophy, *The Matrix* offers yet another

expression of the global culture that is emerging out of our media-interconnected world, and which reflects the more planetary scope of Aquarian thought.

* As mentioned before, the coming Age will be one where the Aquarius/Leo axis will be the dominant polarity, and *The Matrix* expresses this zodiacal dynamic in important ways. For example, at the time of the film's original release during late March of 1999, the Moon's nodes were positioned between these two signs, with the South Node in Aquarius and the North Node in Leo. Simply put, the South Node signifies where one is "coming from," karmically speaking, while the North Node signifies where one is "heading towards," in terms of one's higher calling or unfolding spiritual destiny. (Remember, too, that 1999 also saw a major activation of the Leo/Aquarius axis in the form of the famed "eclipse of the century" during August of that year.) So it's appropriate that Neo's journey of awakening is depicted as a *moving away* from the hi-tech matrix (Aquarius) and a *moving toward* his heroic destiny as the "One" (Leo), with even his name being an anagram for "One." On one level, the movie is therefore a metaphor for each man or woman's struggle to awaken to their own individualistic, "heroic" potentials in the coming Age. It is worth mentioning, too, that both brothers were heavily influenced by the philosophy of Nietzsche and his "superman" concept (as was Stanley Kubrick with *2001).*

* A different perspective on the film's astrological significance lies within the horoscopes of the directors themselves: Larry Wachowski (born June 21, 1965) and Andy Wachowski (born Dec. 29, 1967).[4] Rather than attempt a detailed interpretation of their charts, I'd simply point out that both brothers were born in close alignment with the powerful Uranus/Pluto conjunction of the mid-1960s—a rare planetary conjunction that occurs roughly every 120 years. As anyone who lived through this decade knows, the 1960s were an explosive time of social ferment and revolution, when Rock'n'Roll became the new musical language and the "counter-culture" emerged as a social force. It's often said that one doesn't see the full effects of any major planetary configuration until the children born during it reach their maturity; and works like *The Matrix* represent the fruition of that consciousness birthed during the 1960s. With its aggressive martial artistry, muscular visuals, and pervasive mood of rebellion, this film is clearly fueled by the fiery sentiments that energized an entire decade. One could probably devote an entire article to all the ways *The Matrix* series expresses the qualities of this planetary combination; for instance, also note the powerful subterranean machines, the death and rebirth of lead characters, black leather outfits, metamorphosing technologies, and a whole *lot* of explosions, to name just a few. (In a

different way, the first film *Bound* likewise mirrors the Uranus/Pluto conjunction, but more in terms of an emphasis on alternative sexuality.)

But what does all this have to do with the Aquarian Age? Simply this: the conjunctions of the outer planets, when they occur close to the cusp of a dawning Great Age, can be seen as "cosmic triggers" of a sort, in the way they help to unfold that emerging era. During such "windows" we find the emerging socio-cultural trends bursting forth into consciousness with special force, and for that reason they hold important symbolic and synchronistic clues as to the shape of things to come. That was true of the great Pluto/Neptune conjunction of 1892; it was true of the Uranus/Neptune conjunction of the early 1990s; but it seems especially true of the Uranus/Pluto conjunction of the 1960s, an era that even gave birth to a popular song featuring the refrain *"This is the dawning of the Age of Aquarius..."* In short, it was a decade with an overriding emphasis on freedom and personal liberation—precisely the Aquarian themes expressed within *The Matrix* series, with its stories of humans struggling to break free of traditional structures and powers.

(It may be a testament to the seminal power of outer planet conjunctions that three of the most popular film series from recent years—*Lord of the Rings, Harry Potter,* and *The Matrix*—were all conceived by individuals born during one or another of them: Tolkien was born in 1892; J.K. Rowling was born in 1965; and the Wachowski's born in 1965 and 1967, respectively. We'll have to wait and see what creative visions arise out of the Uranus/Neptune generation!)

On a different note, astrologers like Rick Tarnas and Jeffrey Kishner have pointed out the ways that the original *Matrix* story reflects the psychological theories of Stan Grof in uncanny ways, specifically his views on the individual's emergence at birth from the mother's womb, or "perinatal matrix." Though the brothers were unaware of Grof's theories when writing their script, it's nonetheless striking that Grof first began developing this theory during the Uranus/Pluto conjunction during the mid-sixties—right when the Wachowski's themselves were born!

A final synchronistic tidbit: since the fruit never falls far from the tree, I thought it would be interesting to look at the horoscopes of Larry and Andy's parents for further possible clues into the significance of these films. Lynne Wachowski was born on Oct. 29th, 1938. The most important cultural event of this period? Arguably, Orson Welles' "War of the Worlds" broadcast just one day later—featuring a story about non-human intelligences, in machines, taking over the world. Her husband, Ron Wachowski, was born on April 30th, 1941, during

the extraordinary confluence of planetary energies mentioned earlier in this article. The most important cultural event during *his* first few days of life? Arguably,
the world premiere of Orson Welles' *Citizen Kane* one day later, a film known for
its pioneering technical and stylistic touches, and its unique approach toward
time. (Curiously, also on April 30th the director of *The Great Train Robbery*,
Laurie Dickson, died—a man commonly cited as the father of modern film editing.)

I leave it for the reader to make of this what they will.

*This essay was adapted from the feature article of the April/May 2003 issue of The
Mountain Astrologer, Issue #108.*

1. See especially "Astrology Goes to the Movies," by Ray Grasse, TMA (April
    2000). Also refer to my book *Signs of the Times* (Hampton Roads, 2002) for
    a more extensive discussion of this entire subject.

2. Martin Scorcese's film *Gangs of New York* provides a fascinating look at the
    civic turmoil that accompanied America's first Uranus return in Gemini, not
    only in terms of the Civil War, but the draft riots they sparked.

3. In some ways, the stylistic difference between *Star Wars* and *The Matrix*
    might be thought of in terms of the distinction between Neptune in Libra
    and Neptune in Scorpio. In Libra, the Neptunian imagination takes on a
    more lyrical, idealistic, and "airy" cast; in Scorpio (the Wachowski brothers'
    generation), it assumes more aggressive, sexual, and urban qualities.

4. Birth data obtained from Lynne Wachowski (mother). She recalls that Andy
    was born "around 3:00 AM," in Chicago, Illinois, but could not recall
    Larry's exact birth time. Not surprisingly, both brothers had powerful tran-
    sits firing in 2003; but especially note how the Saturn/Uranus trine that year
    was exactly hitting Larry's Sun at 0 degrees of Cancer (giving rise, among
    other things, to a dramatic solar return chart.)

PART II
The Directors

One cannot underestimate the power of story, and throughout the rise and fall of cultures, the storytellers have given societies and nations their orientation, navigation, and meaning. In our age, the film director has become not only the great storyteller but the meaning maker as well. This section features four great storytellers—George Lucas, Sam Peckinpah, Steven Spielberg, and Stanley Kubrick—who have provided some of the great myths and stories of our time. In this section, the biographies and filmographies of very recognizable directors are contrasted against the background of their astrological birth charts and astrological transits. In each case, the authors demonstrate how archetypal themes as seen in the birth chart are invariably reflected in the director's output.

Astrology as Personal Mythology: An Examination of Star Wars and George Lucas

Glenn Perry, Ph.D.

"Myths are public dreams," wrote Joseph Campbell, "and dreams are personal myths." Just as myths are symbolic of the collective life of humankind, so dreams are symbolic of the personal life of the individual. And dreams, or fantasy, are the stuff of which films are made.

Star Wars is a case in point. The gods within George Lucas take their form in the heroes and villains of his films, battling across the galaxy in a grand homage to their creator, Lucas himself. In this sense, Lucas' "space fantasies" are actually self-portraits, metaphorical expressions of a rich and complex personal life. By making his dreams public, and in so doing creating a new, contemporary mythology, Lucas has unwittingly exposed the bare bones of his own psyche.

The *Star Wars* trilogy has an epic, mythological quality, as if emerging from deep within the collective psyche. Because it touches upon needs and aspirations common to humanity, Jung would call such films *archetypal.* By now it's almost legendary that Lucas purposefully set out to refashion ancient myths for modern audiences. He was reading a lot of Joseph Campbell when he penned the script for *Star Wars.* Yet, while these films have universal significance, they also have a personal significance for George Lucas.

Astrology, of course, has its roots in mythology. The mythological symbols we call signs and planets are the gods within that form the relationships of our psychic life. Planetary relations constitute psychodynamics—the movement and distribution of energies within the psyche. Not only do the structural dynamics of the psyche account for our outward behavior, they shape our artistic creations as well.

That which is created is a metaphor of the consciousness from whence it springs.

In this article, we will examine how the struggles of Luke Skywalker and friends are little different from the struggles of George Lucas. In fact, each character of Star Wars can be seen to embody an aspect of Lucas' own personality as revealed by his astrological chart. More to the point, the conflicts between characters in *Star Wars* symbolize the intrapsychic conflicts of George Lucas.

Charts are Stories

An astrological chart can be thought of as a personal narrative, or life-story. Just as the planets and their various relations symbolize one's character, so they also symbolize the plot of one's story. Plot structure, therefore, is analogous to character structure. In a good story, all the elements are functionally related to each other. Plot structure is the arrangement of materials to give a single effect. The same holds true for the astrological chart, which is an arrangement of archetypes to have a particular effect, i.e., a fate or destiny. Each planetary character represents a type of action. Taken as a whole, the chart symbolizes the structure of action, which is the plot of the story. In other words, chart structure is made up of processes—aspects and dispositorships—that combine to create a larger, more encompassing pattern.

Planetary aspects symbolize the various types of relations—some conflictual, some harmonizing—that exist between parts of psychological structure. An aspect can be thought of as a kind of idea, or mythogem (mythic theme), that emerges out of the relative integration of the planets that make up the aspect. The linking of planets via aspects creates higher-level cognitive structures that tie processes together. Cognitive structures—ideas—predict the likelihood of the individual being able to meet the needs that each planet signifies. The aspect also symbolizes the strategy, or schema, for meeting these needs. For example, if Mars conjuncts Venus, the individual may believe in love at first sight and that intimacy is best attained through bold, decisive action.

> Where both are deliberate, the love is slight:
> Who ever loved, that loved not at first sight?[1]

Fate Is Soul Spread Out In Time

Like any good story, an astrological chart has a pattern; incidents of the same or similar quality keep reoccurring, e.g., an individual continually experiences the same kind of outcomes in his relationships, career, or finances. Ideally, pattern is not simply repetition, but constitutes a path of evolutionary unfoldment. Each incident modifies awareness, which leads toward a progressive development and integration of character. Every new episode has the potential to alter consciousness. People learn, develop insight, and realize their potentials over time. In this sense, plot is an unfolding of character; fate is soul spread out in time. One could even say that fate is the means whereby soul unifies itself.

As the action unfolds, there are invariably conflicts and allegiances that form between the various characters that make up the narrative. As archetypal characters, planets symbolize specific types of action, and every action has the potential for harmonizing or conflicting with other types of action. In other words, planetary characters have relations with one another for good or ill. The challenge of any story is to resolve conflicts and pull all the characters together into a harmonious whole. To the extent this is accomplished, one attains *character*, i.e. integrity and honor.

Conflict is essential to stories. This is as true for the average person as it is for the protagonists of myth and literature. Conflict is what drives a story forward. No conflict, no story. In external conflict, characters struggle against the environment or with each other. In internal conflict, one part of the psyche struggles against another part; motives clash and ideas vie for dominance. In most stories, a strong element of inner conflict balances the outer conflict. To understand a story it is crucial to determine the nature of the conflict and the pattern that the opposing forces assume. Toward this end the astrological chart is an invaluable aid, for almost invariably there is a central conflict clearly revealed in the horoscope. Often, there is more than one. Each conflict constitutes a kind of sub-plot within the overall story structure.

Aspects not only signify the organization of the internal world, they also describe how the external world is structured. Planetary archetypes are non-local entities that manifest simultaneously in both inner and outer events. Just as in stories, inner conflicts tend to be balanced by outer conflicts.

In the beginning of a story, there is generally some situation that entails a lack of wholeness—in other words, a conflict between characters, within a character, or both. Stories can be thought of in terms of problem and solution, conflict and repose, tension and resolution. Whether and how the conflict is resolved constitutes the main question of the drama. This is what creates suspense. A story is a movement through disunity to unity, complication to simplicity, mystery to revelation.

Again, a story can be seen as a metaphor for a person. Just as stories denote conflicts between characters, so every individual experiences internal conflict between the various parts of his own nature. The planetary archetypes make up our inner cast of characters. They are the gods and goddesses within that consti-

tute the ongoing unfoldment of our psychic life. One part of our nature may be quite compatible with another part, e.g., our maternal instinct (Moon) may form an alliance (conjunction) with our inner warrior (Mars) so that we become fierce in our capacity to care and protect. Conversely, other parts of the psyche may be at war, e.g., our impulse for pleasure (Venus) may be at odds (opposition) with the drive for perfection (Saturn) so that we feel undeserving of pleasure. This may show up in the outer world as an interpersonal conflict. One person craves the pleasures of physical intimacy, the other withholds. The outer conflict reflects the inner one while also providing a vehicle for its resolution.

Purely physical conflict does not denote a story. A story requires characterization. There have to be characters that arouse sympathy or antipathy. We have to evaluate the ideas or motives that underlay the external conflict. We may sympathize with one character's perspective, and feel hostile toward another. Sympathy and antipathy, a conflict of ideas, is what makes up the story.

In astrology, too, the horoscope reveals how the native may be more sympathetic toward some planets than others.[2] Conflicting emotions and motivations can easily be portrayed by planetary aspects, e.g., the antagonism between family ties and personal inclination (Moon-Mars), friction between the individual and society (Mars-Venus), disharmony between the aesthetic and the practical sides of life (Venus-Saturn), dissonance between work and play (Saturn-Sun), and strife between career and family (Saturn-Moon).

Conflicts of motive are typically revealed in hard angles between planets, which often emerge as pathogenic beliefs—negative ideas—that express pessimism or fear about the relative likelihood of meeting basic needs. Negative ideas generate self-defeating behaviors that result in external conflicts and frustration of needs, and so the story goes.

The relation between character and events is a fundamental principle of organization in astrology, just as it is in stories. In story, plot is the unfolding of character; in astrology, character is destiny. Just as in every story there is an obvious external conflict and a less obvious internal conflict in the hero's mind, so each planetary aspect has an objective and subjective meaning. An aspect symbolizes a facet of character and a characteristic event.

If an individual believes that he can never truly belong (Moon) unless he achieves distinction in his profession (Saturn), while also fearing that too much work will jeopardize his relations with his family, this internal conflict of Moon-Saturn ideas may emerge externally, for example, as a situation in which his wife accuses him of neglecting the children in favor of his career. Often these conflicts appear as impossible predicaments for which there is no apparent solution. Yet, it is the challenge of the life to integrate the respective planetary functions and, in so doing, bring into being a unique talent or accomplishment that resolves the conflict. Perhaps he builds a company (Saturn) that provides a protective service (Moon) to the community, an accomplishment that ultimately allows him to spend more time with his family.

In every story, there is a key moment that brings into focus all previous events and suddenly reveals their meaning. It is the moment of **illumination** for the whole story, the instant in which the underlying unity is perceived as inherent in the complexity. All the relationships between the elements become clear and the story is seen to have a meaning as a whole. This meaning constitutes the story's key **theme**, which is the principle topic of the story.

The moment of illumination also reveals the story's message or **moral**. Generally, this involves some lesson that the main character has to learn. A story's moral is revealed only after there has been a clear resolution or outcome of the main conflict. Likewise in an astrological chart, there is a potential unity that is inherent in the complexity of the various parts and relations. If the chart is properly interpreted, this wholeness can be illumined. Suddenly the native sees his life as all of a piece; there is an "ah ha!" recognition. Most importantly, the native realizes that the main conflict of his life provides an opportunity for learning a lesson and for actualizing a potential that can only be achieved by working *through* complexity, complication, and confusion—just as in any good story. Pointing the way toward such a "happy ending" is one of the main values of interpreting a chart.

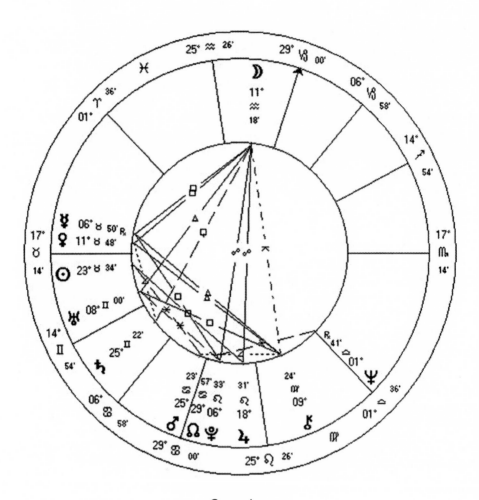

George Lucas
May 14, 1944
Modesto, California
5:40 AM

Conflict In George Lucas

By way of example, George Lucas, the creator and author of the *Star Wars* trilogy, has his Moon in Aquarius in the 10th opposing Pluto in Leo in the 4th (see chart). While it is not possible here to give a full interpretation of Lucas' chart, suffice to say this aspect represents one of the key themes in the Star Wars movies. One might argue that *Star Wars* is just fiction, just a story. But the point is that *every* life is a story, including the life of George Lucas. His Moon-Pluto opposition not only shows up in his fantasy life, it is alive and well in his "real" life, too. If everything is a metaphor of deeper, archetypal forces, it doesn't matter if we analyze Lucas' films or his own, personal experiences. The same archetypal patterns will be there. Suffice to say that "Luke" is an equivalent for "Lucas." Symbolically speaking, the *Star Wars* trilogy is autobiographical.

The Moon, of course, symbolizes one's feelings and dependency needs; it is our capacity for tender, loving relations. It represents the feminine component of the male psyche. The Moon also signifies our experiences with mother, home and family. Pluto, on the other hand, symbolizes one's capacity for transformation through encounters with the shadow, evil, and death. The archetype of the wounded healer is Pluto's role.

When these two planets are in opposition, there is a potential conflict between the functions they symbolize. This often means that the Moon, the feminine, is "killed off" by Pluto, at least initially. One's capacity to love is wounded; feelings and dependency needs are repressed. Ultimately, this is what needs to be healed. To the extent that healing occurs, the individual's capacity to love is powerful indeed. Feelings are potent and deep, and one is able to penetrate others emotionally in a manner that is transformative.

Since Lucas' Moon is in the 10th, and the 10th house signifies father, we can assume that the injury is to the feminine component of the father's psyche, i.e., *father is wounded in his feeling function.* Since Pluto darkens the 4th house, which represents home and family, we can also assume that the problem originated in some crisis, or wounding, to the family. The Moon-Pluto opposition between the 4th and 10th suggests that the native's career (10th) requires him to regenerate a sense of family by healing his capacity to love. Also, he must attain mastery of his emotions and become a protector of the public. This, in effect, is his destiny.

In the beginning of one's life, the core conflict in one's chart is generally at its most disintegrated state. We could speculate that Lucas' Moon-Pluto opposition initially manifested as some sort of loyalty conflict between his mother (4th house) and father (10th house). In other words, loving one parent might be perceived as damaging to the other. Also, an unintegrated Moon-Pluto opposition can signify a fear of being controlled, dominated, or devoured by a caring other. In Lucas' chart, this "caring other" could be mother and/or father, since both parents are implicated by virtue of the houses that are tenanted.[3] This would make lunar needs for belonging and closeness particularly problematic. For example, there may be a fear of never being able to separate from the family, as when a parent appropriates a child for his/her own needs. All of this could lead to repression of the lunar function. Young George Lucas might have found it dangerous to depend on others, trust his feelings, or allow himself to be emotionally close or vulnerable.

The Real Story

There is an abundance of evidence in Lucas' life that testifies to the Moon-Pluto struggle. People who know him have always insisted that the tortured relationship between Darth Vader and Luke Skywalker springs, in many ways, from Lucas' relationship with his own father. George Sr. was a domineering, ultra right-wing businessman who every summer would shave off his son's hair and call him "Butch." Lucas recalls being "incredibly angry" at his father. They had raging arguments over young George's decision not to take over the family stationary business. Even after his son became extraordinarily wealthy, the elder Lucas, while proud, seemed surprised. He never believed his son would succeed at something of his own choosing.

A serious rupture occurred when Lucas went off to Hollywood instead of enlisting in the family stationary store. The elder Lucas tried everything to stop him. "I fought him; I didn't want him to go into that damn movie business," he told *Time* in 1983. "But George never listened to me. He was his mother's pet."[i] This is an interesting statement in that it suggests that the younger Lucas experienced his father's needs for him as too intense. It might also imply that his relationship with his mother was too close. There is at least the suggestion here of two Moon-Pluto themes: (1) a devouring parent (father and/or mother), and (2) closeness with the mother is hurtful to the father.

Lucas admits that his relationship with his father was strained, especially when he refused to go into the family business (Moon in 10th). "My father wrote me off," Lucas confesses, "he thought I wasn't going to amount to anything."[ii] Lucas' father regarded George as an irresponsible dreamer destined for failure. "George was hard to understand," complained George Sr., "He was always dreaming things up."

Difficulty with authority was evident in high school as well. Lucas was a rebellious student with abysmally low grades. His teachers allowed him to graduate only because they thought George was going to die following a serious car accident just before school ended in his senior year. But Lucas fooled his teachers and survived. Later, at U.S.C. film school, he constantly broke rules and challenged the authority of his teachers. Lucas is famous for his hostility toward Hollywood executives, bankers and lawyers—anyone with control over him. After making his first commercial film, *THX 1138,* the filmmaker was infuriated over the "final cut" prerogative of studio executives who had the power to edit and change his film any way they pleased. Again, there is the theme of an intrusive authority (the studio executive) that tries to appropriate George for his own ends.

Lucas' fear of being controlled by studio heads prompted him to break with the industry and set up Zoetrope Studios in San Francisco with Francis Ford Coppola in the late 60's, thus repeating the theme of pushing away the father. The Hollywood grapevine immediately characterized them both as rebels and renegades. "We are the pigs," Lucas ranted in a 1979 interview, "you [Hollywood] can put us on a leash, keep us under control, but we are the guys who dig out the gold."[iii] This statement is telling in light of the fact that Pluto often manifests as a fear of being dominated. Pluto also rules underground riches as in "we are the guys who dig out the gold."

The Leo-Aquarius Theme

While the underlying issue is a Moon-Pluto one, it revolves around themes that pertain to Leo and Aquarius, the two signs that are involved in the opposition. Leo, of course, signifies the need for creative self-expression, while Aquarius pertains to themes of progress, change, technological innovation, revolution, and liberation (independence). On a more mundane level, Aquarius deals with the products and the means to change, e.g., science, advanced technology, and computers. With Moon in Aquarius in the 10th, we can expect to see Aquarian themes played out in his career and in his relationships with authority. For example, it might manifest as an emotional need to break free from the conventions of the past and move toward a broader and more inclusive sense of family (Moon). Family could mean friends of like mind bound together for a common cause (Aquarius), such as the liberation of the masses from authoritarian repression (10th house).

Lucas admits, "There was a lot of rebellion when we came to San Francisco. We moved here in 1961 when I was 23 years old. We thought we were going to change the world."[iv] A decade later, when Lucas set out to create Skywalker

Ranch and his innovative special effects unit, Industrial Light and Magic, nervous Hollywood executives portrayed him as a cunning maverick bent on developing an independent empire to compete with—or even supplant—the major studios. Clearly, the themes of rebellion, innovation, and liberation were already apparent. Lucas' ruling passion was to wrench filmmaking from out of the grip of the past. "The old film studios have never been interested in research and science," complained Lucas in 1980. "We are nearing the 21st century, yet filmmaking is still very crude."[v]

It was Lucas' desire for control—or, perhaps more accurately, the fear of being controlled, that compelled him to establish an independent film research center in Marin County, CA. There, 425 miles north of Hollywood, tucked away in a bucolic valley hidden from view, Lucas and his band of rebels—his Moon in Aquarius family—built Skywalker Ranch and collaborated in new techniques of filmmaking. At Lucasfilm and Industrial Light and Magic in San Rafael, Lucas built what is considered the most technically advanced filmmaking enterprise in the world. Having spearheaded a revolution in the technology and employment of special effects, and having ushered in a whole new era for science fiction, Lucas has indeed changed the world of filmmaking. Again, we see how home and family (Moon) combines with the urge to reform (Aquarius) in the context of career (10th house).

Integration

The integration of the Moon-Pluto opposition is evident in the way Lucas has come to terms with his own dark side, i.e., his fear of dependency and his resentment of authority, and how this, in turn, has brought about reconciliation with his family. Recall that initially Lucas seemed reluctant to do anything but rebel against authority figures. His father worried that he was a dreamer and lacked ambition; Lucas saw his father as suffocating and controlling. It was only by confronting death (Pluto) in the hospital following his accident that Lucas found the incentive to begin his professional career.

After 48 hours in a coma and weeks in intensive care, Lucas' brush with death changed his life. "It was a rite of passage. I felt, now that I have a second chance, I'm going to make the most of it."[vi] The accident, Lucas added, gave him a sense of his own mortality and put him in touch with his *feelings*. "I began to trust my instincts," he said. "I had the feeling I should go to college, and I did. I had the same feeling later that I should go to film school, even though everyone thought I was nuts. I had the same feeling when I decided to make *Star Wars*, when even my friends told me I was crazy."[vii] Here we see the close relationship between

Pluto (death) and the Moon (feelings). Only after facing death was he able to fully open to his feelings.

Following his recovery, he continued to battle authority throughout his college and early professional life. Yet, with the unprecedented success of *Stat Wars*, Lucas became the absolute authority he so feared and resented in others. Jung would call this *enantiodromia,* the tendency for things to revert to their opposites. Lucas admits, "I was a control freak."[viii] His colleagues agree. "I think what drives him as a businessman is control," says Rick McCallum, the producer of the *Star Wars* special editions. "Control over his work. That's primary."[ix] A former attorney of Lucas', Tom Pollock, reveals that he didn't really understand George until he met his father and talked with the elder Lucas about his son. The similarities were startling. "That's when I realized," said Pollock, "George *is* his father."[x]

At his Skywalker Ranch film studio, Lucas is in supreme command. Now it is *he* who makes "final cut" and influences corporate policy in Hollywood. By establishing a home base from which he can work in his own way (Moon in Aquarius in the 10th), Lucas wields a power greater than that previously projected onto superiors. No longer evil, or something to resist, Lucas has integrated the thing he most feared in himself—his own 10th house authority. His success as a filmmaker also allowed him to make peace with his father. "Now he's proud of me," Lucas stated in 1980, "the fact that I actually went to college and am successful at what I do."[xi]

It is worth noting that Lucas and his band of rebels at Skywalker Ranch bear a startling resemblance to the Rebel Alliance in *Star Wars*. First, Lucas had to revolt against his father who sought to appropriate him into the family business, just as Luke Skywalker had to resist Darth Vader's attempts to seduce him into the dark side of the Force. Second, Lucas revolted against the rigid corporate structure of Hollywood and won the freedom to make films his own way. Likewise, a key theme in *Star Wars* involves "freedom fighters"—the Rebel Alliance—that struggle to liberate themselves from the emperor's oppressive control.

In effect, the characters in *Star Wars* recapitulate the struggles and aspirations of Lucas' actual life. The themes of his films and the events of his life are metaphorical equivalents. Both are expressions of conflicting forces in his psyche. Lucas himself confesses the similarity. "A lot of stuff in there is very personal," he said years after *Star Wars* was released. "There's more of me in *Star Wars* than I care to admit."[xii]

Conflict In Star Wars

Recall that a major theme of a Moon-Pluto opposition involves a wound to the feminine function. The need for belonging and closeness is in conflict with the need for transformation and power. With Pluto, whatever needs to be transformed is by definition wounded; thus, very likely there has been some kind of trauma to the lunar function. This suggests that the Moon may be repressed and associated with suffering. Expression of dependency may stimulate a memory of being overpowered, exploited, or violated. Hence all things related to the Moon—family, emotional vulnerability, tenderness, and caring—have been abducted by Pluto into the underworld of the soul. This is the hidden source of shame and pain, the "dark secret" that needs to be redeemed.

In an opposition, each planet is the other's open enemy or partner, depending upon the degree of integration. To the extent that the opposition remains unintegrated, each planet regards the other with animosity, e.g., Lucas' need for closeness (Moon) triggers a perception that the world "out there" is exploitive, evil, or emotionally devouring (Pluto)—especially figures that are associated with the houses tenanted, i.e., father and authority figures (10th), or family and caretakers (4th). However, if the opposition is integrated, then one's capacity for caring and healing are joined in matrimony, so to speak. Feelings run deep and there is an ability to regenerate in others a capacity to love. This occurs by penetrating the other's emotional defenses, containing their pain, and loving in them precisely those places where they are wounded and ashamed. In other words, one transforms the other through an act of caring. *But first one must heal oneself.*

A planet in a house symbolizes both an inner and an outer reality. Accordingly, since the opposition occurs between the 4th and 10th houses, we can assume that 10th house figures, beginning with the father, are potentially wounded in their feeling function; i.e., the feminine component of the father's psyche is damaged. Likewise, with Pluto in the 4th *and* opposing the Moon, this is a signature of double jeopardy in the family. There is likely to be something dark here, some condition that is shameful, frightening, and in need of redemption. To the extent that the lunar wound in the 10th is healed, Lucas will resolve his distrust of authority and become a source of love, support, and protection for families *within the public domain*, i.e., his career is characterized by a capacity for caring that is regenerative. He becomes the master not of disaster, but of family empowerment.

In *Star Wars*, we immediately see evidence of a lunar wound in Luke Skywalker, who is introduced as an orphan living with his aunt and uncle on a dry, inhospitable planet infested with dangerous, dark creatures—sandpeople—lurking in shadows. Luke yearns to separate from his adoptive parents and join the academy to become a pilot, but his uncle insists that he stay on the farm to work for another year. Luke feels trapped and exploited.

By the end of the first act, his aunt and uncle are roasted by the Imperial stormtroopers. We eventually learn that Luke's father has been transformed into the evil Darth Vader, his mother is dead, and his sister, Leia, is a princess yet unknown to him. The family, in short, has been destroyed. Throughout most of this first film, Luke is emotionally upset, angry, and impatient with people around him. He is warned not to give in to the Dark Side, which feeds off negative feelings—fear, hatred, anger, and revenge.

At this point in the story, Luke embodies an unintegrated Moon-Pluto opposition. Obi-Wan Kenobi cautions him, "Don't give in to hate or anger; they lead the way to the Dark Side." The message is clear: certain kinds of feelings are dangerous; you must learn to integrate and control them or they will possess you and turn you into an evil thing, as they did Darth Vader.

Vader, too, embodies an unintegrated version of Moon-Pluto. His pain mirrors Luke's. In fact, Luke and Vader represent two poles of the opposition. Both are equally unintegrated at the beginning of the film. As 10th house authority in the empire, Vader is singularly evil. He represents the Dark Side of the Force, "the quick and easy way," and has a ruthless and seductive power that appears invincible. Cloaked in black robes and body armor, a mechanical monster stripped of his humanity, his true self remains hidden, a dark secret beneath flickering lights and an artificial respirator that keeps him alive. He hasn't even a face to betray a glimmer of kindness. Here we have the perfect symbol of Moon in the 10th opposed Pluto; Darth Vader is "Dark Father," a powerful man who is wounded in his feminine side. He seems devoid of any capacity for feeling or caring. Recall that Vader's mission is to subjugate the rebel planets of the empire into a single *family*—albeit, a family that is controlled through force and intimidation. This itself is a grim expression of the devouring mother, the caretaker that would sooner kill you than allow you to separate from her lethal embrace.

Luke Skywalker, on the other hand, is the wounded Moonchild, seeking to recover that which he lost long ago—a home and family free from the evil and tyranny that Vader symbolizes. The Moon-Pluto conflict heightens when Yoda tests Luke by having him enter a cave "strong with the Dark Side of the Force." Shivering with apprehension, Luke asks, "What's in there?" "Only what you bring with you," is Yoda's cryptic reply. Luke descends into the cave and immediately we see symbols of Pluto—a damp dark underworld inhabited by slithering snakes and assorted reptiles. He moves deeper into the cave and suddenly Darth Vader emerges out of the shadows. In a dream-like sequence, Luke engages in a lightsaber duel with his enemy, whom he decapitates. Vader's mask breaks away and reveals Luke's own face. Later, when he battles the real Vader, we are able to understand the apparition. Just as Luke is about to be slain by the Dark Lord, Vader tells him with horrifying certainty, "*I* am your father," and tempts Luke to join with him and the Dark Side of the Force.

In both sequences it is suggested that the evil that Vader symbolizes is in Luke as well. For Luke to confront Vader is to confront his own dark side—the hatred within that compels him to avenge the destruction of his family. The fact that Vader is Luke's own father again symbolizes that Luke's conflict is an internal one; it is the Vader within that he must slay.

It is interesting to note that it is only through "trusting his feelings" that Luke is able to open himself to the power of the Force. As a symbol of the wounded part of the psyche, Pluto signifies that which we distrust. Whatever it touches, especially by hard aspect, takes on the quality of something dark and forbidden. It is both the wound within the psyche, and the healer of the wound. Its message is simple but never easy: you must die; you must confront your darkness, slay your dragon and be reborn anew.

The Moon, on the other hand, signifies one's feelings and capacity to depend on a loving other. It is only through the integration of these two faculties—Moon *and* Pluto—that Luke is able to trust his feelings and thereby ally himself with the Light Side of the Force. In other words, Luke's real mission is to learn how to contain and ultimately transform the negative feelings that threaten to possess him. To the extent that his identity is predicated upon repression of these feelings, he must *die* to his old self. For his true self can only be restored by integrating that which he fears—his pain and shame. He must learn to accept that Vader *is* his father, but that love is more powerful than hate. He must learn to depend on the Force and regenerate his capacity to love. Only then will he be empowered on an emotional level.

Integration of the Moon-Pluto opposition is prefigured in the characters of Obi-Wan Kenobi and Yoda, two Jedi masters that serve as adoptive parents to Luke, training him in the art of feeling. Over and again he is told to relax, turn inwards, and feel the Force flowing within him. Their love and support provide Luke with a kind of corrective emotional experience that enables him to eventually confront his shadow, personified by Vader.

The Key Moment

In each of the three original Star Wars films—*Star Wars, The Empire Strikes Back,* and *Return of The Jedi*—there is a key moment when the Moon-Pluto theme is fully revealed. Near the end of *Star Wars,* Luke is encouraged by the discarnate voice of his mentor, Obi-Wan, to *trust his feelings* precisely when he is required to shoot the lethal rocket into the interior of the Death Star. But, to trust his feelings he has to *depend* on the Force, which is the supreme intelligence and power of the Universe. "Let go, Luke," says Obi-Wan, "Trust the Force." Luke turns off his computerized targeter, closes his eyes, turns inward and shoots his missile. It penetrates the one vulnerable spot on the Death Star and blows it to bits.

In the sequel, *The Empire Strikes Back,* the key moment is when Luke is told by Darth Vader, "*I* am your father. Search your feelings; you know it to be true. Join with me and together we can rule the galaxy as father and son." Again he is required to trust his feelings in a dangerous situation; he could be seduced by his paternal longings into the Dark Side. Again Luke has to "let go," this time to tumble head over foot into the empty abyss of the reactor shaft in a desperate attempt to escape Vader's hypnotic power. When the Moon opposes Pluto, trusting one's feelings can literally feel like falling into a deep, black hole—a motif that occurs again and again in Lucas' films.[4]

Finally, in *Return of The Jedi,* the key moment occurs when Vader "turns" and rescues Luke from the evil Emperor. Earlier, Luke told Vader, "I will not turn—you will be forced to destroy me....Search your feelings, Father. You can't do this. I feel the conflict within you. Let go of your hate." This time it is Vader who must "let go." Vader emerges as the film's ultimate hero when he realizes that Luke is right; love *is* stronger than hate. And with this realization he forthwith dispatches the Emperor by throwing him into the reactor shaft where he is annihilated in a fitting, plutonic explosion. Although this heroic act ultimately kills Vader, he has already been healed and transformed by his son's love. When Luke cries out to his father, "I've got to save you," Vader replies, "You already have, Luke." And in his final moment, he whispers: "Luke, you were right...you were right about me...Tell your sister...you were right."

The Theme of the Story

In each of these three key moments, the Moon-Pluto theme is fully revealed. Both Luke and Vader had to open to their feelings, let go of control, and face the possibility of death. In so doing, there was healing, transformation, and empowerment. One could argue that evil is born out of a failure to transform, to suffer pain, to die to one's old self and be reborn. The first trilogy hints that this was Vader's original sin; it was *why* he became Vader. He could not tolerate—"let go"—to the pain (Pluto) of his emotions (Moon) when he lost his mother and wife in earlier episodes of *Star Wars*. He did not trust that the way of healing is *through* death.[5]

In the retrospective episodes of I and II, we begin to appreciate the traumas that led to Anakin Skywalker's conversion into Darth Vader. In *The Phantom Menace* we learned that nine-year-old Anakin Skywalker, "Annie," was raised as a slave on the desert world of Tatooine with his slave mother, Shmi Skywalker. The cruel and oppressive slave master, Watto, owned both of them. Anakin never knew his father, and his mother would not reveal his identity when asked by Qui Gon, the Jedi Knight who discovered Anakin.

The secrecy and shame that surrounds the mystery of Anakin's father is itself Plutonian. It is also significant that Anakin's dream to become a Jedi requires him to leave his mother. After learning that his mother could not be freed and would not be leaving Tatooine with him, Anakin was devastated.[6]

> Everything was coming apart inside, all the happiness melting away, all the expectancy fading. But then he felt his mother's hands tighten over his own, and in her touch he found the strength he needed to do what he knew he must...."I'm going to miss you so much," he whispered.[xiii]

And as he was leaving with Qui-Gon...

> He glanced back one more time at his mother. Seeing her standing in the doorway brought him about. He stood there momentarily, undecided, conflicting emotions tearing at him. Then his already shaky resolve collapsed altogether, and he raced back to her. By the time he reached her, he was crying freely. "I can't do it, Mom," he whispered, clinging to her. "I just can't!" He was shaking, wracked with sobs, disintegrating inside so quickly that all he could think about was holding on to her. Shmi let him so for a moment, comforting him with her warmth, then backed him away.[xiv]

Throughout the remainder of the novel, Anakin's pain over the loss of his mother is repeatedly mentioned. Moreover, he fears for her safety and feels guilty for leaving her behind. To separate from Shmi, he must learn to repress his feelings. His mother instructs him, "Now be brave, and don't look back." It is the beginning of a pattern that will ultimately have poisonous consequences, as is typical of an unintegrated Moon-Pluto opposition.

Qui-Gon assumes the role of Anakin's surrogate father and there is a genuine and growing love between them. Soon, however, Qui-Gon is dead, and Anakin's loss of his mother is exacerbated. Qui-Gon—Anakin's first real father figure—is killed in a lightsaber duel with the evil Darth Maul. Hence Anakin's satisfaction at becoming a Jedi is "clouded by the sadness he could not banish at losing Qui-Gon and his mother both." With the Jedi master's death, "Anakin was left adrift. There was no one who could give him the grounding that Qui-Gon had provided….he felt all alone…sick in spirit and lost in his heart."[xv]

Anakin's only consolation is a fantasy that one day he will be a powerful enough to return to Tatooine and free his mother. This is his dream, his life plan. Psychologically, the fantasy of omnipotence compensates for the pain and impotence he feels as a child. Anakin and Shmi's status as slaves symbolize the disempowerment that is a frequent consequence of hard aspects between Moon and Pluto. Disempowerment permeates the ruptured emotional bond between mother and child; it is implicit in the shame and secrecy surrounding Anakin's real father, and it provides the underlying motivation for Anakin's obsession to become a Jedi, for only then would he have the power to free his mother and make his family whole again. "I will become a Jedi," he declared in a small voice. "And I will come back and free you, Mom. I promise."

In *Episode II: Attack of the Clones*, nineteen-year-old Anakin has grown into fledgling status as a Jedi apprentice. But he is headstrong and feels held back by Obi-Wan Kenobi, his Jedi master. Here again we see shades of Lucas feeling held back by his father. Late in the film, Anakin grows increasingly agitated by recurrent nightmares of his mother, whom he senses is in terrible pain. Returning to Tatooine, he discovers she has been abducted by Tuscan Raiders—primitive sand people—and may be dead. Sensing she is still alive, Anakin speeds off to rescue her.

Caked with blood, her ribs crushed, her swollen and battered body hanging from a rack where she has been bound and tortured, Shmi Skywalker clings to life in hopes that Anakin will feel her love for him through the Force.

> She needed that, needed to complete the cycle, to let her son recognize that through it all, through the missing years and the great distances between them, she had loved him unconditionally and thought of him constantly….Without the memories of Annie and the hope that he would feel her love for him, she would surely have given up long ago and allowed herself to die.[xvi]

Indeed, Annie does find her, but it is too late. In the most moving moment of the film, Anakin steals into the Tuscan camp and cuts his way into his mother's tent. Shmi recognizes him and starts to tell him, "I love…" and then goes still. "She looked straight up, past Anakin, past the hole in the ceiling, to the shining Moon." Anakin becomes immobilized by the confusion and unreality of what is happening, and begins to feel "a budding rage and the most profound sense of emptiness he had ever known." He is wracked with guilt that he left his mother on Tatooine, that he couldn't free her, couldn't save her. Consumed with hatred and rage, he gives himself over to emotions that he knows are "of the dark side." Within minutes he has slaughtered everyone in the camp—men, women, and children. At the end of his rampage, "He didn't feel empty any longer. He felt a surge of energy and strength beyond anything he had ever known, felt full of the Force, full of power, full of life."[xvii]

Clearly, this is a turning point in the evolution of Anakin Skywalker's character. Although Padme tries to help Anakin grieve the loss of his mother, his pain and guilt is too much. Rather than open to the full reality of his loss and with it acceptance of his own limitations, Anakin compensates in the opposite direction. Padme gently reminds him that despite being a Jedi warrior, he doesn't have control over death. "You're not *all*-powerful," she says.

> He stiffened at her words and pulled away from her—and angrily, she realized. "But I should be!" he growled, and then he looked at her, his face a mask of grim determination. "And someday I will be!"
>
> "Anakin, don't say such things," Padme replied fearfully, but he didn't even seem to hear her.
>
> "I'll be the most powerful Jedi ever!" he railed on. "I promise you! I will even learn to stop people from dying!"[xviii]

This is the key moment of the film so far as revealing the beginning of Anakin's descent into darkness. His lunar wound is too great. He failed to free and save his mother, which was his primary reason for becoming a Jedi. The only meaning he could derive from this failure was that *he was not powerful enough*. Rather than honoring death and the inevitable pain that it brings in its wake, Anakin resolved to defeat death. It was only through his son—Luke Skywalker—that he ultimately realized his mistake. To heal his wound, Vader had to learn to open to his feelings no matter how grievously painful they might be. For healing is only possible by finding the courage to face death on an emotional level.

In *Star Wars*, Luke faced death when he trusted his feelings and attacked the menacing Death Star without his targeter; in *The Empire Strikes Back* he faced death when he resisted Vader's seductive appeals and jumped into the reactor shaft; in *Return of the Jedi* he faced death when he refused to kill his father and become the Emperor's minion. And finally, it was Vader who faced death when his feelings "turned" and he threw the Emperor into the reactor shaft. While this act of love proved fatal, it was also self-redemptive, enabling Vader to be reborn as his true self—Anakin (and again) Skywalker, a play on words that tells us Vader was meant to be a Pluto symbol of death and rebirth.

A Conflict of Ideas

The *Star Wars* trilogy is also about a conflict of Moon-Pluto ideas. The pathogenic version of the aspect is: "You should not trust your tender feelings, nor should you depend on anyone, for love makes you weak and dark forces will exploit your emotional vulnerability. Therefore repress your pain; give in to your hatred, anger, and revenge, for these pave the way to true power."

Clearly, this idea is embodied in the character of Darth Vader, who literally masks his feelings under an ominous black mask and cloak. The healthy, integrated version is taught by Yoda and Obi-wan, and ultimately comes to be embodied in Luke: "Trust your feelings, open to your capacity to love even at great emotional risk, for the Force will then be with you." Here, the Force is the ultimate Moon-Pluto symbol, for it binds the Universe together, permeates and unifies all things, and can only be accessed by "letting go" of one's thoughts and intentions. This, of course, is how one accesses the Moon, by letting oneself be vulnerable, by turning inward and *feeling.*

The Moon-Pluto theme also contains the moral of the story. For Luke, the lesson he had to learn was to control his angry, bitter, and vindictive feelings and transform them into love, a love so powerful that it can penetrate the darkest evil, eliminate hatred, and heal a soul—that of his father. The moral of the story is "don't give up on the goodness in people; relate to the higher man, good and evil can be reconciled through love."

When Luke surrenders himself to Vader near the end of *Return of the Jedi*, his Moon-Pluto opposition is fully integrated. He addresses Vader as "Father" for the first time, and reminds him, "you were once Anakin Skywalker, my father....It is the name of your true self." Vader resists, but Luke's emotional power has already penetrated his father's defenses. "I know there is good [love] in you," he says, "that's why you could not destroy me." Vader acknowledges his son's ability—which is really the power of his love—when he responds, "Indeed, you *are* as powerful as the Emperor has foreseen." Although the Dark Lord tries to resist, his emotions are moved. That Luke has touched his father's feelings is evidenced by Vader's final statement in the scene, "It is too late for me, Son." One senses Vader's anguish when he has to steady himself against the railing as Luke is taken away. He has resisted Luke for the moment, but it is only a matter of time before he turns completely, i.e., transforms.

In *Star Wars,* the Moon-Pluto theme is at its most disintegrated state. Luke's family (Moon) has been destroyed and evil (Pluto) reigns. Significantly, it was a woman (Moon) in danger (Pluto) that ignites Luke's healing journey, for it was his familial love for Leia, his sister, that inspires him to seek out Obi-wan. Again, the main conflict revolves around Moon and Pluto. Will Luke's family/Moon be reunited, or completely annihilated? Will Luke be turned by the Emperor to the Dark Side of the Force, or will he succeed in killing or perhaps even turning Vader to the Light Side—healing Vader's feminine wound? Luke's willingness to complete his training, a kind of martial arts therapy with Yoda, readies him for the final confrontation with Vader and his own dark side. He does *not* turn; he would rather die (Pluto) than give in to hatred, kill his father, and become the Emperor's pawn.

This is the moment of illumination in *Episode VI: Return of the Jedi.* Luke foils the Emperor's plans, and darkness is transformed into light when Vader throws the Emperor into the reactor shaft where he explodes in a brilliant flash. In that moment, father and son are reunited. Shortly after, when the missile penetrates the Death Star's main reactor, there is again a brilliant explosion, like a fulminant supernova. These are all metaphors of lunar transformation. The Death Star was a dark, evil womb (another Moon-Pluto image) that contained at its atomic core the heart of evil itself, the Emperor. The sole purpose of the Death Star was to hold the planets in place and never let them become independent, self-governing entities.

Whereas in *Star Wars* we witnessed the Death Star shatter Leia's home planet into a billion pieces, by the end of *Return of the Jedi* it is the Death Star that is annihilated. Disunity has been reconciled into a new Moon-Pluto unity. By working through complexity, complication, and confusion, Luke fulfilled his destiny as an emotional master; he transformed hate into love, healed his father, and regenerated his family, newly composed of Han, Leia, Chewbacca, the children (Ewoks and Droids) and the ancestors—Yoda, Obi-Wan, and Anakin Skywalker. Wholeness has returned. Order again prevails in the Universe.

Summary and Discussion

Lucas' *Star Wars* trilogy exemplifies how a single aspect can be a powerful thematic element in a life story. The main psychological conflict within Luke Skywalker, which was mirrored by an interpersonal conflict with his father, was clearly symbolized by the Moon-Pluto opposition. This same aspect also represented the story's primary theme, the core conflict of ideas, the key moment of illumination, and the moral lesson imparted.

In every instance, there is a clear parallel with George Lucas' personal life. At the beginning of Star Wars, Luke Skywalker was struggling to separate from domineering stepparents who pressured him to work on the family farm. Later, he rebelled against imperial domination and fought to overcome the influence of a tyrannical father—Darth Vader. Likewise, George Lucas struggled to separate from a domineering father who pressured him to take over the family business. Later, he rebelled against the Hollywood empire and fought to establish an independent film company far from the reach of Hollywood moguls.

Over the course of the Star Wars trilogy, Luke Skywalker gradually evolved from a rebellious teenager with a bad attitude to a Jedi Master who learned to control his darker emotions. The resolution of Luke's internal conflict was paralleled by the resolution of his external conflict with his father—a resolution that led to wholeness both within and without. There was a "character arc" in George Lucas, too. He evolved from an angry renegade to a powerful magnate that transformed the world of filmmaking. The resolution of his inner conflict, i.e., his distrust of authority, was mirrored by his reconciliation with his father and his unparalleled success as a filmmaker.

In both stories, there is a reoccurring pattern of rebellion, transformation, and empowerment on an emotional level. Yet, this pattern is not simply repetition, but shows how Lucas and his alter ego, Luke Skywalker, traversed a path of evolutionary unfoldment. In both stories, each new episode provided an opportunity to learn, develop insight, and realize lunar potentials. Over time there was a progressive development and integration of character.

Just as there was a "key moment" in each film, so there were key moments in the life of George Lucas. His confrontation with death following his car accident, his severance from his father and decision to enter U.S.C. film school, his break with the industry, his determination to establish an independent studio at Skywalker Ranch, and his decision to write Star Wars, were all pivotal moments where Lucas had to face a kind of death—rupture with his family, retaliation by Hollywood, financial catastrophe, and so on. One way or the other, the lunar theme of belonging was implicit in these moments; Lucas had to find the courage to trust his feelings and create his own family and support system.

If there is a lunar theme in all this, perhaps Lucas sums it up best: "My films have a tendency to promote a personal self-esteem," he says. "Their message is, 'Don't listen to everyone else. Discover your own feelings and follow them. Then you can overcome anything.'"[xix] The key phrase here is discover your own feelings and follow them. Again, this was the overriding theme of Star Wars—trust your feelings—and was the principal moral of the story.[7]

The Leo-Aquarius sub-theme is also equally present in the life of Lucas and Skywalker. Not only is the Star Wars trilogy a testament to the latest advances in film technology, it's about a futuristic society. The film shows an array of computers, druids, robots, bionics, holographs, lasers, and other mechanical gadgets that fairly boggles the imagination. The Moon in Aquarius theme is likewise evident in the warmth and caring that exists between the main protagonists of the film. Like family, there is an emotional bond between Han, Luke, Leia, and their two droids, R2D2 and Threepio. As fellow revolutionaries, their love and commitment to the cause binds them.

Likewise, Lucas and his fellow film revolutionaries at Skywalker Ranch constitute a Rebel Alliance of its own sort. From their base in northern California, they've launched powerful technological fusillades of special-effects brilliance at their Hollywood rivals, who for nearly a century dominated the film industry.

Luke Skywalker's mission to protect and liberate the fledgling republic from imperial domination is a clear expression of Pluto opposed Moon in Aquarius in the 10th. This role of lunar protector is also present in George Lucas, whose fame and power might obscure the fact that his main mission in life has been to develop films, television shows (The Young Indiana Jones Chronicles), and educational materials for the benefit of children. As the prequels make even more clear by telling the story of Darth Vader's youth and eventual fall to the Dark Side, Star Wars is both a family saga and a morality play for children.[8] Long before politicians criticized Hollywood's supposed lack of "family values," Lucas said his "main reason" for making Star Wars "was to give young people an honest, wholesome fantasy life, the kind that my generation had."[xx] Today as a divorced father of three children (two of whom he adopted on his own), Lucas asserts, "The most important thing in life is kids."[xxi]

In addition to opposing Pluto, his Aquarian Moon forms a T-Square to Mercury in the 12th; thus, his caring (Moon) extends to the educational (Mercury) system. Lucas has poured millions of dollars into his subsidiary company, Lucasfilm Learning, to produce innovative software and interactive video games to inject into San Francisco Bay Area classrooms and curricula. Some 18 schools in San Francisco and Marin County served as laboratories for the experimental project. "The way we are educated is based on 19th century ideals and methods," Lucas said. "Here we are entering the 21st century, and you look at our schools today and say why are we doing things this way? Our system of education is locked in a time capsule, and you want to say, 'Hey, you're not using today's tools. Wake up!'"xxii

Again, his Moon in Aquarius in the 10th is evident in his dedication to changing the system for the benefit of children. "I'm interested in the future," says Lucas, "and the future is kids."

Space prohibits a more detailed analysis of how the *Star Wars* trilogy is a metaphor for the struggles and triumphs of George Lucas. Suffice to say that an astrological chart depicts a story—a personal myth. And within any good myth there is conflict; conflict is what drives the story forward. Whether it's Luke Skywalker defying the empire, or George Lucas defying Hollywood tradition, the external conflict provides a vehicle for resolving an internal one. Resolution of the inner conflict leads to outer harmony. This was clearly depicted in Lucas' Moon-Pluto opposition. As the tension between these two forces was slowly resolved, each function enriched the other. For Lucas, this meant learning to express powerful feelings of caring concern for the welfare of future humanity—today's children. Toward this end, he has bequeathed us a remarkable gift in the myth of *Star Wars*.

◆   ◆   ◆

Adapted from an chapter originally published in "An Introduction To AstroPsychology"(1998) published by The Association for Astrological Psychology.

References

i. Bruce Handy, "The Force Is Back," *Time,* February 10, 1997, 74.

ii. Joanne Williams, "Sun Interviews George Lucas," *Pacific Sun,* February 8, 1980, 7.

iii. Michael Pye and Lynda Myles, *The Movie Brats* (New York: Holt, Rinehart, and Winston, 1984) 9.

iv. Paul Chutkow, "The Lucas Chronicles," Image Magazine in the *San Francisco Chronicle,* March 21, 1993, 15.

v. Alice Yarish, "George Lucas—hell-raiser to millionaire," *Independent Journal* (Marin County, CA), March 2, 1980, 14.

vi. Paul Chutkow, "The Lucas Chronicles," Image Magazine in the *San Francisco Chronicle,* March 21, 1993, 15.

vii. Bernard Weinraub, "Luke Skywalker Goes Home," *Playboy Magazine*, July, 1997, 174.

viii. Ibid, p. 12.

ix. Bruce Handy, "The Force Is Back," *Time,* February 10, 1997, 72.

x. Bernard Weinraub, "Luke Skywalker Goes Home," *Playboy Magazine*, July, 1997, 120.

xi. Joanne Williams, "Sun Interviews George Lucas," *Pacific Sun,* February 8, 1980, 7.

xii. Bernard Weinraub, "Luke Skywalker Goes Home," *Playboy Magazine*, July, 1997, 176.

xiii. Terry Brooks, *Star Wars, Episode I, The Phantom Menace* (New York: Ballantine, 1999) 188.

xiv. Terry Brooks, *Star Wars, Episode I, The Phantom Menace* (New York: Ballantine, 1999) 191.

xv. Terry Brooks, *Star Wars, Episode I, The Phantom Menace* (New York: Ballantine, 1999) 322.

xvi. R.A. Salvatore, *Star Wars, Episode II, Attack of The Clones,* (New York: Ballantine, 2002) 271–272.

xvii. R.A. Salvatore, *Star Wars, Episode II, Attack of The Clones,* (New York: Ballantine, 2002) 274–278.

xviii. R.A. Salvatore, *Star Wars, Episode II, Attack of The Clones,* (New York: Ballantine, 2002) 283.

xix. Paul Chutkow, "The Lucas Chronicles," Image Magazine in the *San Francisco Chronicle,* March 21, 1993, 15.

xx. Bruce Handy, "The Force Is Back," *Time,* February 10, 1997, 73.

xxi. Paul Chutkow, "The Lucas Chronicles," Image Magazine in the *San Francisco Chronicle,* March 21, 1993, 16.

xxii. Ibid, p. 10.

Endnotes

1. Christopher Marlowe (1564–1593), English dramatist, poet. *Hero and Leander*, "First Sestiad."

2. The "native" is the person for whom the chart is cast.

3. A planet is said to "tenant" that house.

4. The Moon-Pluto motif of the devouring mother occurs in a variety of guises throughout the *Star Wars* trilogy, as well as in all the *Indian Jones* films (also by Lucas). For example, in *Star Wars* there is the garbage compactor on the Death Star, replete with a devouring dragon that pulls Luke down below the surface of the foul water. Then the compactor walls begin to close in on Luke, Han, and Leia. In *The Empire Strikes Back*, Luke plummets down the reactor shaft toward what seems certain death. Also, Han Solo flies the Millenium Falcon into a cave that turns out to be the open mouth of a monstrous Jonah-like creature. In *Return of the Jedi* there is the underground lair of the Bantha monster who nearly swallows Luke, and again, later, there is the Sarlaac creature in the desert that is a virtual hole in the ground with teeth and tentacles that reach up and pull unwilling victims into its belly where they are "digested over a thousand years." All of these images attest to Lucas's preoccupation with being devoured by large, powerful entities.

5. Admittedly, this part conjecture, for we will not know the fate of Anakin's marriage to Padme until Episode III, due for release in 2005.

6. In the novel, *Episode I: The Phantom Menace*, the full extent of this trauma was more fully explored than in the film, which omitted many significant scenes. Likewise, the novel, *Episode II: Attack of the Clones,* reveals much

more of Anakin Skywalker's inner world. The remaining quotes in this section are taken from those two books, both of which are based on the story and screenplay by George Lucas.

7. Of course, no one part of a chart is entirely responsible for key themes in the native's life. In the end, the whole chart is implicated. Certainly Lucas' 1st house Sun, which is sextile Mars, gives him a "can do" attitude that is reflected in the action heroes of his films. In this article, however, we are principally interested in how his lunar wound manifests within the context of his career, and how learning to trust his feelings has been a key to his success.

8. One could make a case that his Sun square Jupiter in the 4th house is the astrological signature of his focus on "family values." Lucas has a compelling sense of moral obligation to the community. He feels that children today are being corrupted by television because it has no sense of morality (Jupiter). Consequently, he made *Star Wars* as a post-contemporary myth in order that children would again have access to the great mythological traditions and the moral lessons they impart. The point is, he cares about children. And this is an expression of the Moon.

The Violent World of Sam Peckinpah: The Pluto Archetype in Action

John M. Whalen

In the opening shots of maverick film director Sam Peckinpah's *The Wild Bunch* (1969), soldiers on horseback ride slowly into the town of Starbuck, passing by a group of children playing in the street. Compared to the tough-looking soldiers, the children seem innocent enough, gathered in a tight circle, playing with something we can't see yet. They look up at the soldiers and smile at them shyly. Then Peckinpah moves the camera in so we can see what the children are playing with—two scorpions fighting for their lives on a swirling pile of red ants.

As the scene progresses, we learn that the soldiers are really a disguised band of outlaws—none other than the infamous Wild Bunch. We also discover that on the rooftops of the town a posse is waiting in ambush for the Bunch. At the same time, Temperance Union marchers singing "Shall We Gather at the River?" stride up the street toward the bank. The Bunch, detecting the ambush, decides to use the marchers for cover. They charge out of the bank, guns blazing. All hell breaks loose on the screen as the Bunch and the posse fight it out with the helpless teetotalers caught in the middle of the bloody, chaotic battleground. A scene of total carnage.

Only five of the Bunch manage to escape, and as they leave town they pass by the children again. It is here, after all this, that Peckinpah fills the screen with perhaps the most searing visual representation of the Pluto archetype ever committed to film. We see the dying scorpions, their stingers jabbing furiously at the hungry ants, now enveloped in flame as the laughing children toss burning straw on them.

The Wild Bunch opened in 1969 to cries of outrage, protest, and critical confusion. At its premiere, some patrons walked out, sickened by the violence. Critics either loved the film or hated it. But despite the turbulent reaction, and whether or not you agree with Peckinpah's artistic sentiments, *The Wild Bunch* changed forever the way action films are made.

While symbols of the Pluto archetype may be strongest in *The Wild Bunch*, all of Peckinpah's movies deal with Plutonic themes—themes of betrayal, revenge, self-destruction, trust, paranoia, selling out, power (those who have it and those who don't), and ultimately redemption, resurrection and transformation.

Peckinpah's real life was just as turbulent and full of passionate struggle as any of the movies he made. As an artist, he refused to compromise himself, and fought a brazen battle with the impersonal studio system in which he worked. Despite constant interference from the bean counters who run Hollywood, he managed to turn out films that were both personal and true to his own vision. As a man, he struggled most of his life with addictions to alcohol and later cocaine; his relationships with women were violent and destructive; and he had more than his share of real life brawls and fistfights. Yet one concludes that at the end he lived up to the sense of purpose expressed by a character in one of his films—Steve Judd, in *Ride the High Country*—who says: "All I want is to enter my house justified."

With so much of his life and creative output colored by the tumultuous energy of Pluto, you might be tempted to guess that Peckinpah was born under the sign of Pluto's rulership—Scorpio. But you'd be wrong. He was born Feb. 21, 1925 at 2:15 p.m. in Fresno, California. He was born with the Sun in Pisces, the Moon in Aquarius, and Cancer was rising on the Ascendant.

The Pisces Sun tells us that it was Peckinpah's nature to be someone who would be imaginative, creative, someone who deals with imagery, possibly a film maker—but it offers no hint at all of the deep subjects he would commit to film. Peckinpah's Aquarian Moon made him a rebel, and someone who valued friendship and enjoyed camaraderie. But it provides no indication of the dark themes that would obsess him as an artist. Cancer rising gave him a tough exterior mask to hide behind. But still no hint of Pluto. To what, then, can we attribute the dark and gritty nature of Peckinpah's films and the equally turbulent and stormy nature of his life?

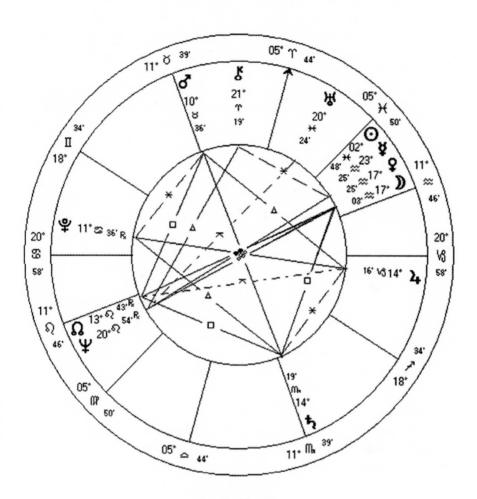

Sam Peckinpah
February 21st, 1925
Fresno, California
2:15 PM

Before we look for the Pluto factor in Peckinpah's chart, it might be well first to discuss the Pluto archetype in general—what it is, how it appears in the horoscope, and how it manifests in life and the world.

Pluto is the archetype of intensity, depth analysis, penetration, evolution and transformation. It is the planet that pushes us over the abyss, in the sense that it forces us to face inevitable and irrevocable change—change brought on by necessity. What usually makes Plutonic changes necessary is the death and decay of existing forms. All things in the universe have a certain life expectancy, beyond which they can no longer continue to exist. When time runs out—whether it be for a plant, an animal, a person, an institution, a government, or an idea—it is Pluto that is pushing it toward the abyss of extinction so that something new can be created.

In the natural world of plants and animals, this process goes on continually without much fuss. But to the mind of man, this kind of change—the kind that involves letting go of things that we prize—is abhorrent. What we love, we want to keep. Even the things we don't love, we often do not want to lose. We cling to what we know. We stay in jobs and relationships beyond the point of all reason, in some cases, afraid to let go of what is no longer satisfying. We fear the abyss of the unknown and we struggle to maintain the familiar at all costs.

On a psychological level, Pluto acts mainly on the plane of the unconscious mind. Part of the Pluto process consists of a certain buildup in the psyche of unconscious resentment and anger over existing situations. Things that make us feel we've been had, or people who are rude to us, and don't want to acknowledge our worth, create a feeling of animosity in us that can slowly build up. Pluto often acts through the emotion of disgust, when circumstances and situations finally become intolerable and we feel that we would rather die than continue with them one minute longer. Finally, something snaps. There's an internal explosion and we act or are compelled to act to make a change, no matter what.

Pluto is also about power, and many of the scenarios described above come down to whether an individual has the power to make changes in his life and world, or whether someone else holds that power. The Alcoholics Anonymous prayer goes: "God grant me the serenity to accept the things I cannot change, the courage to change the things I can, and the wisdom to know the difference." There is no greater definition of individual power. Finally, Pluto is a healer. When we finally decide to leap into the abyss and let go, the transformation process of Pluto can occur, healing can begin. The process of elimination may be painful, but the result is ultimately rehabilitating and restorative.

These are some of the typical manifestations of the Pluto archetype in action. The strongest expression of this archetype in the astrological chart is the planet itself. Pluto's location in the chart tells us where the most powerful changes and transformations are likely to be experienced, where power will be an issue, where unconscious resentments lie waiting to be triggered. Next is the Sign of Scorpio. The house of the horoscope where Scorpio lies shows which area of life will be charged with strong emotions—positive ones like passion and commitment as well as negative ones like rage and jealousy. Here too we will experience the need for change.

Last but certainly not least is the 8th House—the battleground of life. In the 8th House we encounter the most intense experiences life offers. Sex, death, intimacy, emergency life and death situations, and resources shared with others. The resources referred to in the 8th House are not solely physical resources, such as money or jointly held assets. They include emotions that are shared with another. Whether you are considering physical or emotional resources, the stakes at risk in this house are usually very high.

◆   ◆   ◆

Now, let's take a look at Sam's birth chart. First impressions are key in chart analysis. Just as everyone you meet makes an initial impression the first time you meet them, so do their horoscopes. The first thing you notice when looking at Peckinpah's horoscope is the fact that four of his ten planets are located in his 8th house—the house naturally associated with Pluto. And it's not just any four planets. Sam's Sun, Moon, Mercury and Venus—the most personal of his planetary makeup—are bottled up, as it were, here in this most intense sector of the chart. Let's take this planetary package one planet at a time, and see what they tell us about the man some called "Bloody Sam."

The Sun represents one's sense of oneself. It is the ego, our source of identity and power. It indicates our potential and all that we can become. The person with Sun in Pisces is, above all else, imaginative and sensitive. Pisceans are dreamers and many of them are gifted with the ability to express some of the finest, and most sublime human emotions. Poets, painters, musicians, and composers of all stripes are born under the Sign of the Fishes.

Pisceans are extremely sensitive people. They seem to lack the normal sense of separateness and boundary that most of us have. They are often described as "psychic sponges," absorbing others' feelings, picking up emanations and vibrations of which most of us are unaware. As a result many of them have difficulty coping with the sometimes painful and hurtful circumstances around them. One way some Pisceans try to shut down the impressions coming in at them from the outside world is to use mood-altering substances. Addiction to drugs, both legal and illegal, and alcohol can become a serious problem for them. According to biographer Marshall Fine, author of "Bloody Sam, The Life and Films of Sam Peckinpah," Peckinpah had a drinking problem most of his adult life.[1]

"On *The Wild Bunch*," Fine writes, "as on other films, Peckinpah's drinking was constant and occasionally heavy." The drinking did not affect his work at that stage of his career, although it would later, when the alcoholism was combined with cocaine use. In later years, Fine writes, "alcohol would be one of the causes of Peckinpah's chronic respiratory and heart problems."

While the Sun Sign tells us of the person's substantial nature, it is the House the Sun occupies that tells us about the circumstances and life situations that will be key to the development of that nature. Those with the Sun in the 8th House seek to expand themselves and transcend their personal limitations and separateness through some form of union and interchange with other people. Some people with this position of the Sun draw to themselves other people's money and possessions.[2]

This is certainly true in Peckinpah's case. As a filmmaker, his life depended on other people investing their money to back his films. And it was this touchy subject of other people backing him, and then wanting to control the product they were investing in, that caused most of Peckinpah's problems in the Hollywood power structure. He clashed continually with his bosses, and blamed them for some of his failures, claiming that the studio heads, in an effort to protect themselves, made cuts in his films that he considered disastrous.

His work on *Major Dundee*, starring Charlton Heston, is a clear example of this. The film went over budget, and the studio threatened to pull the plug, but Heston invested his own money to finish the picture. Still, when the crew returned from filming in Mexico, the executives at Warners cut the film mercilessly. The result was a commercial as well as artistic failure.

Sometimes those with the Sun in the 8th have a fascination or preoccupation with death. Killings abound in Peckinpah's films. And it may have been this fascination with violent death that led Sam to be the creator of the "squib" and the slow motion fall. Peckinpah was the first to use squibs—plastic bags containing red fluid that are set off by a small explosive charge, creating the impression of blood spurting from a gun shot wound.

Peckinpah's stylistic treatment of death included one element for which he became well known—the slow-motion fall. Whenever someone in a Peckinpah film is shot, he falls to the ground in slow motion. The fall is usually interrupted by multiple jump cuts to other parts of the ongoing action, creating a sensation of expanded time—a visual poetry of death in motion.

Eighth Housers also usually have a great interest in taboo subjects. As a film-maker working in the 1960s through the early 1980s, Peckinpah continually dealt with subjects that were definitely not for the squeamish. His films depicted rape, grave desecration, decapitation, sadism, and moral depravity of various types. These subjects usually provided the background for the dramatic dilemmas facing Peckinpah's anti-heroes.

Let's look next at Peckinpah's Moon. The Moon shows our strongest emotional need. It symbolizes what we require to feel secure and defines our comfort zone. The Moon stands for one's mother. It shows how we respond emotionally to other people, as a result of the kind of nurturing we received as small children. In a male chart it also characterizes one's attitude toward women.

With the Moon in Aquarius, there is a strong emotional need for friendship, to belong to a group. Friendship, the importance of camaraderie and male bonding are major themes in Peckinpah's work. *The Wild Bunch,* by its very title, says it all. The film about a group of outlaws, society's outcasts, now growing old and obsolete in a changing West is all about the importance of loyalty to the group.

"When you side with a man, you stick with him," William Holden as Pike Bishop, leader of the Bunch, says in a crucial scene. "If you can't do that you're nothing but an animal. You're finished. We're finished."

The powerful humanism of this sign also inclines toward an identification with the underdog.[3] Peckinpah always sided with society's misfits. His films all focus on characters out of step with mainstream society: down and out losers, men who have lived past their time, women of questionable virtue, drunks, thieves, and outlaws.

Those with the Moon in Aquarius also have a great need to be different, individualistic, and special. This is often because mother treated them as something special when they were children. In Sam's case, his mother, Fern, treated him as something *very* special—favoring him over his brother Denver. According to biographer Fine, in Fern's eyes, Sam "could do no wrong."

The Moon's position in the 8th House took Sam's rebellious and humanistic instincts and directed them toward Plutonian issues. This position of the Moon made him extremely open to hidden forces operating personally or collectively.[4]

As a child, he would have been highly sensitive to undercurrents in the home environment, especially the mother's deeper feelings, moods, and frustrations. The feelings evoked by his mother would have left lasting impressions. Peckinpah had major problems with his mother, and his attitude toward women, which has been described by some critics as "misogynist," stems directly from his relationship with her.

According to Fine, in the 1940s, Sam's father, David Peckinpah, was a well-known activist attorney in Fresno. He was well respected in his community, but he was cowed in his own home. Peckinpah's mother, Fern, was the real power in the family. Sam was torn between the father he loved and respected and Fern who pampered and spoiled him.

When Sam's father decided he wanted to run for Congress, Fern, whose father had been a Congressman, opposed the idea. According to Fine, as far as she was concerned there would be only one Congressman in the family and that was her father. She threatened to leave Sam's father if he ran for office.

David Peckinpah caved in and declined the invitation from the Republican Party to be nominated. Fern later covered her tracks by convincing the family it was really his idea not to run. According to Fine, it was several years before the angry Sam estranged himself from his mother.

"But the damage was done—long term damage in his attitude toward women," Fine writes. "Here was the most important man in his life being emasculated by the most important woman. His father was the Boss—and yet he had caved in to a tiny, manipulative female."

Katy Haber, one of Peckinpah's long time associates, is quoted as saying, "He said that when she died, he was going to piss on his mother's grave. All his love/hate feelings for women were based on his mother."

Looking next at Venus, we note it is in extremely tight conjunction with the Moon in the 8th House. Venus is in charge of our relationships and partnering. In a man's chart, it is another indication of one's dealings with women. Everything we have just said about Peckinpah's Aquarian 8th House Moon can be repeated for Venus. But now those feeling and attitudes apply to Peckinpah's ability to love and form relationships. Obviously there will be spillover and confusion coming from his relationship with his mother. Peckinpah might have difficulty distinguishing women as capable of being or behaving differently than his mother. Venus in the 8th House by itself indicates that relationships would be deep, soul searching, complicated, and stormy.

Venus is also in Aquarius, indicating that the women in his life would be unique, and different. It is a classic textbook description of Venus in Aquarius that it often indicates marriages to foreigners or people of a different race or nationality.

Peckinpah had three wives and several women that he lived with over the years. His first wife was American, but the second, whom he married three times, was Mexican. The third wife was British. Katy Haber, with whom he had an off and on love/business relationship that lasted for years, was also from England.

Last but not least among the quartet of planets in the 8th House is Peckinpah's Mercury, the planet of thought and communication. Mercury governs our mental processes and perceptions. Mercury is our five senses, our capacity to take in experience and to learn. Our intellectual approach to life is indicated by Mercury's sign.

Sam's Mercury is in Aquarius, so he thought like an Aquarian. His thinking was highly individualistic and prone to seeing things in his own way. Mercury in Aquarius holds stubbornly to its own point of view and the viewpoint that is taken is often offbeat and not in step with the status quo.

Mercury rules communication and writing, and the scripts Sam wrote for TV and film often took offbeat, eccentric turns. His stories dealt with Aquarian themes of belonging to a group, friendship, and sticking with your friends, and most of his characters were society's misfits and outcasts.

Placed in the 8th House, Mercury took those themes and focused on the darker side of them. As often as he wrote about friendship, his stories usually depicted the betrayal of friendships. His scripts often present two old friends who find themselves in a position where one of them is tempted to sell the other out for a price.

In *The Killer Elite*, Robert Duvall plays the treacherous intelligence agent who betrays his friend, played by James Caan. Duvall can't resist the highest price ever paid for selling out—two years in Bora Bora and a million dollars. In *Ride the High Country*, Randolph Scott turns on Joel McCrea in order to try to steal a gold shipment. In *The Wild Bunch*, Deke Thornton, played by Robert Ryan, is the former friend of Pike Bishop, leader of the bunch, played by William Holden. Thornton is now the Judas Goat leading the posse hired by the railroad to bring the Bunch to justice. In *Bring Me the Head of Alfredo Garcia*, Peckinpah presents Warren Oates as a man so desperate he's willing to sever the head of his dead and buried friend in order to collect one million dollars.

◆　　◆　　◆

Zooming back now from the intense energy of Sam's 8th House, let's get an overview of the entire chart. We can see that Sam has four planets in the emotional water signs: The Sun and Uranus are in Pisces, Pluto is in Cancer, and Saturn lies in Scorpio. This emphasis on the signs of emotion further indicate a sensitive nature—one easily bruised and prone to seeking self-protection.

His Cancer Ascendant emphasizes the emotional quality of his nature and adds to the tendency toward self-protection. Cancer can be expressed in two ways. One way is to be very caring, solicitous, kind of like a mother hen. We see this more often in female charts. The other way, more often seen in male horoscopes, is to use Cancer's crab-like outer shell to project a hard, crabby exterior personality. The person, in an effort to protect the tender inner feelings, acts in a hard-bitten manner, as if to show the world that nothing bothers him.

Sam appears to have used the second approach to the Cancer energy. His hard Cancer exterior was used to protect the inner vulnerability of his emotional inner self. He projected a hard-boiled kind of personality—a tough, hard nose with something of a chip on his shoulder.

He professed having been raised like a cowboy in the Old West, while in reality he was a city boy who only took vacations in the mountains near Fresno with his dad and grandfather. He was short in stature, but swaggered and acted tough, especially around other men. He liked to carouse and drink with male friends, and his shoots on location in Mexico or the American Southwest were often described by participants as macho-oriented endurance contests.

The tough exterior, however, was a double-edged sword. On one hand it protected his inner sensitivity, but on the other it isolated him from others. Although he was constantly surrounded by people, both on the movie set and after hours, Peckinpah was at heart a loner.

On the set, he was the boss, but, as they say, it's lonely at the top. He frequently got into quarrels with his cast members and would deliberately instigate fights and arguments to get a better performance. During one such incident while filming *Major Dundee*, Peckinpah so angered Charlton Heston by calling him "a lying S.O.B.," that the actor, while on horseback, literally charged at him with a drawn sword. Peckinpah was sitting on a camera crane and yelled at the operator to lift him up out of the way.

After hours, he liked to gather with friends. But there was always a separateness, a wall between Peckinpah and those he associated with. As he grew older, he drew more and more into his tough Cancer shell. Isela Vega, the Mexican actress who starred in *Bring Me the Head of Alfredo Garcia,* recalls phoning him on the opening night of *The Osterman Weekend,* the last film he would ever direct.

"He was sitting home by himself," she says. "He was a lonely man."

◆   ◆   ◆

Another significant feature of Sam's chart is a number of planets in the fixed signs of Taurus, Leo, Scorpio, and Aquarius. His Moon, Venus, and Mercury, as mentioned earlier, are together in rebellious Aquarius. Saturn, the planet of discipline and lessons surrounding your limitations, is in suspicious Scorpio. Neptune the dreamer is in dramatic Leo. Mars, the planet of assertion and action, is in Taurus, a sign known to act only when something of value is at stake. Six planets all set in signs marked by their propensity for willfulness and determination, and all at odds with each other.

This emphasis on fixed signs is indicative of someone who lives life by a certain, unchangeable set of values. Their lives are often marked by conflicts with others over questions involving those values. In a Peckinpah film, the most important value for a man is the integrity of his word. This is one of the major themes in *The Wild Bunch*.

In one scene, Bishop (William Holden) tells Dutch Engstron (Ernest Borgnine) that their former friend Deke Thornton (Robert Ryan) is riding with the railroad posse. When Dutch can't understand why, Bishop says:

"What would you do in his place? He gave his word."

Dutch: "Gave his word to a railroad."

Pike: "It's his word."

Dutch: "That ain't what counts. It's who you give it to."

The tense dynamics of Peckinpah's fixed planets also indicate problems with self worth and being able to give and receive love. The Moon, Venus, and Mercury oppose Neptune across the 2nd House-8th House axis—the houses associated with self-worth and sharing the worth of others. The placement of Neptune in the 2nd house may have provided Sam with highly idealist values, but it also probably weakened his own sense of self-worth.

Even more telling in Sam's chart is the presence of Saturn in the 5th House–the house of love given. Saturn's presence in this sector of the chart in the sign of Scorpio made it very difficult for Peckinpah to give love easily. His love affairs were marked by dark suspicions, jealousy, and violence.

Saturn stands for the father's psychological impact on the individual. Saturn is in apparent retrograde motion in Sam's chart, and indicates problems with the father. Retrograde Saturn usually means that somehow the father is ineffective in providing the kind of loving protection and role modeling that a child, especially a boy, needs growing up.[4] We've seen how Sam was filled with resentment at the way his mother emasculated his father. To Sam, his father appeared weak. Since Saturn is in Sam's 5th House of love given, it would have had an inhibiting effect on his ability to express love at a personal level.

The 5th House is also the sector of the horoscope where our creativity can be found. The Pluto archetype expressed through Saturn in Scorpio yielded creative works of dark intensity and emotional impact. Saturn would tend to produce "serious" films, and indeed, he only made one really successful comedy, *The Ballad of Cable Hogue*.

◆   ◆   ◆

We've covered quite a bit of Sam's horoscope, and how it manifested in his life. We've seen how the Pluto archetype expressed itself in different, subtle ways. But what about the planet Pluto itself? Where is the Lord of the Underworld in this chart, and why is it the most powerful force in this horoscope? We've saved the most important part of our study for last.

Pluto lies in Peckinpah's 12th House—the house of the unconscious mind. Traditionally, the 12th was known as the House of secret enemies, and it is true that if not properly understood and managed, planetary energies here can manifest as forces that seem to sneak up on you from behind and attempt to undo you, or rather, help you undo yourself.

In modern astrology, the emphasis is on psychologically integrating all the elements of the chart, and we attempt to explain 12th House planets as parts of ourselves that can turn us into our own worst enemies, if we let them. The task is to become aware how energies in the 12th may be unconsciously undermining our lives. But the problems associated with planets in the 12th are not strictly related to one's personal psychology. There is a universality associated with them.

Pluto here must deal in some way with what Jung called the collective shadow—those things that most people just don't want to think about, much less make movies about. People with Pluto in the 12th have to transform an ancient anger and rage, and they must either act out the collective shadow or find a way to redeem it. One way of redemption is through art.[5]

Is there a more apt description of what Peckinpah was trying to do with his art? All of his films are about people who are exposed to the dark underbelly of life. Peckinpah's Plutonian anti-heros are people whose souls are corroded by the muck of existence. They've seen too much, lived too long. All of these characters reach a point where sheer disgust at the sorry state of the human condition builds up to a volcanic eruption—a Plutonic explosion of violence that is actually a final, desperate act of redemption.

As noted earlier, Pluto is the planet that pushes us over the abyss. At the climax of *The Wild Bunch*, the outlaw band, seeing they have no options left, and disgusted with the butchery of one of their members by a Mexican general, face that abyss and leap into it. They commit a Plutonic act of self-immolation by starting a shoot-out with an entire army.

Pluto's most significant aspect in Sam's chart is its opposition to Jupiter in his 6th House of work and health. Jupiter governs our ethics, moral standards and principles. People who have Jupiter in opposition to Pluto are people who simply cannot compromise their principles. They have standards and they will not give them up no matter what. So we can see how Pluto, operating from the most unconscious part of his chart, the 12th House, may have compelled Peckinpah unwittingly to buck the system he worked in (6th House), spending most of his life in battles with studio bosses over everything, including finances, writing, casting, and editing of his creative output.

The stories of his fights with studio executives are legendary. And the retaliation that the bosses took, by re-editing his films before they were released, failing to distribute them properly, and in at least one case, firing him (Jupiter in the 6th House of employment), all resulted from his inability to compromise.

The essence of the Jupiter-Pluto opposition is a clash between those who live by a certain code of behavior and those with no scruples at all. In terms of artistic subject matter, themes generated by Pluto opposite Jupiter permeate all of Sam's films. His stories are all about men who live by a code (Jupiter) pitted against big, ruthless forces that operate on an impersonal level (Pluto). Whether it's the railroad; a ruthless Mexican general in charge of an army of cutthroats (*The Wild Bunch*); a family of degenerate gold miners (*Ride the High Country*); a CIA official working for both sides and ultimately only for his own self-aggrandizement (*The Killer Elite*); or an imperious German aristocracy that ruthlessly sends its young men out to be killed so they can obtain the Iron Cross for themselves (*Cross of Iron*), Peckinpah kept his focus on the battle between those brave enough to take a stand based on personal values versus the blind forces of unscrupulous ruthlessness and inevitable change.

In *Pat Garrett and Billy the Kid*, Billy (Kris Kristofferson) asks Garrett (James Coburn), his former friend and fellow outlaw, who now wears a badge, how it feels to be working for the other side.

"It feels," Garret says, "like times are changing."

"The times, maybe," the Kid says. "But not me."

Pluto opposing Sam's Jupiter also stimulated his search for faith in a greater order in the universe. It created a search for meaning through transformation.[6] This theme is no more strongly portrayed than in the final scenes of *The Wild Bunch*.

After the Battle of Aqua Verde, and after the Bunch have all been killed by the army of Mexican general Mapacahe, the railroad posse descends on the town like vultures and carries the Bunch away, their bodies tied over their saddles. But the bounty hunters are ambushed by the peasant guerillas who have also been fighting Mapache, and who will eventually succeed in their revolution.

Paul Seydor in *Peckinpah: The Western Films, a Reconsideration*, notes that the peasants identify with the Bunch, because of what they perceive as the outlaw's suicidal "heroism" in fighting Mapache to the death.[7] In their eyes, the Bunch become heroes of mythic proportions.

Peckinpah ends *The Wild Bunch* with clips of each of the four, laughing as they did in life, and then, dissolves to a reprise of an earlier scene, in which the Bunch rode through the streets of Angel's poverty stricken village. The villagers, lined up on both sides of the dirt road, throw flowers in the path of the outlaw gang and sing for them—it's almost a religious procession. Peckinpah has shifted perspective and we now see the Bunch as the villagers see them, through child-like, but not childish, eyes, transformed, "illumined," Seydor says, "by a radiance if not celestial then at least transcendent..." Like the Phoenix, the mythological bird most often associated with Pluto and the sign Scorpio, they have risen anew out of the ashes of their own self-immolation.

◆   ◆   ◆

The tense energies in Peckinpah's chart gave him the drive to pursue his art as a film maker, but the same energies also were the demons that possessed him as a man. To quell the fury of his demons Peckinpah resorted to the use of alcohol, marijuana and eventually cocaine. The substance abuse provided temporary relief but created long term problems that eventually undermined his health. His physical constitution became weakened. He died in 1984 at age 59 of heart failure caused by complications from pneumonia contracted while in Puerto Vallarta, Mexico.

After *Osterman Weekend*, his last feature film project, Peckinpah seemed to be trying to reestablish himself professionally, but after that film his only other work was limited to directing two music videos for Julian Lennon. He had quit drinking, but it was too late. The excesses of his life had by now caught up with him.

He flew down to Puerto Vallarta from San Diego the day before Christmas 1984 for some relaxation. Two days later, his former wife Begonia Palacios received a phone call from Sam canceling plans to have her meet him on the 28th in Mexico for her birthday. Then on the 27th she received a call from a government hospital in Mexico saying Sam had been admitted with chest pains and vomiting blood. She flew him in an ambulance plane to a hospital in Inglewood, California.

"Why did God do this to me," Peckinpah asked her, as she signed his admission papers. "I stopped drinking for a year. I was good and now look at me."

At one point, referring to the Julian Lennon videos, he said, "Do you know the last film I made was five minutes long?"

Begonia watched as doctors and nurses tended to the failing director. Finally his breathing stopped and could not be restored. He went into cardiac arrest. He died on the morning of his ex-wife's birthday, on December 28, 1984.

Peckinpah's chart at the time of his death was receiving a number of stressful aspects by transit, though possibly there were none that a healthy man would not have survived. The transiting Sun was square his Midheaven and transiting Venus conjuncted natal Uranus (ruler of 8th House of death). Mars conjuncted his Sun, often an indicator of heart attack and Jupiter opposed his Ascendant (the health center). In addition, Saturn squared his Mercury (difficulty breathing), and Pluto trined his Sun, indicating, perhaps, a sense of surrender to the final transformation. Also significant is the fact that during the preceding month a solar eclipse, often an indicator of death, had squared his 8th House Sun. The Mars transit to his Sun at the time of death triggered the November eclipse into activation.

Two weeks after his death, at a memorial ceremony in Hollywood, actor James Coburn, in one of several eulogies given that day, said Sam Peckinpah was a director "who pushed me over the abyss, and then jumped in after me. He took me on some great adventures."

It was a fitting epitaph for a man who had spent a brief, but passionate lifetime not only leaping into the abyss but exploring it and sending back to us films that could only have been made from there.

A Table of Events in the Life of Sam Peckinpah

Sept. 1958—Transiting Pluto opposes Sun: Premiere of *The Rifleman*, Sam's first television series. He created the character and wrote several of the episodes. He had his own offices at Four Star Productions.

Sept. 1960—Transiting Pluto inconjunct Midheaven: *The Westerner* premiers on NBC television. Peckinpah wrote and directed episodes, created the character played by Brian Keith.
—A solar eclipse trines his natal Pluto and natal Saturn. Transiting Saturn opposes natal Pluto: *The Westerner* fails after one season. Peckinpah's first marriage ends in divorce. His father dies.

Sept.—Oct. 1962—Transiting Pluto trines natal Mars: *Ride the High Country* with Randolph Scott and Joel McCrea opens. The film is a critical success, but suffers because of poor studio editing and distribution.

July—Dec. 1963—Transiting Saturn opposite Neptune. *Major Dundee*, with Charlton Heston, a major disaster.

Dec. 1964—Solar eclipse in Sam's 5th House inconjunct natal Pluto: Fired from *The Cincinnati Kid*, over artistic differences with the studio.

April—July 1968—Transiting Pluto opposes natal Uranus. *The Wild Bunch* is in production. This proves to be Sam's masterpiece, and ensures him a place in film history. The Pluto/Uranus themes, so strong in his chart, are now activated and the film embodies both Pluto and Uranian archetypes.

April 1971—Transiting Neptune squares natal Sun. Ill health, caused by drinking and smoking, results in pneumonia, and Peckinpah is forced to leave location site in Cornwall, England, where *Straw Dogs* is being filmed. He goes to London and enters the hospital. The studio nearly fires him, but he recuperates and completes the film.

Feb. 1975—Transiting Jupiter conjuncts natal Uranus. Transiting Uranus trines natal Sun. Filming of *The Killer Elite* begins. Transiting Saturn conjuncts natal Pluto in the 12th House of addictions. Peckinpah begins first use of cocaine.

May 15, 1979—Transiting Uranus squares natal Moon and Venus in the 8th House. Neptune on cusp of 6th House, inconjunct Ascendant. Transiting Jupiter inconjunct natal Sun. Peckinpah has first heart attack.

Oct.—Dec. 1982—Transiting Jupiter conjuncts natal Saturn in 5th. Transiting Uranus squares natal Sun. Creative activities resume with filming of *Osterman Weekend*. But film is weak effort, showing Peckinpah's physical and mental deterioration.

1.   Marshall Fine, *Bloody Sam, The Life and Films of Sam Peckinpah* (New York: Donald I. Fine, 1991) A good, concise biography of the director.

2.   A good discussion of the meaning of planets in houses, some of which is included here, can be found in *The Twelve Houses* by Howard Sasportas, 1985, The Aquarian Press.

3.   For clear interpretations of the meaning of planets in signs, see, *Character and Fate*, Katharine Merlin, 1989, Arkana.

4.   The interpretation of retrograde Saturn as indicating psychological problems resulting from relationship with the father are discussed fully in *Synthesis and Counseling in Astrology*, by Noel Tyl, 1994, Llewellyn Publications, St. Paul Minnesota.

5.   Pluto in the 12th House is discussed brilliantly by Howard Sasportas in *The Twelve Houses*, 1985, The Aquarian Press.

6.   Jupiter-Pluto aspects are explained authoritatively in *Exploring Jupiter: The Astrological Key to Progress, Prosperity, and Potential* by Stephen Arroyo, 1996, CRCS Publications, Sebastopol, CA.

7.   Paul Seydor, *Peckinpah: The Western Films, A Reconsideration* (Urbana, Illinois: University of Illinois Press, 1999). The best critical analysis of Peckinpah's western films. •

Steven Spielberg: Archetypal Journey of the Artist and Entertainer

Bill Streett, M.A.

For both good and ill, Steven Spielberg has both created and defined the face of America and movie-making in the latter half of the twentieth century. Through movies of wild fantasy, he has captured the American family lifestyle: suburban tract houses, divorces, adults looking for the inner child, children looking to grow up too fast. In movies of unwavering realism, Spielberg has allowed us to reflect upon the defining moments of the twentieth century that defined the nation's character. By tapping into collective dreams, Spielberg allows us to build a future nation. Spielberg's movie empire and entertainment machine may represent the last bastion of anti-postmodern, irony-free filmmaking in which history is black and white, with winners and losers, and with a universe that is easily dichotomized between good and evil. In a sense, mainstream America and Spielberg have co-existed in a dialogue of mutual admiration for each other, with Spielberg becoming America's greatest ambassador to the world, evolving into the P.T. Barnum of late twentieth century cinema.

A cursory and critical assessment of Spielberg could legitimately accentuate his lesser contributions to film: overemphasis of technical wizardry at the expense of character development and story; a lack of depth, realism, and nuance pervading his oeuvre; the inadvertent spawning of Spielberg clones and one-offs, pollution of the American film market with would-be blockblusters of rampant superficiality and high-gloss ephemera, leading to what critic Pauline Kael called the "infantilization of the culture."[1] In essence, Spielberg has too easily succumbed to style over soul, sensory onslaught over the subtlety of substance.

An equally critical, but broader view of Spielberg would retain the preceding but add the following appraisal: a master craftsman who has never failed to grow and develop when the temptation to rest on popularity and mega-success have been great; an individual courageous enough to imprint his child-like innocence and awe on celluloid in an industry notoriously known for its ability to destroy dreams as quickly as they are made; an unsurpassed entertainer with an innate and uncanny intuition of pacing, image creation, and storytelling; and finally, at the pinnacle of his success, a young man willing to transform from a gadget-obsessed Peter Pan to a mature father, from hard-bargaining mogul to philan-thropist, and from entertainer to artist. The simple, unambiguous narratives that Spielberg injects into the majority of his movies belies the complexity of their cre-ator. Spielberg's meandering journey towards psychological wholeness is not unlike others inspired to actualize their deep potentials, the only difference is that Spielberg has left grand visions of his journey, impressing themselves in the imag-inations of millions.

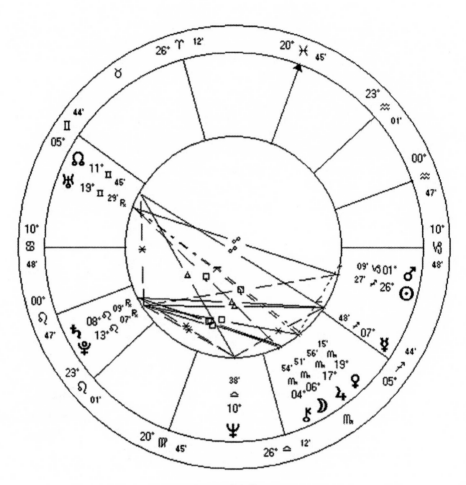

Steven Spielberg
December 18, 1946
Cincinnati, Ohio
6:16 PM

The Birth Chart

Through unearthing the details of Spielberg's childhood, the potentials of his astrological birth chart already manifest themselves in his early biography. Born under a Uranus-Sun opposition, Spielberg exuded many of the positive traits of this potent combination from an early age. People born with Uranus and Sun in angular relationship often feel compelled to accentuate their own individual uniqueness and feel an obligation to stand out and use their strong wills to fit outside of prescribed molds. This specialness, this reveling in one's own distinctive creativity, is often misunderstood and is quickly labeled as "weird" and "strange."

Spielberg was no exception; his passion for film at an early age and his experimental exuberance toward life made him stand out from the crowd and earned him the labels of "wacky" and "bizarre." As Spielberg himself describes, "I think I was never considered really weird, the way the philosophy majors were weird. But I was considered different."[2]

Not only are Sun-Uranus people likely to stand out in youth, but they are more inclined to follow their own creative spark, or pursue what the Greeks called one's "daimon." Spielberg took his family's storytelling tradition and his father's love of electronics and poured them into a love of the relatively new art of movie-making. So obsessed was he by film that by the time he entered high school, academics were a mere afterthought in relation to his passion. Much like his recent collaborator Stanley Kubrick (who also possessed a Sun-Uranus aspect in his birth chart), Spielberg was in serious pursuit of his vocation and dream when others were debating college choices and pursuing prom dates. It is this intractable need to follow their own calling, often at the admonishment of parents and friends, which is the mark of a strong Uranus in the birth chart.

With Uranus in Spielberg's natal 12th house, Spielberg acts as a conduit to channel deep, archetypal images and myths that strongly resonate with the collective unconscious of society-at-large. Aliens, UFO's, artificial intelligence, poltergeists—strangely we are drawn into this world of imaginal possibility through Spielberg's unparalleled ability to realize these dreams on screen. As Roger Ebert stated in a recent article for *Time*, Spielberg's great strength is "his direct line to our subconscious."[3] Like strange attractors from a dimension that interfaces with our world on a subtle level, Spielberg's visions of possibility attract us somewhat hypnotically and instinctively.

However, the fantasies of mythical beings from other dimensions represent only half of Spielberg's repertory. These ethereal, often benign and adorable beings are counterbalanced by primordial creatures designed for death and destruction. The sharks, dinosaurs, and wartime psychopaths found in Spielberg's films spring from a very different part of Spielberg's psyche indeed. However, like his fascination with a utopian future filled with peaceful and spiritual beings, the seeds of his interest in the darker, crueler side of reality are evidenced in his childhood. In his youth, Spielberg had an attraction toward war, monsters, and innocent forms of torture. As a childhood friend has said, "Stevie had a surprising kind of morbid streak."[4] The specific archetypal combination responsible for his infatuation with atrocity, violence, and the horrific is the Saturn-Pluto conjunction in Leo. With Saturn and Pluto in combination, the primal force of destruction and regeneration is compacted, actualized, and tinged with dread and fright. Thus, the creative and obliterative functions of the universe are concretized in vessels of tremendous potency that strike fear in the hearts of onlookers—T Rexs, great white sharks, S.S. concentration camp guards.

It is this same archetypal combination that has driven Spielberg with such obsessive power to achieve success in the world of film. As this combination was awakened and stimulated by a transiting conjunction by Uranus at the age of twelve, Steve's hobby became a vocation. He states, "I've been really serious about [filmmaking] as a career since I was twelve years old. I don't excuse those early years as a hobby, do you know what I'm saying? I really did start then."[5] Fueling an intense ambition and allowing for incredible powers of focused, sustained passion, it is the Saturn-Pluto combination which has allowed Spielberg the power to make his dreams a reality.

The Films

Since Spielberg is in the minority of directors working in Hollywood who have attained artistic control of their movies, his personal vision and the workings of his own psychology are more likely to manifest in the movies he directs. The succession of movies he has directed, then, should reflect the personal ideas, experiences, interests, and passions that occupied Spielberg during the time of their creation. In addition, astrological transits should correlate with Spielberg's experience of creating a motion picture and should mirror the main themes and content explored in each movie. Hence, a threefold dialogue—a trialogue—occurs between archetype, Spielberg, and his creation, each accurately reflecting and affirming each other's condition.

Jaws (released 1975)

One the most grueling and technically demanding productions in motion picture history resulted in the greatest box office success of its time. *Jaws* was a masterpiece of suspense and fear that put Spielberg on the map as a noteworthy director. When outer planets have conjoined Spielberg's natal Mercury, Spielberg has been inspired to not only direct stories but create them in the form of screenplays and scripts. As Neptune conjoined Spielberg's Mercury for nearly three years in the early seventies, Spielberg fashioned the stories for *Sugarland Express* and *Close Encounters of the Third Kind* and made critical revisions to Peter Benchley's novel of *Jaws*. Known for it's inspiring qualities, writer's block is anything but the case when Neptune conjoins Mercury.

The symbol most often associated with the archetype of Neptune is the ocean. Acting as the literal embodiment from which creation springs forth, the ocean potently captures the matrix of creation that archetypal Neptune signifies. However, the Neptunian waters that connected with Spielberg's thoughts were not of the sort that led to experiences of oceanic bliss. As Benchley's novel used the great white shark as a secondary device around which to devise a tale of morality, Spielberg, to his credit, focused primarily upon the shark and crafted scenes of chilling suspense and terror as a result.

Spielberg's natal chart illustrates that he was undergoing the generational transit of Pluto conjoining Neptune. Individually manifesting as an intensification of dream life and fantasy or as transformation in consciousness itself, Pluto conjoining Neptune received its perfect realization in the image of the killer shark terrorizing a U.S. resort town. Pluto represents the revolution and renovation of life by processes of intense and extreme transformation; whatever archetypal Pluto contacts is irrevocably changed. That which evokes extreme conversion and metamorphosis—death, sex, birth—are Pluto at work at its most actualized level. The killing machine of the shark is not necessarily "Plutonic" *per se*; however, the pain of extinction and annihilation that a shark attack represents is deeply metaphorical of the process of Pluto. Thus, Spielberg's *Jaws* is a symbolic manifestation of the transformative powers embedded within the collective unconscious (Neptune).

Going over budget and one hundred days beyond its original production schedule, Spielberg assumed that *Jaws* would destroy his professional reputation. Reflecting upon the experience, Spielberg stated, "No one is ever going to see this picture, and I'm never going to work in this town again."[6]

However, within two months of its release, *Jaws* became the most successful motion picture in history, surpassing Coppola's *The Godfather*.[7] Upon *Jaws's* release, with Jupiter firmly entrenched in Spielberg's 10th house, the house of career and public reception, Spielberg began his quarter century domination of the worldwide box office and was widely known outside of Hollywood circles and cinemaphiles. Jupiter's ability to expand and bring triumph is very much in evidence here, as Spielberg achieved financial independence through the film's box office generation, gained tremendous creative leverage and bargaining power in the industry, and received wide critical acclaim through his directorial efforts.

Close Encounters of the Third Kind (released 1977)

As much as *Jaws* tested Spielberg's ability to direct under difficult production circumstances, *Close Encounters of the Third Kind* was the film that truly challenged Spielberg's ability to work under a very strained and pressure-filled state of affairs. In his own words, Spielberg believed that the experience of filming *Close Encounters* was "twice as bad—and twice as expensive as well."[8] French filmmaker Francois Truffualt, who acted in the film, remarked, "In the face of overwhelming hardships and innumerable complications that would, I suspect, have discouraged most directors, Spielberg's perseverance and fortitude were simply amazing." [9]

Close Encounters was made under Spielberg's Saturn Return. Of this most perplexing and complex of transits, one thing could be said unequivocally—it is a time of challenge, a time of frustration, and it is first and foremost *hard*, like the archetype of Saturn itself.

Since Spielberg's specific Saturn Return inflected his natal Saturn-Pluto conjunction, the transit manifested this archetypal combination in very concrete and real terms. Saturn and Pluto together often translate into an indefatigable work effort under circumstances of limited resources. Spielberg's work effort and ability to keep cool under strained situations had been noted before, yet it is was really proven on the set of *Close Encounters*. Spielberg also found that realizing his grand vision under budget and time constraints was a monumental task for which he was not fully prepared. The experience of *Close Encounters* matured Spielberg as a filmmaker and also made him more sensitive to focus on the pragmatics of filmmaking, as he made a commitment to stay within budget and shooting schedule after the headaches of the production.

More than any other film, *Close Encounters* comes closest to expressing Spielberg's personal outlook on the cosmos. Of the movie, Spielberg states that it is "my vision, my hope, and philosophy." [10] Arguably more than any other narrative film, *Close Encounters* realizes the essential and deep-seated need of human beings to create meaning in the universe, the will to surpass earthbound limitations, and the unshakeable conviction that "we are not alone." After viewing, Ray Bradbury insightfully stated, "this is a religious film, in all the great good sense, the right sense, of that much-battered word."[11] *Religious*, derived from the Latin "religio" meaning "to bond," is the word that refers to humans' relationship to the infinite.

Close Encounters, as author Joseph McBride states, is Spielberg's "spellbinding dream of the transcendence of mundane reality,"[12] perfectly reflecting the archetypal configuration informing Spielberg's psyche at the time of the movie's creation. Jupiter, Neptune, and Uranus, were either actively transiting his birth chart or the recipients of major transits themselves. Taken together, these archetypes represent the transcendent (as opposed to immanent, and earth-bound) religious impulse. Forcing our gaze heavenward, Neptune, Jupiter, and Uranus symbolize the inherent capacity to dream about the absolute nature of reality (Neptune), form systems of belief and faith in those dreams (Jupiter), and the reason to reflect on the ability to create technology to transcend limitations to better experience those dreams (Uranus). More than any other combination, Uranus, Jupiter, and Neptune are associated with the peak and mystical experience. Uranus shocks and stimulates the Neptunian capacity to alter ordinary experience and perception. Finally Jupiter expands and elevates the religiously transcendent principle to reach unheard-of heights and aspirations.

At the time of *Close Encounters'* release in late 1977, Neptune was opposing Spielberg's natal Uranus, Uranus conjoined his natal Jupiter, Pluto conjoined his natal Neptune, and finally, Jupiter squared his natal Neptune. The hyperstimulation of these three archetypes reflects the awe-inspiring and benign view of the universe that is captured in the film. As a point of reference, arguably the only other major commercial hit that so inspiringly captures the need for humans to explore the cosmos, spurned by the religious impulse is *Contact*, released under the triple conjunction of Uranus, Jupiter, and Neptune in 1997.

E.T. (released 1982)

Regardless if you buy into the plausible theory that *E.T.* is the Christ myth repackaged, this is a story of higher love and the ability to create union through friendship. More than a sci-fi movie, *E.T.* is a movie of relationship. With a once-and-a-lifetime chemistry between director and ensemble cast, Spielberg explored the nature of communion between two beings and the result was deeply touching and satisfying for Spielberg and audiences alike.

At the time of *E.T.*'s creation and release, Spielberg was experiencing a Neptune conjunction of his natal Sun placement. The inspiration, longings for authentic connection, and yearnings for deliverance that Spielberg was sure to be feeling shone through in *E.T.* Spielberg turned down the technical aspects and special effects magic—correlations of his Sun-Uranus conjunction—so that the heartfelt centerpiece of the story, the friendship between E.T. and Elliot, could carry the movie.

The central image and the most memorable line of the movie epitomize the archetypal themes associated with Neptune. The movie poster featuring the outstretched fingers of E.T. and Elliot evokes the similar image of the extended digits of God and Adam on Michelangelo's mural on the Sistine Chapel. The core motifs remain the same: the yearning to touch the infinite, to be healed, to dissolve boundaries—all central Neptunian issues. Similarly, E.T.'s pitiable repeated groveling to "phone home" captures the longing in all of us to return to an undifferentiated state of union with the divine, the oceanic womb, the condition of unbroken wholeness.

The Color Purple (released 1985)

A remarkable shift occurred in Spielberg's filmmaking with the creation of *The Color Purple*. Spielberg began to create movies less reliant on technical prowess and more involved in high drama, intense conflict, deep emotional impact and the profound themes of human existence—movies the Academy usually smiles upon. Films like *The Color Purple*, *Schindler's List* and *Saving Private Ryan* are much deeper in scope, heavier in emotional content and more darkly dramatic than the early Spielberg. Very simply, Spielberg made a shift from the heights of spirit to the depths of soul. This transformation is paralleled in a major transit to Spielberg's birth chart. As transiting Uranus ended its seven year stay in Spielberg's planet-rich 5th house—the house of creativity—in 1984, Pluto entered the same house for a much longer sojourn. The "Uranus period," a period of dazzling spectacle, soaring heights, heroic journeys, and cutting edge technique, can be contrasted with the serious tragedy, mournful loss, and power-charged confrontations of the "Pluto" dramas from 1984 onward.

The Color Purple was the first full manifestation of this change. Slight hints at Spielberg's transforming aesthetic could be seen in 1984's *Indiana Jones and the Temple of Doom*. The memorable ritual scenes of a Kali sect in "deepest India" could not be considered lightweight fare for all audiences and earned the film the newly instated, controversial rating of PG-13.

The Color Purple, however, more markedly delineated the transition as Spielberg left the popcorn universe of extra-terrestrial fantasy and action epics for the gritty realism of human relationships with their attendant corruption, immorality, and cruelty—the "fallen state" of earthbound reality.

In an interview in 1985, a prescient Spielberg noted his own shifting interests. "It's as if I've been swimming in water up to my waist all my life—and I'm great at it—but now I'm going into the deep section of the pool."[13] The depths he is referring to is Pluto.

With *The Color Purple*, many critics believed that Spielberg was entering into a domain reserved for more serious directors. As an established director in action-adventure, fantasy, and suspense, Spielberg, they believed, had no business delving into the realm of a tight human drama. Even the confident Spielberg had some trepidation. Agreeing that he was a director of "Big Movies. Movies about out there [referring to outer space]," Spielberg admitted that, "I didn't know if the time was right to do a movie that was about in here [tapping his chest]." [14] However the timing was right, as the "in there" was being intensified and deepened by a Pluto transit to his natal Moon.

On its most literal level, the Moon represents the feminine aspects of the psyche, and, fittingly, *The Color Purple* has been the only feature film he has directed to not only feature multiple female protagonists but is his only film from the female characters perspective. The Pluto-Moon complex can represent someone who is witness and privy to powerful emotional states; abusive, enmeshed affairs; and transformative, soulful relationships. *The Color Purple* centers principally around the journey of Celie, a woman who is brought up in a abusive situation only to repeat the pattern later on as an adult. First and foremost, however, those with the Pluto-Moon constellation are survivors and their journeys are journeys of emotional fortitude, strength, and wisdom. Principally, *The Color Purple* is not a movie of abusive relationships but is a journey of the heart and emotional transformation through the survival of racism and abuse.

Schindler's List and *Jurassic Park* (released 1993)

The transformation that Spielberg documented in *The Color Purple* awaited him in the creation of *Schindler's List*. In the year of both the production of *Schindler's List* and *Jurassic Park*, Spielberg's progressed Sun, representing his ego and core personality, opposed his natal Saturn-Pluto conjunction. For this year-long period, Spielberg had the privilege and burden of carrying this Saturn-Pluto archetypal combination with its associated attributes: work ethic, maturity, high seriousness, and the highest and lowest of human potentials.

With the saccharine sentimentality of *Always* and the overindulgence of *Hook* recently behind him, Spielberg needed to find projects that would allow him to return to form. *Schindler's List* was the vehicle that not merely restored his reputation but would be the struggle of his personal and professional life. Prior to the production of *Jaws*, Spielberg acknowledged his reluctance to take on the project because it threatened to turn him into a commercial director and not the auteur he longed to become; he would be a director, in his words, of "movies" and not "films." At long last, *Schindler's List* represented the opportunity to become the artist that was Spielberg's original intention. The effort to transcend his commercial success was compounded by the equally demanding need to return to his Jewish heritage and to immerse himself in the difficult recreation of the mass annihilation of his people.

In essence, *Schindler's List* was the complete transformation of Spielberg as director and individual, and the archetypal configuration of Pluto, Saturn, and Sun parallels this theme of annihilative metamorphosis. As author Joseph McBride writes, "*Schindler's List* became the transforming experience of Spielberg's lifetime. Making the film after a decade of hesitation and avoidance was the catharsis that finally liberated him to be himself, both as man and as artist, fully integrating those two, sometimes distinct-seeming halves of his personality."[15] As Spielberg himself commented on the process of his psychological transformation during this production, "It was so bloody painful."[16]

Not only could the archetypal manifestation of Saturn-Pluto be seen through Spielberg's rapidly changing character but also through the films themselves. Saturn and Pluto symbolizes the polarization of good vs. evil, of the peaks and valleys available to the human condition, as Saturn concretizes and manifests Pluto's tendency toward extremities. In *Schindler's List* we see Oskar Schindler, an enterprising capitalist, caught between the saintly morality of his accountant and the immoral monster S.S. Untersturmfuhrer, Amon Goeth. It is this excessive schism between forces—angel versus devil, madness versus holiness—under the harshest and most extreme of circumstances—war, poverty, famine, plague—that typifies Saturn and Pluto in combination.

Jurassic Park's computer animated dinosaurs symbolize yet another aspect of the Saturn-Pluto grouping, the fear and problematic side of the primal, instinctual, and biological. Like the great white shark of *Jaws,* the dinosaurs brought to life in *Jurassic Park* represents nature at its most creative and destructive. Saturn can render problematic and impose fear on whatever it contacts. In this case, Saturn makes the transforming, primal side of nature—Pluto—something which evokes terror and fright in others. All transformative processes have a degree of threat involved as that which is transformed necessarily surrenders its previous state; however, some of these processes are incredibly alluring, seductive, and appealing. Saturn, by contrast, makes these transformative processes dark and ter-ror-inducing.

And, of course, what of the critical and commercial success of these films? *Jurassic Park* earned Spielberg more money off one film than any other director in history. *Schindler's List* garnered critical accolades and gave Spielberg the much-deserved first time Oscar for Best Director. It was, as they say, a vintage year. When one observes success at this level and magnitude, one must hunt for Jupi-ter's position in the sky relative to the birth chart.

Not only was Jupiter in the aforementioned 5th house, but Spielberg was expe-riencing the coveted Jupiter Return at the time of his Oscar win. The Jupiter Return occurs approximately every twelve to fourteen years (his previous Jupiter Return coincided with the release of *E.T.* and *Poltergeist* in 1982, which he pro-duced). It is correlated with success; however, the amount of hard work, dedica-tion, perseverance, and determination one is willing to put forth is often correlated with the size of the Jupiterian bounty.

Saving Private Ryan (released 1998)

Unrelenting, uncompromising, heroic, and deeply moving, *Saving Private Ryan* is, by many accounts, one of the handful of truly great war films. Revisiting the material of World War II for a third time behind the camera, *Saving Private Ryan* is Spielberg's most unobtrusive look into the horror of war, relying upon ensem-ble acting and film technique to tell the story without any preconceived notion of right answers and justifications for war. The result is a visceral tour de force that is overpowering without offering contrived answers and without manipulating audience expectations.

As Spielberg's progressed Sun opposed his natal Saturn-Pluto conjunction for *Schindler's List*, for *Saving Private Ryan*, Spielberg's progressed Mars opposed the Saturn-Pluto conjunction. Mars in its most crude form usually conjures up images of a naïve, aggressive, quick-tempered and untested warrior looking for action. In *Saving Private Ryan*, little does Mars know that the energizing skirmish he is looking for to prove his courage and inflate his ego is nothing but the epic struggle between light and dark for which individual action proves inconsequen-tial—the archetypal combination of Saturn-Pluto.

Spielberg's genius—and what separates *Saving Private Ryan* from other war movies—is the realism that numbs and yet engrosses. In order to capture the level of authenticity needed to evoke such a powerful reaction, Spielberg and cinematographer Janusz Kaminski completely abandoned their usual plan of attack by abandoning storyboards, cranes, and dollys and chose to have hand-held cameras capture action without much directorial interference. This unexpected revision of technique gave brilliant, shocking, and original results. Paralleling this tactic, Uranus by transit was opposing Spielberg's natal Saturn-Pluto conjunction. Being the archetype which is related to technology and original, creative thinking, Uranus awoke the "thinking outside the box" which was necessary to recreate the now legendary sequence of the allies landing on Omaha Beach that opens the film.

A.I.: Artificial Intelligence (released 2001)

When Neptune conjoined Spielberg's Mercury in the mid-seventies, the script for *Jaws* was the result. As Pluto conjoined Spielberg's natal Mercury, Spielberg was attracted to the ideas of *A.I.* and wrote the screenplay. Pluto-Mercury is the aspect for penetrating ideas and thoughts that probe to the heart and depths of any matter. (Spielberg's collaborator on the project, Stanley Kubrick, possessed a Mercury-Pluto conjunction by birth.) *A.I.* addresses the fundamental questions of any age that are sure to have concrete implications for the 21st century: What is the true definition of life? Is the animating principle, the élan vital of biological life, something that can be reproduced by human creation? If so, what are the positive and negative potentials of tampering with the fundamental building blocks of creation? The questions run deep in *A.I.* and Spielberg doesn't run away from them, but interweaves them in an engrossing, perplexing, and complex narrative.

For nearly three years, Neptune, the planet of imagination, idealism and illusion opposed the dark magus in Spielberg's natal chart, Saturn. If Saturn manifests in our life as strict definitions of form, boundary and structure, Neptune, by contrast, represents the amorphous, the oceanic and the ever-changing fantasy life of the unconscious emerging subtly into our day-to-day awareness. When Saturn and Neptune meet, our visions, hopes and dreams tend to take a turn toward the grim.

In movies, Saturn and Neptune are often evidenced in starkly beautiful sets. Grays and blacks are the color palette of choice, and only the essentials are needed in terms of props, backdrops and acting. In terms of direction, Saturn-Neptune films tend to be hauntingly quiet, allowing the power of nuance and suggestibility to be as present as anything explicitly stated. Thematically, Saturn and Neptune beg the question, "What is real and what is not?" *A.I.* is Spielberg's darkest fantasy to date. Scenes of Rouge City and the Flesh Fair recall the dark sets and dystopic settings of movies like *Dark City* and *The Matrix*, produced under a recent Saturn square to Neptune in 1999.

For *A.I.*'s release, Jupiter made a conjunction to Spielberg's natal Uranus in the 12th house. If there is any planetary combination that is associated with all-time classic films and movie breakthroughs, it's Jupiter-Uranus. Often when Jupiter travels past Uranus' placement in a director's natal chart, a signature film, or even masterpiece, is released. Examples include George Lucas's *Star Wars*; Milos Foreman's *One Flew Over the Cuckoo's Nest*; John Schlesinger's *Midnight Cowboy*; Stanley Kubrick's *Dr. Strangelove*; Cecil B. DeMille's *The Ten Commandments* and Elia Kazan's *On the Waterfront*. The common denominator with all of these films is that they are classics that improve with each passing year. Often the Jupiter-Uranus movie is too ahead of the time of its release to be fully appreciated by the movie-going public, and so is the case with *A.I.*. Some critics have appreciated the brilliance of this film upon first-viewing. Others expecting not to be challenged have come away perplexed, expecting not to be so stirred emotionally and intellectually.

Stanley Kubrick waited so long to initiate *A.I.* because he believed that the state-of-the-art in special effects couldn't do justice to the futuristic world he envisioned. The CGI effects in the film, without being overproduced, are stunning. Realizations of an underwater New York and a decadent future city are beautifully crafted and one has the sense that the creators really have their pulse on plausible appearance of the future.

1. Pauline Kael, "The Greening of the Solar System," *The New Yorker*, November 28, 1977.

2. Lester Friedman and Brent Notbohm, eds. *Steven Spielberg, Interviews* (Jackson, MS: University of Mississippi Press, 2000).

3. Roger Ebert. http://www.multimania.fr/general/pub/popup/perso.phtml?

4. Joseph McBride. *Steven Spielberg: A Biography* (New York: Da Capo Press, 1997) 61.

5. Ibid, 61.

6. Ibid, 253.

7. Ibid, 254.

8. Ibid, 269.

9. Ibid, 269.

10. Ibid, 262.

11. Ibid, 289–90.

12. Ibid, 262.

13. Lester Friedman and Brent Notbohm, eds. *Steven Spielberg, Interviews* (Jackson, MS: University of Mississippi Press, 2000) 121.

14. Joseph McBride. *Steven Spielberg: A Biography* (New York: Da Capo Press, 1997) 367.

15. Ibid, 414.

16. Ibid, 415.

Steven Spielberg: Analysis of Individual Films

Jeffrey Kishner, M.A.

E.T.

The Twentieth Anniversary Edition of Steven Spielberg's *E.T. the Extra-Terrestrial* was recently re-released, with digital enhancements and never-before-seen footage. At the time of its original release, *E.T.* was the biggest grossing film in history. Twenty years later, it is still a powerful film, combining great special effects with a heart-warming ending.

Great filmmakers act as channels through which the energies of the planets express themselves. The friction resulting from hard aspects in a director's natal chart results in creative energy that he puts into his movies. Hence, there are many correspondences between the hard aspects in Spielberg's chart and the plot of *E.T.* The aspect that represents the most tension is the Moon square his Saturn-Pluto conjunction.

A square is an aspect that usually manifests as a struggle between the expression of the planets involved. In *E.T.* one can see a battle ensuing between the Moon and Saturn. The Moon symbolizes the child, the home and one's sense of belonging. Saturn is the principle of restriction and authority—the Establishment. Throughout the film, there is a struggle between the children (Moon) hiding E.T. and the throngs of adults trying to find and get him. The images of police cars and the giant white tent limiting access to and from the house are all expressions of Saturn. Pluto's role here is to intensify the energy of Saturn. This outermost planet gives the suffocating quality of Saturn all the more power; instead of a few secret service agents coming to the door to collect the alien (which would be an adequate Saturnian experience), we see what seems like hundreds of people merging in on one home.

This aspect also manifests as E.T.'s separation from the other aliens. Saturn, being the furthest planet from the Sun that can be seen with the unaided eye, is

155

the boundary-maker, beyond which reside the transpersonal planets. Saturn cuts E.T. off from his home (Moon), his physical connection to the aliens who had to leave him behind. The heartbreak is so strong that he dies on the operating table, after having lost his life force from not being with them. The Moon is also E.T.'s childlike wonderment at everything on this new planet he came to explore. In his vulnerability and need to be taken care of, E.T. also exhibits qualities of the Moon.

Jupiter conjuncts Venus in Spielberg's chart. The planet of expansion and good fortune, Jupiter lends abundance to the Venus principle of love and relationship. It is no surprise that everyone who meets E.T. feels great affection for him. This conjunction also relates to the unforgettable image of E.T.'s heart chakra glowing red after Elliott tells him he loves him.

Spielberg also has Uranus opposite his Sun. Uranus is the principle of independence, of breaking free. The archetype of the Sun, usually understood as one's sense of self, is also the literal Sun. E.T. is a being who is independent of our solar system. (Spielberg's preoccupation with aliens also manifests in *Close Encounters of the Third Kind* and *AI*). Uranus lends an "out of this world" quality to the stranger from another planet. On a more mundane level, the Sun represents Elliott's father, who left his wife and kids and moved to Mexico. He presumably experienced the Uranian need to break free from the confines of his home life.

A.I.

The story of David in *AI* is an accurate reflection of Spielberg's natal Pluto-Saturn conjunction square his Moon. David, a Mecha (the mechanical Saturn combined with the biological Pluto) child (Moon)—who malfunctions (Saturn) when he eats food (Moon)—is abandoned (Saturn) by his mother (Moon) after it becomes evident that he may inadvertently harm or kill (Saturn-Pluto) her biological son (Moon). He is left alone in the woods with Teddy, his supertoy. A truck comes into the forest and dumps a load of robot parts. Out of the woodwork come deformed (Pluto) robots seeking parts to make them complete, or at least more presentable. The moon rises, only to be a deceptive image of the real thing. Beneath the moon-balloon is a cage that houses captured robots. (Deceit is associated with Scorpio, which is ruled by Pluto; the capture and restriction of robots is Saturn.) David is then transported into a journey into the underworld (Pluto). He first is transported to the Flesh Fair, a "blood" rite that appeals to the basest instincts of humankind, taps into their rage, and indulges in extreme violence (all Pluto): robots are shot from canons through hoops of fire and then chopped up by a rotating blade, or boiling oil is poured upon them. This latter fate is to befall upon David and his prostitute (Pluto) companion Gigolo Joe, but they are saved because the crowd cannot reconcile the image of a child with their hatred of Mecha.

Gigolo Joe and David escape and begin David's compulsive (Pluto) pursuit of the Blue Fairy (Moon). David hopes that, as the Blue Fairy turned Pinochio into a real boy, she will do the same for David; then David's mother will take him back into her home. (Although David is a Mecha, his thoughts are patterned after the mythic logic of children.) Gigolo Joe, knowing that the Blue Fairy is a woman, takes David to Rouge City (the sexual underworld), because, from Joe's perspective, that's where the women are. They consult Dr. Know, who was programmed, upon hearing the right question, to inform them through riddle that the Blue Fairy was to be found in Manhattan.

This latter section of the movie transforms into a Neptunian vision. (During the filming of the movie, as well as the release date, transiting Neptune in Aquarius was squaring Spielberg's Moon in Scorpio.) Manhattan has been submerged into the ocean (Neptune). Only the tops of skyscrapers are visible. David and Gigolo Joe find Professor Hobby's office through the help of Teddy's instincts. Entering the office, David sees a replica of himself. All along, David thought he was unique and special. Seeing otherwise, he destroys his replica in a narcissistic rage. When he further explores Professor Hobby's lab and sees racks and racks of "Davids" ready for sale, he sinks into a depression so severe that he attempts suicide by falling into the ocean.

Here at the bottom of the ocean he encounters the fairy tale world (Neptune) of Pinocchio, and finally finds the Blue Fairy. (David is immersed into the collective unconscious, and meets the archetypal Mother.) He asks her for several human lifetimes to turn him into a real boy. Within 2000 years, the ocean freezes over—a symbol of the rigidity (Saturn) of his obsession (Pluto) to become human (Moon)—and space aliens unearth him. He alone has memories of the human race, and for this reason the space aliens find him unique and special. They want to make him happy. He finds himself in his original home (Moon), but the soft, fuzzy quality (Neptune) of the image suggests that it is an illusory (Neptune) re-creation. He is reunited with his mother for one day, and he blissfully has her all to himself; she tells him she loves him and she has always loved him, and he falls asleep with her, and dreams (Neptune) for the first time.

Minority Report

Minority Report features a dystopic future in which the State knows the whereabouts of its citizens via eye scanning, and advertisers custom-design their pitches to customers via the same technology. In mid-21st century Washington D.C., a pre-crime division of the police helps cops arrest murderers before they commit their crimes, thanks to the work of "precogs"—young adults born of drug addicts who can foresee murders. The images from their brains are extracted and downloaded, and the police put the pieces together to stop future murders from taking place. The murder rate in the capital has decreased substantially, but at what cost? An investigator from the Attorney General's office is trying to find out if there are any flaws in the system.

The protagonist is John Anderton (Tom Cruise), a pre-crime cop whose son was kidnapped and never found. John's motivation for working in the division is to prevent crimes like this from happening again. He has also been a dope addict since that horrible event. His day of reckoning comes when he witnesses a precognitive vision of himself murdering a man he doesn't know. The investigator and John's colleagues go after him, while he goes on the run and tries to find out who set him up.

During the filming of *AI*, Neptune's transit through Aquarius squared Spielberg's natal Moon. This transit correlated with David (the Moon child) submerged in the Neptunian ocean, looking for the mythic Blue Fairy. Both *AI* and *Minority Report* have similar cinematographic styles, incorporating foggy blues and greys, a gauzy feeling that coincides with the unreality of Neptune.

While *Minority Report* was in production from March to July 2001, Neptune was exactly opposing Spielberg's natal Saturn. This archetypal combination permeates the film. Neptune is water, image, visions, mysticism, drug use. Saturn darkens and brings out the negative in planets it contacts in hard aspect. This combination manifests in the following ways:

- John Anderton attempts to transcend the painful reality of his child's abduction through the use of narcotics.

- Several people question the reality (Saturn) of the precogs' visions (Neptune), i.e., does not the "minority report" challenge the validity of the pre-crime program?

- John pulls the female precog out of the "temple," thus traumatizing her. Saturn is separation. The "temple" is the name for the pool of water in which the three precogs are submerged, while being constantly pumped up with endorphins to bliss them out. Neptune correlates not only with the water, but with the drugs and the spiritualization of the "temple" by the pre-crime unit. Saturn-Neptune is also the disruption of the oceanic consciousness of the baby in the womb. The precogs are in a toxic womb experience: being exposed to horrific images and emotions, yet being unable to escape (Saturn).

Another negative water experience occurs when John's child is abducted while John is trying to beat his child's record of staying underwater in the swimming pool. The abduction itself relates to Spielberg's natal chart. Spielberg has Pluto square Moon, which is activated by transiting Neptune by virtue of being in natal aspect to his Saturn. Pluto (Hades) is God of the Underworld, who abducted Persephone into his domain. Pluto-Moon correlates with bringing a child into the underworld. (The same happened to *AI*'s David, who witnessed the underworld elements of the Flesh Fair and Rouge City.) The assumption is that John's son was molested and murdered; two core themes of Pluto are sex and death.

The essays on *E.T.* and *Minority Report* were originally published for StarIQ.com.

Stanley Kubrick, Or, How I Learned to Stop Worrying and Trust Astrology

Bill Streett, M.A.

After viewing *Dr. Strangelove: Or How I Stopped Worrying and Learned to Love the Bomb*, Martin Scorsese said of the film's director, "By that time I knew that Kubrick was the one." Jack Nicholson, who worked with Kubrick on *The Shining*, said of the filmmaker, "Everyone pretty much acknowledges that he's the man."[1] With Scorsese's and Nicholson's endorsements, we have the case of two luminaries, often credited as being the greatest director and actor of their generation, placing Stanley Kubrick at the zenith of cinematic greatness and achievement. Kubrick may not have been the most influential director, certainly not the most popular, and by all means not the most prolific, but by the measure of many in the industry, he was the one director that elevated the Hollywood movie into an art form by which all other films would be judged.

Envied by other filmmakers that yearned for his creative autonomy, and revered by students and serious filmgoers as a creative genius, Kubrick combined artistic sensitivity, penetrating insight into the human condition, and a notorious perfectionism to create landmark achievements of film. Other filmmakers may have possessed equal amounts of Kubrick's intensity, his innate photographic eye, his thoroughness, or his depth of vision, but no director—in Hollywood or otherwise—had the talent and perseverance to match all these gifts simultaneously.

Kubrick films were not ordinary releases. The irreverent and taboo subject matter of his films, the painstaking craft he demanded of his collaborators, the groundbreaking technology he employed, the absolute secrecy on his sets, and the long passages of time between his films suggested that his movie openings were *events* rather than merely releases. The increasing legend that surrounded Kubrick made each new film in his oeuvre a major milestone in film history rather than an easily forgotten movie pumped up by ephemeral hype.

Although not a recluse by any means—Kubrick enjoyed human contact and loved company—his privacy allowed him to penetrate both the visionary, ecstatic heights as well as probe the nadir of the human condition. Kubrick's need for seclusion and his innate farsighted and questioning genius allowed him to make films that have, and will, continue to stand the test of time. Brash and bold, Kubrick established his autonomy away from Hollywood at a very early age. Without his independence from the studio system, Kubrick would have remained a respected, if not remarkable, director, producing large Hollywood epics such as *Spartacus* and the like for the rest of his career. However, it was ultimately the freedom he attained in conjunction with his extraordinary visionary and intellectual gifts that would allow him to produce films that would cement his reputation among only a handful of truly great film directors of the twentieth century.

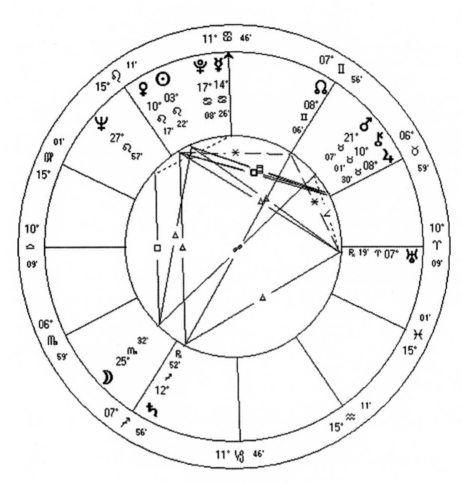

Stanley Kubrick
July 26, 1928
New York City, New York
Rectified to 10:30 AM

The Birth Chart

Of Kubrick's legacy, biographer Michel Ciment commented, "His is an oeuvre that both demands and defies analysis."[2] When approaching Kubrick and his films, one is immediately struck by impressions, images, and feelings that later must be translated into words. As Ciment suggests, encountering Kubrick necessitates the need to admire his work as irreducible, and yet there remains the compulsion to dissect the man's heritage into its components. Perhaps when confronting Kubrick and his films, we enter into his mode of perceiving and working: gestalts and impressions strike the first chord, but as we enter more fully into his legacy, the more the need to penetrate, investigate, and obsess over the material we have been privy to.

The images and impressions that are first to enter consciousness when mentioning Kubrick include some of the most iconographic and memorable film experiences of the twentieth century: the intense, brooding, and penetrating stares of his protagonists; the extraordinary blend of classical music and editing; exquisitely framed and photographed scenes; extraordinary use of tracking shots; shockingly irreverent and dark humor; mystery; images that evoke awe and religiousness; cold and inhuman interiors. The images and impressions of a Kubrick film strike deep resonances in all of us; they are brilliant not just in terms of their composition and technical mastery but because they insinuate and suggest rather than deliberately expose or reveal. Like Kubrick's famous tracking shots, the visual impressions of his films seduce and invite, alluring us deeper into a shared depth of field. The power and profundity of Kubrick's filmic impressions do not necessarily satisfy or enliven; in fact, they usually disturb, provoke, and perturb. Kubrick's ability to shock and penetrate jolts the viewer into a heightened state of awareness and disquietude about things—an uneasiness and agitation results from viewing his films.

Entering into Kubrick's birth chart is an attempt at analyzing and dissecting the man and the indelible cinematic impressions that he left behind. As Kubrick's cinema is truly irreducible and eludes analysis on some level—his film legacy has its own logic and grammar—an analysis of Kubrick's birth chart is both enlightening as it is confounding. Although the man and his films stand alone, examining his birth chart can assist in giving important supplementary information, unfolding the main mythic themes and structures which permeated his art and life.

In the classic sequence of *2001: A Space Odyssey*, "The Dawn of Man," one particular proto human is struck by an incredible idea. As this apeman is fumbling about with the skeletal remains of a recently deceased carcass, he receives an incredible insight—the bones he holds can be utilized to manipulate, control, and otherwise dominate his environment and improve his condition. The bones the apeman holds, with the addition of insight and application, are transformed into a tool and technology. The apeman is not just delighted by his discovery, but elated, discharging primal screams of joy into the African plains. The viewer can deduce from the images and sequences on screen that the apeman is in the throes of quasi manic elation, the "eureka" high or peak experience that accompanies the discovery of radical inventions and ideas.

In Greek mythology, this creative elation and the ability to liberate the collective through technology is associated with the Titan Prometheus. It was Prometheus that defied the pantheon of gods on Mount Olympus and liberated humanity through the gift of fire. The Titan Prometheus upset the balance and order of the universe by harnessing vision, creativity, and insight for humans, and thereby bridging the gap of the worldly and the divine.

Like the apeman in *2001*, Kubrick was the most Promethean of creatures—a visionary, a genius, an agent of cultural change, and a rebel against tradition. With movies like *Lolita* and *Dr. Strangelove: Or How I Stopped Worrying and Learned to Love the Bomb*, Kubrick pushed cultural tolerance limits into uncharted territory. With films such as *2001: A Space Odyssey* and *A Clockwork Orange*, he created bold visions of the future utilizing state-of-the-art technology that redefined film as we know it. However, more than these examples, Kubrick was a maverick, an outsider who didn't play by the rules, so that he could create his own. He defied the Hollywood studio system, gaining unheard of freedom and autonomy to create as he saw fit.

As noted by cultural historian Richard Tarnas, the boldly Promethean quest—this drive toward creation, liberation, and cultural change—is most easily identified with the archetype of the planet Uranus.[3] Closely paralleling the myth of Prometheus, those that are born with a significant Uranus in the chart are cultural creators—those who defy tradition, liberate themselves or humanity into a new order, and bring about sweeping change. Looking at Kubrick's birth chart, we witness his Sun in trine aspect to Uranus. Thus, Kubrick's essential identity as symbolized by the Sun was heavily intertwined with the meanings and associations with Uranus and Prometheus: brilliance, innovation, irreverence, autonomy, creativity, boldness, uniqueness, and defiance. The trine aspect between his Sun and Uranus suggest a relative ease, a harmony, and comfort between his identification as a rebellious outsider and culture-bringer. There is little indication that Kubrick's maverick rebelliousness brought him suffering or discord; on the contrary, he seemed to easily fit the part. Moveover, the trine aspect can be seen in the relative ease with which he attained his own autonomy—his contemporaries were amazed at the effortlessness with which the studio system granted Kubrick creative and financial freedoms. This unrestrained move toward autonomy and the relative comfort Kubrick had at breaking norms reinforces the notion that the trine aspect in astrology suggests flow, harmony, and mutual enhancement.

Typically, signs and suggestions of a rebel streak are seen at an early age for those born with Sun in aspect to Uranus, even though it may not fully manifest until later in life. Like Steven Spielberg, who was also born with the Sun in aspect to Uranus, Kubrick was labeled as different from his contemporaries—his interests and passions deviated from the norm early in his schooling. Before high school, Stanley was pouring much of his time and passion into photography, a hobby that would develop into an early career for Kubrick. Moreover, Kubrick displayed little if any interest in what was expected of him socially or academically; he was following the beat of his own drummer—a typical manifestation of those born with Sun in aspect to Uranus. Kubrick's underachievement in school was a rare example of someone who simply put effort into that which captivated or interested him. His extraordinary work effort and intense grasp of philosophical and technical ideas demonstrated that Kubrick lacked neither discipline nor intelligence. On the contrary, Kubrick was a highly motivated and brilliant individual who bucked the system because he already had an intuition of what he wanted—or indeed, needed—to do in life.

Broadening our view on Kubrick's birth chart, we witness a Grand Trine between the planets Venus, Saturn, and Uranus in fire signs. A Grand Trine occurs when planets in similar zodiacal elements form a triangular pattern in the sky. The aspect is related to gifts, harmony, and ease surrounding the planets involved. With Kubrick's particular Grand Trine involving Venus, Saturn, and Uranus, his aesthetic tastes were balanced between tradition and progress, classicism and the new. We can observe this tendency most profoundly in Kubrick's usage of music in film. Kubrick frequently employed the use of established classical music in innovative and novel ways. The stunning juxtaposition of Strauss's *Also Sprach Zarathustra* relative to the image of the Starchild in *2001: A Space Odyssey* is indicative of utilizing tradition and classicism (affiliated with the archetype of Saturn) in novel and innovative ways (associated with Uranus).[4] As Kubrick said, "However good our best film composers may be, they are not a Beethoven, a Mozart or a Brahms. Why use music which is less good when there is such a multitude of great music available from the past and from our own time?"[5]

Since Saturn is involved in the Grand Trine, Kubrick's film taste and sense has an enduring significance to it. Kubrick loved to experiment with his film aesthetics; however, he intuitively knew when to push the envelope and when to remain rooted in tradition. Thus, the Grand Trine involving the planets of revolution and stasis formed a partnership, allowing Kubrick to create lasting film revolutions. Although Kubrick himself may have been very much the rebel and aligned more with the rebelliousness associated with Uranus, his films had a stateliness, a poised balance, and a beautiful symmetry that transcends the time in which they were made.

We can also see the Grand Trine expressed through Kubrick's love of technology, and, in particular, the urge to aestheticize technology. Saturn and Uranus in angular relationship often manifests as adeptness at technical matters and technology—a sort of engineering facility, or an ease with gadgetry and tools. Kubrick, unlike other directors, had a mastery of cinematography and the movie camera. Kubrick knew nearly all technical facets of his productions, a skill which came from both an intrinsic interest in these matters but also from his pursuit of perfection. The archetype of Saturn acts to ground, limit, and give practical application to Uranus's visionary and brilliant intuitions, channeling the liberating and creative instincts of Uranus into useable form.

The technical brilliance of the Saturn-Uranus combination in Kubrick's chart was also evidenced in the cold aesthetic that pervaded all of Kubrick's films. The striving for aesthetic perfection—from lighting, to set design, to costumes, to scene composition—gave Kubrick's films a harshly austere, though radiant, look and feel. The overall effect of Kubrick's aesthetic lent an impersonal, if not dehumanizing, aura to his output, often dwarfing the contributions of his actors. One need only to conjure remembrances of the famous "war room" set from *Dr. Strangelove*, the surreal interior of the closing moments of *2001*, or the bar room sequences of *The Shining* to evoke the cool, minimalist perfection that inflected all of Kubrick's productions.

Perhaps the greatest single characteristic of Kubrick's birth chart was his possession of a Pluto-Mercury conjunction.[6] On so many levels, this particular archetypal combination informed both the personality and output of Kubrick. The guarded sense of secrecy in his life and on his films, his dictatorial level of control on the set, the intensely obsessive penetration into the deepest subject matter, his strategic approach toward life, the intensity and profundity which pervaded his films, and, finally, the exposure of the taboo can all be seen as undeniable demonstrations of Kubrick's Pluto-Mercury conjunction. Yet perhaps the single greatest expression of the planetary combination that was potentially the fundamental theme of all of Kubrick's films was the sense of *threat*, the terror of annihilation and breakdown. Although Kubrick was praised for never getting comfortable with one particular genre, regardless of whatever category of film he was directing—be it horror, drama, war, or science fiction—the sense of threat, decay, and breakdown was all-pervasive. In films like *Paths of Glory, Dr. Strangelove*, and *Full Metal Jacket*, Kubrick investigated the terror of existential annihilation through war or nuclear catastrophe. In *The Shining* and in *2001*, Kubrick examined the possibilities and consequences from the threat of mental breakdown (in *The Shining* through Jack Nicholson's collapse into "cabin fever" madness and in *2001* through the breakdown of the perfect brain, the HAL 2000 computer). In *Lolita, Barry Lyndon*, and *Eyes Wide Shut*, Kubrick examined the possibility of the breakdown of relationships and the threat of collapse of societal reputation and standing.

The sense of threat, this sense of the possibility of breakdown, corruptibility, or decay, are all manifestations of the archetypal Pluto. The force of Pluto threatens death, or more appropriately, transformation and regeneration through breakdown and resurrection. This process is part of nature, and although it is indeed a "natural" process, this doesn't mean that the process that Pluto symbolizes is at all invited or welcome into one's life. On the contrary, Pluto's archetypal dynamics are on the one hand energizing, titanic, and profound, but on the other, painful, overpowering, and annihilative—and Kubrick was well aware of this dimension of life, if not obsessed with it.

When one studies Kubrick's biography, one is left with the impression that this foundational theme of threat that pervaded his movies also consumed his life and structured how he perceived reality. From an early age, Kubrick became a master chess player, spending hours strategizing moves that would allow him to overcome and beat his opponents. Reality, for Kubrick, was not unlike a chess match—a game of winners and losers, and moreover, a game of intensely deliberative strategy. As Jack Nicholson commented on Kubrick, "[he] felt everyone was an opponent."[7] That is, Kubrick perceived the world as one of aggressive strategy, where everyone's covert approach was to ultimately undo and break down the other.

If indeed Kubrick saw the world as a macrocosm of his chess matches—with hidden agendas, strategy, manipulation, and antagonism as dominants—then it is logical that he demanded such tremendous control and privacy in his personal life and as director. Both of these qualities garnered Kubrick a notorious reputation, but as his legend grew, it is likely that the stories concerning his privacy and dictatorial control also grew. Due in parts for his desire for artistic perfection and his assumption of external threat, Kubrick did gain obsessional control over his productions—to an extent that no other director in the history of cinema commanded. Moreover, Kubrick's mastery of the technical aspects of film allowed him an all-pervasive quality control into all facets of his filmmaking. Little if anything remained left to chance, for chance, in Kubrick's eyes, was synonymous with the threat of chaos, which was synonymous with death.

As much as the Pluto-Mercury combination created an all-pervasive dynamic of threat and control in Kubrick's life and films, the planetary duo could also be seen through his intensely penetrating and obsessing mind. As we've seen, Pluto correlates with the threat of annihilation, dismemberment through chaos, or the terror of the primal side of life; however, it also deepens, intensifies, and makes profound whatever it contacts in the natal chart. Kubrick's films not only investigated deep and dark themes—tackling subject matter that was often off-limits from popular discourse—but he saturated his films with a primal intensity through image, dialogue, and sound. Every facet of his movies and directorial style was rendered profound and concentrated, from colors, to acting, to plot development.

When looking at the Moon in Kubrick's birth chart,[8] we are predominantly concerned with his portrayal of the feminine. In Kubrick's chart the Moon in Scorpio forms a square, or ninety-degree aspect, to Neptune in Leo. When the Moon forms an angular relationship to Neptune, the feminine side of one's psyche is rendered sensitive, impressionable, refined, and idealized. Neptune categorizes an entirely different set of gestalts than Pluto. If Pluto is the submergence into the terror and horror of the underworld, Neptune is the innocent and untouched state that is captured by mythic places such as Eden, Heaven, utopia, or paradise. If Pluto puts us in touch with the demonic and dark, Neptune makes one reconcile the transcendent, beatific, and pure. Often in a male's birth chart, Neptune's aspect to the Moon colors one's experience of the feminine so that the qualities of Neptune are perceived, projected, and attracted into one's life via the feminine and females.

Although Kubrick's is a masculine oeuvre, when the feminine is cast in a significant role in his films, female characters are conduits and carriers of the archetypal Neptune. Ranging from idealized beauty, to helpless victims, to saintly innocents, the female invariably is the bringer of the pacific and transcendent. Certainly, the sacrificial victim of "Wendy"(Shelley Duvall) in *The Shining*, the sensitive and refined "Lady Lyndon" in *Barry Lyndon*, and the numerous ideally beautiful redeemers in both *A Clockwork Orange* and *Eyes Wide Shut* come to mind. However, arguably the clearest example of Kubrick's women carrying the archetypal Neptune is within the film *Paths of Glory*. In the closing moments of the movie, a despondent and destroyed Colonel Dax (portrayed by Kirk Douglas) wanders the streets of France after seeing men of his own company executed by the French military for a wrong that they didn't commit. Presumably enraged, embittered, and stripped of good faith, Colonel Dax rambles aimlessly across the night to console his weary soul. In his meandering, he hears a voice emanating from a tavern. Peering inside, he witnesses a young, innocent woman (ironically portrayed by the future wife of Kubrick) sweetly and courageously singing a German folk tune before an audience of soldiers. So moving is her rendering of the song that it moves the soldiers to tears, as seemingly the song evokes remembrances of a sweeter, innocent time that existed before war. With the female, we have the saving and redeeming force of Neptune portrayed via a woman to provide soothing balm to soldiers, wounded from the atrocities and insanity of war.

The Films

Paths of Glory (1957)

Considered to be one of the all-time great war films (or to be more precise, anti-war films), *Paths of Glory* marked the emergence of Kubrick as a major young director in Hollywood. *Paths of Glory* would not be his first major motion picture—Kubrick gained attention for his heist film *The Killing* and to a lesser extent *Killer's Kiss*—however, the film's strikingly distinct style, the powerful story, and wonderful performances from an ensemble cast got Kubrick noticed. By the time of the release of *Paths of Glory*, Kubrick was considered one of a handful of new directors that threatened the established studio system within Hollywood.

During the shooting and subsequent release of *Paths of Glory*, Kubrick was undergoing a conjunction of Uranus to his natal Sun by transit, a once-in-a-lifetime experience. As mentioned previously, Uranus is a liberating influence, allowing barriers and obstacles to suddenly and quickly dissolve and recede. However, more importantly, a Uranus transit such as the one Kubrick received during the filming of *Paths of Glory* is a powerful release of unique self-expression and authenticity; this particular transit is the releasing mechanism for what may be called *personhood*. It is during this rare transit that the self orients to an inner call, to the motto, "to thine own self be true."

For creative types like Kubrick, a Uranus transit to the Sun can be the time when one's own unique original and inventive impact is released to the world-at-large. This is often the time when one's creative stamp or calling card is impressed firmly into collective consciousness. Secondly, a time in which Uranus is highlighted is often a time of dawning, emergence, or breakthrough. So, too, are Uranus transits representative of the genesis of one's authentic self-expression into the outer environment.

Not only does a Uranus transit signify a bold birthing of one's true authenticity into the outer environment, but it also corresponds to a time of creative stimulation. A notable Uranus transit generates a need for experimentation, increases intuition, and urges novel solutions to old problems. Through the electrifying creativity of the Uranus transit, *Paths of Glory* was the first film in which Kubrick's innovative style began to express itself. Kubrick's earlier films were solid productions but lacked a distinct style that would be identified as a product of a bold auteur. Elements in *Paths of Glory*, however, marked the origins of an approach and style that would gain full manifestation in Kubrick's later masterpieces. The wide-angle shots, the famous tracking sequences, the meticulous attention to detail, and the unconventional camera setup—practices that would become synonymous with Kubrick's directorial style—materialize to full effect in *Paths of Glory*.

Spartacus (1960)

After *Paths of Glory's* critical triumph, Kubrick began to attract established stars and big producers from Hollywood. Enduring a failed collaboration with Marlon Brando, Kubrick was asked to direct *Spartacus* as a stand-in director. Stanley, a boyish looking thirty year old from the Bronx, looked out of place among the glitterati of Hollywood. However, forever aloof and detached, Kubrick took advantage of his outsider status and did a highly respectable job directing a project that held very little personal interest.

During the filming and release of *Spartacus*, Kubrick received a ninety-degree square transit from Uranus to his natal position of Mars. The synchronicity with this particular alignment can be seen on at least two different levels. The subject matter of the film revolves around the legendary slave revolt led by the gladiator in the title role. Spartacus's role in the history of the Roman Empire is not a minor one; the slave and gladiator led the greatest internal insurrection in the history of the Empire. Approximately seventy years before the birth of Christ, Spartacus and a band of nearly 120,000 disenfranchised followers revolted against the Empire. Due to the sheer size of the rebellion and Rome's initial casual dismissal

Leeds Trinity University
Tel: 0113 283 7244
Fax: #### ### ####

Borrowed Items 07/02/2014 11:16
PARI KARIMINIA

Item Title	Due Date
* The astrology of film	21/02/2014
* Ego and archetype	21/02/2014

Amount Outstanding: £0.60

* Indicates items borrowed today
Thank you for using this unit. See you next time!
PLEASE REMEMBER TO SWIPE YOUR DVDs THROUGH THE DETACHER AT THE ENTRANCE TO THE LIBRARY

Service and opening hours details at:
http://intranet.leedstrinity.ac.uk/CampusServices/helpdesk

of the insurgency, the revolt lasted for nearly two years and produced serious injury to the Roman troops.

Spartacus is a prime exemplar of the pairing of Uranus and Mars—the archetypal warrior who fights for freedom and independence. Mars—the Roman god of war and the astrological symbol—have obvious parallels. Like the Roman god, the astrological Mars is the energy and expression of assertion, belligerence, aggression, and, in some cases, violence. The most undiluted (and arguably unconscious) manifestation of the astrological Mars is to be found in competitive physical exertion of will—war, battle, fights, and combat. With the addition of Uranus added to the archetypal Mars, we see the assertive and aggressive tendencies of Mars augmented with Uranus's willfulness toward freedom, independence, and idealism. Although Spartacus may not have been the champion of social reform that legend has assumed, his extraordinary and courageous uprising was motivated by an intense desire to set slaves free from the harsh and oppressive conditions of the Roman Empire. The intrepid will towards freedom that Spartacus displayed makes him one of history's paradigmatic illustrations of Uranus's pairing with Mars.

Synchronistically speaking, Kubrick directing *Spartacus*—a motion picture that simply landed in his lap after the first director was fired from the movie—is a fascinating complement to the Uranus transit that Kubrick was receiving to his natal Mars at the time. However, the Uranus transit has more dimension to it when realizing the difficulty that Kubrick had on the set of the film. The transiting square that he was receiving suggests discord, strife, confrontation, and an imperative towards resolution. Thus, the relationship between these two archetypes was a tense and difficult one for Kubrick. Any square transit to Mars can often insinuate a clash of egos—willful personalities with conflicting agendas. With a set full of Hollywood's greatest stars—Tony Curtis, Lawrence Olivier, and Kirk Douglas among them—Kubrick's directorial agenda was in constant odds with the actors' intentions. In particular, Kubrick and Kirk Douglas were notoriously opposed on the set. *Spartacus* was a Douglas production, but Kubrick, as director, wasn't willing to let go of his extreme desire for meticulous control. The two entered the film as creative collaborators with mutual admiration for each other; they exited *Spartacus* severing ties from each other personally and professionally.

Up until *Spartacus*, Kubrick was an iconoclastic outsider who was being primed for larger and larger Hollywood spectacles and productions. However, after *Spartacus*, with its egos jockeying for position and political machinations, Kubrick would never again enter a project as a "man for hire" nor as a director without complete command and power. Kubrick lamented in an interview shortly after the film, "*Spartacus* is the only film on which I did not have absolute control."[9] Like Spartacus himself and mirrored by his Uranus transit to Mars, Kubrick threw his own rebellion of sorts. In many ways, Kubrick became the first truly successful and revered independent filmmaker, pioneering the path for so many after him who would crave independence from the Hollywood system in the decades that followed *Spartacus*.

2001: A Space Odyssey (1968)

2001: A Space Odyssey was a technical and aesthetic masterpiece that revolutionized and advanced the science fiction film to levels that have rarely been equaled. Although current technology and special effects have evolved since the making of *2001*, it's arguable that no film has so wedded technical brilliance with a virtuosic symphony of images, sound, and profoundly deep subject matter. However, beyond just its special effects luminosity and its impact on the science fiction genre, *2001* both defined the countercultural ethos of the 1960s and transcended it. The film was one of a handful of iconographic statements that defined that turbulent and creative era while simultaneously connecting the period to timeless, eternal, and even spiritual ground.

After the success of *Lolita* and *Dr. Strangelove: Or How I Learned to Stop Worrying and Love the Bomb*, Kubrick was given ever more creative control over his movie-making process. Whereas before these films, Kubrick made his own decisions but with his own money, after his early 1960s triumphs, the Hollywood studios essentially gave him carte blanche to develop, produce, and direct projects as he saw fit. Little did studio executives at MGM realize that Kubrick's next project after *Dr. Strangelove* was to be the enigmatic *2001*.

Since the 1950s, Kubrick had been interested in making a science fiction movie, however, contracts and other material prohibited him from investigating the matter until the 1960s. A friend of Kubrick's suggested that he contact the author Arthur C. Clarke for material for a science fiction film, as the writer was one of only a handful of authors whose material would truly interest Kubrick. After several amicable meetings and phone conversations, the two highly intelligent individuals decided to collaborate on what would become a masterpiece of twentieth century cinema.

During the conception and materializing of the script, both transiting Pluto and Uranus formed a sextile, or sixty-degree aspect, to Kubrick's natal Mercury. Known for its stimulating qualities, the sextile aspect added excitation to the extreme creative potency of Pluto and Uranus simultaneously transiting

Kubrick's Mercury.[10] The mental creativity at the time of the collaboration was intense. Borrowing material from vastly different sources and collaborating with such notables as Carl Sagan, Kubrick and Clarke birthed the novel from which the film would be adapted.

The usually reserved and restrained Kubrick was highly thrilled by the results of the collaboration. After reading the finished first draft, Kubrick exclaimed, "We've extended the range of science fiction."[11] However visionary and creative the results of the script were, realization of the concepts for the movie screen proved to be yet another matter entirely. The broad scope of the project wedded with Kubrick's now infamous perfectionism and meticulousness translated into a technological and logistical mountain of gigantic proportions.

Throughout the majority of principal photography and the creation of special effects, transiting Saturn conjoined Kubrick's natal Uranus. Although considered archetypal forces that are principally at odds with each other, the problems, delays, constraints, and sheer hard work that is affiliated with Saturn can impress its energy into the creative genius associated with Uranus, forcing innovative and novel solutions to extremely demanding problems. The force and weight affiliated with Saturn can press down and insure the manifestation of extraordinary inventiveness and originality. As related specifically to *2001*, this Saturn transit to Kubrick's Uranus mirrored the pressure and determination needed to come up with advances in technology to render Kubrick's original vision.

As befitting such a transit, *2001* was a quantum leap not only in look and feel but in technology as well. Kubrick had succeeded in harnessing a type of transcendent vision that had never been realized on screen. With a team of twenty-five special effects specialists and a huge conglomeration of technical advisors, photographers, modelers, and artists, Kubrick demanded his crew bear a new level of technological sophistication. Some under Kubrick resented the taskmaster; others enjoyed the challenged. The end result made the vast majority of science fiction films before *2001* look simply amateurish in appearance. In particular, the two sequences that formed bookends for the film—the "Dawn of Man" sequence and "Jupiter and Beyond the Infinite"—brought film technology a great leap forward. Shot not on location but on a studio set, the extraordinary realism of the "Dawn of Man" sequence was due, in part, to front screen projections that, in this instance, utilized transparencies of Africa. At the end of the film, Astronaut Bowman's psychedelic journey into the heart of creation was created through an innovative slit-scan technique, an application never before used in feature-length film.[12]

More than just the product of collaboration between Clarke, Kubrick, and a talented crew and cast, *2001: A Space Odyssey* was a document that captured the archetypal dynamics and spirit of the times of the 1960s. Throughout the entire decade of the 1960s, Uranus and Pluto formed a potent and rare conjunction. The dynamics of the decade simply speak of the motifs associated with the archetypal pairing of these planets: cultural revolution; creative and technological awakening; challenge to old structures; quantum leaps in nearly every facet of society; heightened eroticism and liberation of sexuality; chaos, disruption, and the threat of violence and destruction. However, Kubrick's film seemed to articulate the dynamics of this conjunction between Uranus and Pluto at its most profound, even spiritual, level. Taking the larger view of history as Kubrick did for *2001*, the 1960s represented a radical evolutionary advance and turning point in global culture. As suggested in the film itself, periodically through history, evolution is quickly and radically shifted through a sort of initiation, rite of passage, or death-rebirth sequence. Just as apes and astronauts were awakened, transformed, and liberated by the presence of the monolith in the film, 1960s culture—and particularly the youth of the decade—was initiated into a great, mysterious rite of passage whereby new expressions, attitudes, values, creativity, and behaviors manifested—and all of this was mirrored by the conjunction of Pluto to Uranus.

The three-note clarion call at the beginning of Strauss's *Thus Spake Zarathustra* (the often-parodied music used throughout *2001*) is symbolic of the three great evolutionary sequences seen in the film. From ape to man to Starchild, Kubrick suggests that a tremendous force (as symbolized by the use of the monolith) breaks apart, initiates, and gives birth to a new, higher and advanced evolutionary state at particular moments throughout the historical process. *2001* suggests that man is the middle stage between the evolutionary steps of ape and Starchild. To borrow a quote from Nietzsche, who served as philosophical inspiration for Kubrick, "[man is] a rope stretched between the beast and the Superman, a rope over an abyss."[13] Translated in the context of the film, man is the connecting point between the apes of the African savannah and the Starchild witnessed at the end of the film.

Given Kubrick's rather pessimistic brilliance and complexity of thought, he suggests through the film that although these evolutionary leaps are indeed dramatic and awe-inspiring—if not spiritual—they are not without their problematic consequences. The acquisition of tool-making gave the proto-humans (and eventually humans) the power to control and dominate their environment; however Kubrick suggests that the reliance upon technology has unforeseen consequences. Throughout the bulk of *2001: A Space Odyssey*, Kubrick presents a possible future where technology is dominant in our species' environment. As a result, humans are portrayed in the film as disaffected, detached, coldly rational, and suffering from a sort of psycho-spiritual ennui. Kubrick suggests that tools have liberated humans but have also made them more reliant upon them, where humans are forced in a relationship of mimicry, parroting the hyper-rationality of their creations. In the end, humans are forced into an intense death-rebirth sequence, needing to kill off their technology so they that they may be reborn. Astronaut Dave Bowman destroys HAL, the androgynous and coolly reasonable mainframe in the film, and is reborn into an entirely new state of being—the Starchild. Kubrick insinuates that this initiation or transformational rite is anything but mundane but rather an awe-inspiring, metaphysical revolution.

Like Kubrick's Dave Bowman, the 1960s generation was being shuttled through a death-rebirth mystery as mirrored by the Pluto-Uranus conjunction of the time. Society was in need of a great death-rebirth, as the disaffected pleasantry and artifice of the 1950s was in trouble of divorcing the human spirit from its deeper, more liberated potentials. Thus, with its positive and negative polarities, a transformational rite of passage was engaged throughout the 1960s, liberating a heightened sense of creativity, eroticism and sexuality, and new social expressions.

Befuddled by the film or despising the painstaking length of the movie, some critics believed that *2001* was simply a smorgasbord of incoherent spectacle and that the ending, in particular, was not the result of design but happenstance and whimsy. This is highly unlikely, in that, like his films themselves, Kubrick's pacing and decision-making were deliberate, staid, and strategic. As friend Jack Nicholson said of the director, "What I love about his films is that they are completely conscious."[14] Without question, Kubrick's intentions of creating a science fiction film that explored the transcendental possibilities of the power of evolution were thoroughly conscious on his part. The use of Strauss and the homage to Homer were not accidental or coincidental but premeditated, implying that Kubrick was well aware of the philosophy he was trying to reveal on screen (but secretive and cryptic about revealing it verbally with anyone). Whether or not Kubrick was influenced by more esoteric teachings—as some have insisted—remains to be conclusively seen.

Kubrick's intent was not to give a morality lesson or philosophical teaching; rather, his main motivation with *2001* was to speak to an unconscious part of the viewer and to convey a depth of meaning and a sense of transcendence through images and sound—an assault on the senses. By most accounts, he was extraordinarily successful. After several viewings, many sensed that the movie was saying something of immense importance, although it defied rational analysis. His epic motion picture not only spoke to a deep and profound mystery but also resonated with the archetypal ground of the times. Thus, for many viewers *2001* was a religious experience that served as an initiation into the profound and mysterious workings of the cosmos. [15]

A Clockwork Orange (1971)

If prior to *2001* Kubrick had gained the stature of an independent filmmaker, then after *2001* he would attain the status as an independent artist working as a director. After *Spartacus*, Kubrick began breaking convention after convention, pushing the envelope thematically and technologically. The entire span of *Lolita* to *A Clockwork Orange* can be viewed as one extreme push on societal conventions—in sexuality (*Lolita*), politics and military defense (*Dr. Strangelove*), myth and technology (*2001*), and violence and its potential for reform (*A Clockwork Orange*). Although philosophically *2001* and *A Clockwork Orange* may arrive at separate conclusions (*2001* suggesting the possibility of spiritual evolution whereas *A Clockwork Orange* presenting the irredeemable and primal violence in man), from a creative standpoint they remain congruent. The novelty and originality that was displayed in *2001* receives an even greater amount of dynamism in *A Clockwork Orange*.

A Clockwork Orange is Kubrick at his most radical, rebellious, experimental, and ingenious. Whereas *2001* is balanced in its bold, creative originality and stately, elegant classicism, *A Clockwork Orange* is unrestrained in a phantasmagoria of sex, violence, and creativity. Some might argue that Kubrick pushed the barriers too far with this film, with the buzzing novelty actually overwhelming the plot and acting; however, Kubrick was undergoing the generational Uranus opposition transit. Occurring at midlife, Uranus opposing Uranus is *the* transit of creative regeneration and breakthrough. During this transit, from the wellsprings of the unconscious come radically rebellious ideas, an almost frenetic state of free play and chaos, inspired rejuvenation, and an almost wild state of independence and mania.

The Uranus opposition transit represents an influx of mental fire, where possibility, novelty, recreation, and inspired "what ifs" are nearly uncontainable. During this time, it is likely that previous inhibiting boundaries (self-proscribed or otherwise) will be broken. In its most positive outcome, the transit brings forth expression, freedom, and rejuvenation that borders on exuberance. In its negative consequences, the transit brings forth a burning of bridges, an obstinate refusal for any and all previously held traditions or proscriptions, or a radical acceptance of the new and exciting without a cautious deliberation of the consequences.

Throughout *A Clockwork Orange* we see the free play, whimsy, and experimentation affiliated with the Uranus opposition transit punctuated throughout the film. Like *2001: A Space Odyssey*, Kubrick continued to employ classical music as an accompanying score; however, in this instance, much of the masterpieces from previous centuries were synthesized. Kubrick used the talents of composer Wendy Carlos's electronic renderings of classics to great, albeit controversial, effect. Here we can witness the archetype of Uranus in both the experimental reworking of tradition but also in the fact that Kubrick wanted a technological, electronic reappraisal. Uranus is affiliated with ever-increasing technological sophistication and wizardry; the high energy "buzz" of electronic music relative to the more earthy, organic acoustic music is a typical expression of the archetype.

More than just Kubrick's use of music, *A Clockwork Orange* is the film where Kubrick takes his free license as director to maximum effect. Throughout the film, Kubrick consistently plays with and bends traditional filmmaking techniques. High-speed film, slow motion film, editing set to music, and unconventional camera angles all create the effect of creative maelstrom that carries the story along. If *2001* is the film equivalent of a stately ballet, *A Clockwork Orange* is a frenetic dance with jagged rhythms and alternating tempos. The overall impression the film makes in style is to express the convention breaking, experimental pulsations of Uranus's manic-like high.

The Shining (1980)

In a particularly memorable sequence of *2001*, astronaut Dave Bowman disassembles the mainframe computer, HAL, to ensure his survival on his space mission. Slowly and deliberately, we witness the breakdown of the computing capacity of HAL. A once logical and rational mind is destroyed and undone. The pivotal sequence in Kubrick's science fiction epic intimates the central theme of his classic horror film, *The Shining*. Kubrick's reworking of Stephen King's successful novel explores the possibility of mental disintegration and collapse. The threat that Kubrick would so often explore in his movies was now rendered from within. The enemy, evil, and threat to be found in *The Shining* was to be found within one's self, in the recesses of one's own mind.

Although *The Shining* has elements of a typical horror movie, ranging from evocations of the supernatural and murder, it is primarily a psychological mystery. After the frenetic pacing of *A Clockwork Orange*, Kubrick once again returned to his more familiar style of a slow, deliberate, and methodical tempo. *The Shining* follows a measured, unhurried arc of descent into mental insanity. Jack Torrance (Jack Nicholson) is submerged into the dark inner recesses of his own psyche, eventually leading him into a state of murderous psychosis.

Shot in England in 1978 and 1979, Kubrick was undergoing a lengthy square transit of Pluto to his natal Mercury-Pluto conjunction. The parallels between the archetypes involved and the storyline of *The Shining* are extraordinary. Pluto transits are notorious for initiating whatever it contacts in the birth chart into the underworld, the shadow, and the darkness. For approximately a two to three year period, Pluto transits plunge whatever archetype it contacts into the terrain of the dark side of the psyche. That is to say, Pluto lets us come in contact with the sinister and demonic potentials of any facet of our being. In this instance, transiting Pluto was initiating Kubrick's already compulsive and rather darkly-attuned mind further into the mysterious underworld ruled by Pluto. *The Shining* and, in particular, the character of Jack Torrance, allowed Kubrick a sort of cathartic safety valve for the deep shadow terrain that Kubrick's mind must have entered into during this particular transit. In Torrance, we have a man possessed by his own inner demons, and, in the end, the depraved and murderous side of Torrance's psyche completely and utterly possess the character.

However, more than just a descent into the underworld, we can see the potentials of Kubrick's Pluto transit to his natal Pluto-Mercury conjunction manifest in other ways in *The Shining*. Pluto represents not only a process of submergence into the dark and often demonic sides of self, but it is also symbolic of a process of transformation. As alluded to earlier in this essay, Pluto marks a course of development of decay, corruption, annihilation and, ultimately, resurrection and rebirth. In an unapologetic fashion, Pluto obliterates and exterminates so that new potentials and growth can ultimately surface. In *The Shining*, Nicholson's Torrance is not only slowly inundated into the shadow elements of his unconscious, but his rational, conscious mind is ultimately broken down. Toward the conclusion of the film, any and all elements of Torrance's former sanity and ego consciousness are simply and utterly discarded. In its wake, a murderous and monstrous force latent within Torrance wreaks havoc and destruction. More subtly, we see the Pluto transit to Kubrick's natal Pluto-Mercury conjunction in the form of "shining" itself. Essentially, another name for telepathy, "shining" is the ability to receive and transmit information psychically. Both Torrance's son, Danny, and the hotel chef, Dick Hallorann, have the gift to "shine" and the characters rely upon this sixth sense towards the film's conclusion. Pluto is often affiliated with hidden, psychic abilities, and, in this instance, adjoined with Mercury, the combination is known to wield gifts of mental intuition and psychism.

Perhaps the most significant manifestation of Kubrick's Pluto transit was an increasing extremism that surrounded his already obsessional control and perfectionism in his role as director. Pluto transits tend to exert a tremendous, compelling force on the archetype it is informing. In Kubrick's instance, the Pluto transit was simply adding an additional power and compulsion to his need for control and his striving for perfection, manifestations of his natal Mercury-Pluto conjunction. Anne Jackson, who played a psychiatrist in the film, said of Kubrick, "He was the most meticulous director I ever worked with."[16] If Kubrick was demanding on his crew and cast, he was most challenging with the two leads, Jack Nicholson and Shelley Duvall. In order to get the heightened sense of emotional and psychological shock that envelopes the couple, Kubrick pushed the two actors near the brink of exhaustion. Shelley Duvall took Kubrick's intensity particularly hard, as she stated, "I resented Stanley at times because he pushed me and it hurt. I resented him for it."[17]

Eyes Wide Shut (1999)

The unintentional final film of Kubrick's legacy, *Eyes Wide Shut* explores one man's descent into martial infidelity and the consequences of his actions. *Eyes Wide Shut* remains unique in Kubrick's oeuvre for its resolution. Unlike the stunning, triumphant birth in *2001*, the monstrous breakdown in *The Shining*, or the dark irreverence of *Dr. Strangelove* and *A Clockwork Orange*, *Eyes Wide Shut* concludes in the most conventional and realistic of ways. After flirting dangerously close to marital collapse, a New York couple (portrayed by Nicole Kidman and Tom Cruise) decide to bear the consequences of the recent past and continue with their marriage. *Eyes Wide Shut's* ending is neither redemptive nor destructive but realistically bittersweet. It is an amazing irony that Kubrick's final film ending—so balanced and quietly authentic—would conclude a career whose brilliant crescendos would match that of any other director.

Like *The Shining*, throughout the filming of *Eyes Wide Shut*, Kubrick endured yet another Pluto transit, yet this time to his natal Saturn. In both films, we observe the sense or terror of "threat" of breakdown, yet set in very different terms. In *The Shining*, Jack Torrance faces the threat of extinction from within, as forces siege his waking consciousness and terrorize his sense of mental health (reflected in Kubrick's Pluto transit to Mercury). In *Eyes Wide Shut*, Dr. Bill Harford (Tom Cruise) is also threatened, but unlike the possibility of mental breakdown, the annihilation is more aimed at Cruise's sense of identity, security, marriage, career, and reputation in his community. What is threatened for Bill Harford is the Saturn function in astrology, as mirrored by Kubrick's transit of Pluto to his natal Saturn at the time. Saturn rules the personality structure concerned with how one interfaces with society-at-large, with tradition, and, in particular, structures (like career or relationship) that maintain self-preservation. From the opening moments of the film, we observe Bill Harford as a member of the New York elite and establishment, undoubtedly a person who has worked hard to obtain a position of respect in his community. However, as the plot elements unfold, these cherished security patterns and structures (Saturn) become endangered as repressed fantasies roar to the surface of consciousness (Pluto). As Michel Ciment comments, "The odyssey of William Harford, a well-known doctor, married for nine years to the beautiful and intelligent Alice and father of a seven-year-old daughter, resembles those of a number of Kubrick's protagonists. These characters, with their appreciation of a life that is well balanced, comfortable, devoted to order and logic, suddenly confront an unexpected event that unsettles their convictions and causes the ground to slip from beneath their feet."[18]

Although thematically we witness the destructive powers of Pluto threatening to break down the structures associated with Saturn, we also witness the concentrated power of Pluto intensifying and compelling the expression of Saturn through other elements in the film as well. Stylistically, the film has a Saturn-Pluto resonance: chastising and judgment from authority, weighty and sonorous colors and atmospheres, guilt and gravity, a journey of isolation, heavy moral dilemmas, the urban landscape in the dead of winter, and the expectations and traditions of the societal elite. The style, pacing, tone, and mood of *Eyes Wide Shut*, somber and slightly melancholic, are nearly diametrically opposed in expression to the wild experimentations and exuberance of *A Clockwork Orange* (which is more exemplary of the archetype of Uranus).

Stylistically, the Pluto-Saturn quality of *Eyes Wide Shut* is best expressed by the ritual sequence in the middle of the film. The deep, heavy hues of crimson and black, the ominous intonations of the ritual leader, the sense of formality and custom that pervade the ceremony, the grave sense of foreboding and impending fate all give stunning realization to the synthesis of Saturn and Pluto. However, the entire film is saturated with stylistic elements of the meeting of these two archetypes: the plodding, onerous piano motif that carries the film; the tremendous outpouring of guilt and grief from Bill Harford as he integrates his experiences of near-infidelity; the weightiness and burdens that results from the customs of old wealth; the desolate gray and darkness that results from the city in the dead of winter.

◆   ◆   ◆

Astrology suggests that individuals stand as mouthpieces and conduits to timeless, archetypal expressions. Kubrick's remarkable heritage heightens and strengthens our understanding of the symbols of the astrological grammar. By pushing artistic expression into unknown territory, Kubrick amplified and added to our understanding of the pantheon of astrology. His futuristic visions hone our understanding of the creative genius associated with Uranus. His uncanny sense of the destructive impulses latent within humanity gives us a fuller appreciation of the astrological Pluto. His ability to convey the transcendent and sublime through images wedded with music gives an unparalleled expression of the archetype of Neptune.

Kubrick was a singular visionary who raised the possibilities of filmmaking into unknown and vaulted territory. In our current era of directors who imitate many legendary filmmakers, perhaps the greatest testament to Kubrick's legacy is the total lack of clones working to emulate his style. Although imitation may be the sincerest form of flattery, the absence of Kubrick protégés and impersonators suggests that his style was truly inimitable. Kubrick's oeuvre of thirteen feature films stands alone as an unique and stunning chapter in the history of moviemaking.

1. *Stanley Kubrick: A Life in Pictures.* Warner Bros., Los Angeles, 2001.

2. Michel Ciment, *Kubrick: The Definitive Edition* (New York: Faber and Faber, 1999) 3.

3. Richard Tarnas, *Prometheus the Awakener* (Woodstock, CT: Spring Publications 1993)

4. Insights expressed in Richard Tarnas's course, "Psyche and Cosmos," November 9, 1999.

5. http://kubrickfilms.warnerbros.com/mainmenu/mainmenu.html

6. Because of the pervasiveness of the Pluto-Mercury combination in Kubrick's life and film, it is assumed that this combination is angular, that is, receiving greater potency and importance in the birth chart.

7. *Stanley Kubrick: A Life in Pictures.* Warner Bros., Los Angeles, 2001.

8. Although we do not have Kubrick's exact birth time, we do know that, given a seven degree orb of influence, the Moon would have remained in square aspect to Neptune throughout the entire date of his birth.

9. Vincent LoBrutto, *Stanley Kubrick: A Biography* (New York: Da Capo Press, 1999) 193.

10. Perhaps the mental creativity that was energizing Kubrick was potentially too intense. According to biographer Vincent LoBrutto, Kubrick apparently witnessed a UFO in mid-1964. Upset that the finding might potentially destroy his film concerning extra-terrestrial intelligence, Kubrick filed the standard UFO-report with the Pentagon. Abuzz with the spirit of the times, stimulated by the burgeoning space race, and as always an element of paranoia, what Kubrick thought was a UFO was merely a transiting satellite, *Echo I.*

11. Vincent LoBrutto, *Stanley Kubrick: A Biography* (New York: Da Capo Press, 1999) 268.

12. The technique had its first appearance in experimental filmmaker Jordan Belson's work. Although Belson rarely worked on commercial, feature length films, his special effects would have a lasting influence in Hollywood in the latter half of the twentieth century.

13. Friedrich Nietzsche, *Thus Spake Zarathustra* (1891)

14. *Stanley Kubrick: A Life in Pictures.* Warner Bros., Los Angeles, 2001.

15. According to biographer Vincent LaBrutto, "At one screening a young man ran down the aisle during the Star Gate sequence and crashed through the screen screaming, 'I see God!'" *Stanley Kubrick: A Biography* (312)

16. Vincent LoBrutto, *Stanley Kubrick: A Biography* (New York: Da Capo Press, 1999) 429.

17. Ibid, 442.

18. Michel Ciment, *Kubrick: The Definitive Edition* (New York: Faber and Faber, 1999) 260.

PART III
Individual Films

In the first section of this anthology, films were selected to demonstrate and express the essence of astrological symbols. In this section, individual films are explored in-depth, taking into account the astrological symbolism for world events, directors, actors, actresses, and screenwriters surrounding the making and release of a particular film. In *Double Indemnity*, Deb McBride analyzes the various astrological synchronicities of the making of this classic noir mystery. Jeffrey Kishner illustrates how *The Matrix* is exemplary of several planetary archetypes and the stages of birth as developed in the work of pioneering psychologist Stan Grof. Finally, Bill Streett analyzes *The Lord of the Rings* and demonstrates how the trilogy resonates with the symbolism surrounding the Saturn-Pluto cycle.

Double Indemnity

Deb McBride

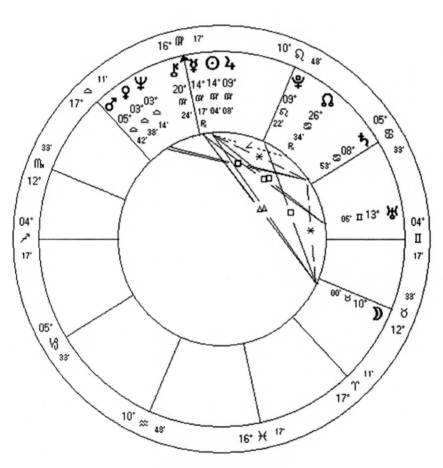

Release for *Double Indemnity*
September 6, 1944
Los Angeles, California
12:00 PM

Neptune is the planet traditionally associated with film, the movies and the glamour of Hollywood. But everyone's life has been under the influence of Neptune at one time or another, and it undoubtedly has affected both personal and professional relationships. Neptune can heal, inspire or create, but it can also blind, beguile, and cause addiction. In matters of the heart Neptune can make it or break it, but it always takes us on a journey and drops us off somewhere we've never seen before. When the journey is over, we scratch our heads and wonder how we got there.

While under the spell, Neptune renders it nearly impossible to gain distance and realize what is happening. It may be love or it may only be seduction. The spell is so infatuating that one's spirit is willing to follow the scent of Neptune right into hell. So sweet, so intoxicating, how could one know that murder sometimes smells like honeysuckle?

That's the question asked by Walter Neff, the anti-hero of *Double Indemnity*. Neff's experience in the film was a Neptunian one on many levels, and it is not surprising when one considers the astrological dynamics involved in the making of this film. The day the film was released and had its public birth, Neptune was in the relationship sign of Libra. Since Neptune is an outer planet, its journey though a sign lasts for many years and has an extensive influence on the collective unconscious. On the one hand, Neptune in Libra was highly romantic and this was quite evident in many of the films of the 1940s, especially those dealing with romance during World War II. On the other hand, in certain films of the 1940s Neptune in Libra indicated a relationship where all was not as it seemed and a man was gravely duped by a woman.

The horoscope for the release date of *Double Indemnity* shows Neptune in Libra in close conjunction with Venus and Mars. Venus conjunct Neptune in this case indicates the deceptive, double dealing woman, and in Libra, an illusory relationship. The addition of Mars designates the themes of violence, danger and ulterior motive. This conjures up a morally complex situation in a shadowy relationship where the leading male is not certain whether he is being cherished or hoodwinked. And so it went: *Double Indemnity* was the story of jaded insurance salesman Walter Neff, played by Fred MacMurray, who worked for the Pacific All-Risk Insurance Company in Los Angeles. The film began with Neff walking into his office after hours, injured from what appeared to be a gunshot wound. He told a story into a dictation machine that began with his confession of a murder and continued as a narration for the entire film. Walter Neff worked for and with Barton Keyes, portrayed by Edward G. Robinson. Keyes was a dogged insurance investigator with a knack for sniffing out fraudulent cases and solving them. On one of Walter Neff's daily sales calls, he met Phyllis Dietrichson, played by Barbara Stanwyck. Neff was immediately attracted to Phyllis, and she used her feminine wiles to seduce him into helping her dispose of her husband. The two plotted to murder him in her automobile and made it look as though he had accidentally fallen from a train so they could benefit from the double indemnity clause in Mr. Dietrichson's accident insurance policy. It was the perfect crime until Barton Keyes and Phyllis' stepdaughter, Lola Dietrichson (played by little-known actress Jean Heather) suspected Phyllis of the murder. Keyes' instincts and persistent examination of the case led the murderers to panic and eventually destroy one another.

During the release of the film, a cluster of planets is to be found in Virgo, including Jupiter, the Sun, and Mercury. Virgo is a sign that pays great attention to detail, is diligent and loves vocabulary and words. Neff and Phyllis engage in several scenes of fast-talking, sharp-witted banter that can also be seen as sexual foreplay. Every step of her husband's murder was planned thoroughly 'straight down the line' as Phyllis and Neff said to one another several times. The Sun and Jupiter together indicate an inherent faith in a favorable outcome, but the lower expression of this aspect can manifest in the form of gambling or taking high risks because one feels that one cannot lose. This brought in the element of arrogance as the characters felt they could beat the system. They were overconfident and self-satisfied with their plans and were counting on the insurance money. Given the challenging aspect the Sun and Jupiter make to Uranus in Gemini, eventually their perfectly organized scheme would become undone as the forgotten details tripped them up and called attention to their crime. The nature of Uranus in Gemini can bring about abrupt turnarounds in situations where details and communications are paramount.

Saturn was in Cancer during the release of the film and shows the leading characters as unfeeling, hardhearted, and unsympathetic. An innately cold planet such as Saturn does not have its best expression in a warm, watery, sensitive sign such as Cancer. As it is in challenging connection to the Neptune-Venus-Mars conjunction in Libra, Saturn acknowledges that Phyllis and Neff are not realistically together with feelings of deep and profound love.

As the story unfolded we saw the struggle between obsessive, enthralling, mysterious passion versus genuine emotion and friendship. There were unspeakably magnetic feelings going on for Phyllis and Neff as they acted out the lower instincts of Venus and Neptune by indulging the self-destructive relationship. The power of seduction and danger intrigued both of them. They would not have committed this crime without each other, as it was the thrill of acting together that drove them. Neither of them really wanted to know the truth of their association, as Neptune sways one to see and believe only that which one *wants* to see and believe. They preferred to continue living out the illusion that Neptune had brought them.

It is the nature of Neptune to lack boundaries, which allows for great creativity and inspired artistry. But when entangled with Venus and applied to relationships, Neptune may also operate inappropriately thereby bringing about triangular affairs, as there is no moral structure to Neptune's energies. In the manner of Venus and Neptune, Phyllis and Walter Neff's relationship was always triangular, which not only enhanced the thrill, but also provided the necessary hook on which the devious couple could hang all their problems. They failed to realize that when the third party was removed, the relationship didn't have legs. At the outset, it was Phyllis' doomed husband who was their hook. Since he never caught them in the act, their sense of danger remained. Once they got rid of him, they needed a replacement and they found it in Barton Keyes. Only this time the danger was genuine, as the dogged Keyes was a sharp inspector bound to discover the answer to the crime's riddle. Furthermore, Neff had a greater investment in his relationship with Keyes than Phyllis did with her husband.

Keyes and Neff performed the Venus-Mars-Neptune relationship where they had unconditional love for one another up to and including the moment when Neff died and Keyes lit his bloodstained cigarette. The addition of the Mars principle shows this level of love happening between two men in their friendship. This revealed the authentic relationship in the movie. They also acted out the Sun-Jupiter in Virgo by the apparent loyalty that was the basis of their bond.

This chart not only explains the film but also the emergence of a new type of movie experience known as "film noir" or "dark film." Despite our victories in the war abroad, the pessimism that surrounded our involvement and the condition of the world was present in certain films. When motion pictures from the United States were imported to Europe during the war, the French, seeing this darkness, coined a name for this mood of film. *Double Indemnity* was one of the first instances of the then new style of film noir and to this day is considered to be the standard.

Film noir described the mood or feel of the film, which was commonly oppressive. It was mostly shot in grays and black and white and was almost always a crime film. Also, wartime budgets caused many movie sets to be stark and this contributed to the shadowy elements on screen. These films reflected society's evils and generally involved a confusing morality issue. Any description of the mood of film noir is what we associate with Neptune such as disillusionment, disenchantment, ambiguity, moral corruption, guilt and paranoia. The lighting and skewed camera angles, the use of silhouettes, circling cigarette smoke and disorienting visual schemes are all very Neptunian. These factors generated a feeling of uncertainty, an early instinct in the films that something was about to go wrong. Film noir seemed to have its own pathology, that being the fatal sexual magnetism between its characters. The protagonists are generally driven to the point of no return by weaknesses or a tragic flaw that caused them to repeat mistakes.

Pluto in Leo correlated with the creative flourishing of the movie industry. As Pluto is an outer planet and spends many years in a particular sign, it has great influence over collective movements. Leo is a sign that desires to be a source of energy for others. Leo wants to radiate like the Sun, and therefore has a strong need for personal recognition and strives for great self-expression. Pluto in Leo was a generation that had a great collective need to put people on the big screen to express their lightness and darkness, fears and anxieties and joys and redemptions. It was a new way for the masses to experience the projection of their unconscious feelings. Pluto in Leo would also be appropriate to something new called a 'dark film.' Murder is always a Plutonian subject as Pluto deals with what is hidden or mysterious. While Pluto was moving through the sign of Leo, actors were more willing and able to conjure up a darker and more honest element for their portrayals. This deep creativity birthed a wide range of cinema experiences.

Double Indemnity began as a detective novel by James M. Cain, based on a true murder story that happened in Brooklyn in the 1920s. Mr. Cain had three planets in Cancer, the Sun, Mercury and Venus. Using his Cancerian talents, which include sensitivity to one's environment, he could emotionally process this information by creative story telling. The Pluto-Neptune conjunction in Gemini under which he was born also shows the genre of writing (Gemini) as a dark one.

Among other novels, his most famous include *The Postman Always Rings Twice* and *Mildred Pierce*, both of which were turned into Hollywood films and were considered to be part of the film noir genre. The Venus in his chart was retrograde in Cancer, indicating a skewed perception of love, women, and relationships. The appearance of Venus retrograde in a natal chart generally does not allow a person enough detachment to skillfully comprehend and handle the love principle in his or her life. Cain did not know great fortune with women as he was married four times, the last time being in 1947. And it is no surprise that his most successful novels were about a man undone by a woman.

Cain stated that he made no conscious effort to be tough or grim and that his stories were about the average man and his circumstances, although many of his novels were on the subject of murder. He had Uranus in Scorpio, which inspires an intense desire to understand and discover life in all of its lightness and darkness. From this sprung his ability to write detective novels, since there was always a character that was going to get to the bottom of the puzzle and figure out how the crime was committed. There was usually one person in the story who had a relentless need to get an answer, mirroring Cain's need to unravel a mystery.

The film *Double Indemnity* was born of the collaboration between Billy Wilder and Raymond Chandler, who took Cain's book and turned it into a screenplay. It's interesting to note that both Chandler and Cain were born in the late 1800s when Pluto and Neptune were conjunct in the literary and sometimes gossiping sign of Gemini; these men together were called the poets of the tabloid murder.

Screenwriter Raymond Chandler was a Leo with the planets Venus and Saturn conjunct in Leo as well. Leo has an innate understanding of performance and stage work and is likely to get directly involved with film and screenplays. A Venus-Saturn conjunction can be considered to be harsh, cold or insensitive; "hard-boiled" is a phrase most commonly used to describe Chandler's stories and characters. Chandler had made a name for himself as the writer of detective novels featuring the famous character Private Investigator Philip Marlowe. Marlowe made it to the silver screen and was portrayed by Humphrey Bogart in the film *The Big Sleep*, based on Chandler's novel of the same name. Most of his crime novels were set in Los Angeles and were derived from pulp stories he was writing for magazines. The settings and characters were shadowy and the stories were dark, which was suitable as Chandler's edge came from his Mars in Scorpio. Mars is a sharp and fiery energy. Scorpio has an innate desire to dig deep into darkness in order to facilitate a transformation. Together they are intense and tenacious. Chandler's work on *Double Indemnity* altered Cain's novel as the characters became more provocative and insensitive. In his screenplay, Phyllis was far more unloving and calculating than Cain's depiction of her.

As Pluto transited the sign of Leo, it moved through Chandler's planets and gave him a fresh artistic edge, and therefore made him a famous name in writing and in Hollywood. As Pluto will darken anything that it touches, his creative ideas became more extreme. In the case of this film, Chandler rewrote the ending of the novel by having the lead characters violently undo one another. When Neff arrived to settle the score with her and she had the gun tucked in the chair ready to shoot him, the background music playing was the song "Tangerine"—a song that describes a woman whose heart only belongs to her.

Billy Wilder secured the rights to James M. Cain's novel. This was Wilder's first big Hollywood success in directing, after working on other Hollywood projects as a writer. Wilder had a stellium of five planets in Cancer: Sun, Moon, Mars, Neptune and Mercury. This is a clear indication of someone who is multi-talented in the arts. Water signs such as Cancer are naturally artistic because they find it easier to act on their emotional instincts and put primitive internal feelings into creative activities than to express them through words. During his very long career, he grew from writer to director and eventually to producer. All of the great sensitivity and passion he experienced was channeled through his Uranus in the opposite earth sign of Capricorn, grounding it so that it could be expressed as creative genius. Since Uranus sits alone in his horoscope, it is a strong placement and therefore it figured greatly in his life. Wilder was quite confident with his artistry and in the case of *Double Indemnity*, he turned the portrait upside down in true Uranian fashion to create a meaningful film. He told the story in hindsight—he begins with a confession—so we opened knowing who committed the crime and what the murderer believed his motives were.

The stellium in Cancer in Wilder's chart also serves to draw the audience into the emotional experience of the tale being told. As a result, the viewer experiences the sick, queasy feeling at every moment that the murderers may be exposed. We root for them to succeed and, in essence, experience their emotional roller coaster. The glamour, their romance and the excitement pull us into the tide of Neptune and take us on some escapist ride, as a masterful film should.

Wilder used the genius of Uranus and surprised the viewer as the movie turned a corner. It happened when Lola Dietrichson was going to turn Phyllis in to the police for her father's murder, and Neff spent time with Lola to keep an eye on her and cool her fever. He subsequently found out about Phyllis' role in Lola's mother's death, and her relationship with Nino Zachetti coming to the house every night. Neff realized that she had set him up and was setting up Nino as well. For the moment, Neptune's haze was lifted and he was able to clearly see Phyllis for the iniquitous woman she really was.

In the early 1940s, Fred MacMurray (who played Walter Neff) was the highest paid and most sought after actor in Hollywood. In the manner of his Virgo Sun, his specialty was portraying nice guys who get the girl in romantic comedies. These roles were not a stretch for him; he felt comfortable with these characters. Typical of Virgo, MacMurray appeared on screen as a charming, completely natural, easygoing guy—one of the boys. Billy Wilder convinced him to play Walter Neff, a role no actor wanted, as the role was too unsympathetic and taking it on would be a career risk. MacMurray felt the part of Neff required something his previous roles did not—acting. He brought the Virgo personality to Neff by making him a regular guy on a regular day at work and exhibited all the good qualities about Virgo: reliable, loyal, hardworking, and deserving of promotion until something unforeseen happens. This also emphasized James M. Cain's belief that he was writing about an ordinary person and his situation.

MacMurray's Venus-Neptune conjunction in Cancer echoed the release chart of the film, underscoring the fact that his character was easily misled by the thrill and promise of a woman's love. This was the leading male type in film noir: a jaded, down on his luck, bored with everyday life kind of guy, who happens upon a woman who takes advantage of his vulnerability. Its opposition to Uranus in Capricorn truly gave him the versatility to change the types of characters he played, from a romantic lead to a morally conflicted soul on a downward spiral. Later in his career he would repeat edgy roles highlighting his many acting talents.

Edward G. Robinson was known for playing gangsters (remember *Key Largo?*) and in fact he was the actor in Hollywood history who set the type for gangsters early on in talking films. He has Mars and Uranus conjunct in Scorpio, making his characters sharp, skilled, tough, smart, and resilient. This time he took the role of an insurance investigator who solved the mystery of the crime. Just as James M. Cain used his Uranus in Scorpio to create the detectives who needed to get to the bottom of the riddle, Edward G. Robinson brought that same energy to his role as Keyes. Robinson had great understanding of the characters he played, yet his Sagittarius Sun made it all appear effortless. Sagittarius has a constant outpouring of fiery energy as it seeks maximum self-expression. Anyone born under this sign, such as Edward G. Robinson, feels his or her expressiveness is part of a larger social context and raises consciousness.

Once again the viewer sees evidence of Billy Wilder's strong expression of Uranus in his casting of the two leading men. Uranus' creativity lies in viewing the plan backwards or upside-down. Wilder cast MacMurray as the murderer and cast Robinson as the man on the side of justice, a role reversal for both of them, and developed their camaraderie as the most anchored relationship in the film. While there was a fatal mistrust between Neff and Phyllis that leads to the destruction of both of them and the seemingly perfect crime, Keyes and Neff's bond was still a strong one, despite the latter's weakness. The film would be a lot harder to digest if it were not for the genuine friendship between Barton Keyes and Walter Neff. Keyes was a good man, and he didn't judge Neff; he was above and beyond whatever lies Neff had told; he was looking out for Neff all along, like a father figure. And in that sense, Keyes has deepened their attachment even when Neff felt he did not deserve Keyes' affection.

Film noir introduced audiences to the female character type known as the femme fatale. *Double Indemnity* is the first instance in which this type of woman appears: callous, manipulative, double-crossing and desperate. She could only be trouble for the leading man. In the case of Phyllis Dietrichson, she described herself as "rotten to the core." Barbara Stanwyck's characters are usually tough women—cardsharps, chorus girls, gangster molls, even Annie Oakley was a tough cookie. When asked by Billy Wilder to play the role of a murderess, she loved the thought of it, but was hesitant just as Fred MacMurray had been. She, too, was fearful that a role this extreme would harm her image and career. At that moment she was the highest paid actress in Hollywood. To be the leading lady and play an out-and-out killer was a huge risk, as it hadn't been done before. Upon approaching Wilder with her concerns, he asked her if she was an actress or a mouse. He changed her mind; she took the part and was always grateful to him.

Stanwyck's Mars-Uranus conjunction in Capricorn opposite her Venus-Neptune conjunction in Cancer is a powerful combination that she drew from in a masterful way, especially in this film. She took the amalgamation of these four planets and turned out a treacherous character in Phyllis. Mars-Uranus can have a hot temper, be impulsive, cunning, disloyal and violent. This aspect, when not used creatively as in acting, could become explosive and is often indicative of a murderous rage. Due to Neptune's ability to operate behind the scenes, Venus and Neptune together can play out as a deceptive female. A Mars-Uranus conjunction involved with Venus and Neptune has all the makings of a premeditated murder. When placed in Capricorn, Uranus and Mars generate intelligent and well contemplated plans. For the actress, her planets in Capricorn produced in her a desire for perfection and sheer professionalism. The combination of Mars and Uranus usually designates a person with a vast knowledge of a highly mechanical skill. This placement in her chart is an indicator of her strong technical ability and brilliant use of props that she had always exhibited in her film work. Her gestures, posture and movements all enhanced her character, as she knew how to control and direct (Capricorn) her energy (Mars-Uranus). Her Neptune-Venus conjunction manifests in her ability to be a convincing actress. The artistic qualities associated with Venus placed in an emotional sign such as Cancer combined with Neptune's traits of imagination, illusion, and shape-changing point to someone who can creatively mold a character just by envisioning and owning that character's qualities. Her audience was transported into the story, experiencing that world as if they, too, were a part of it. Clearly, she knew this dame very well. Early in her life, Stanwyck had met people from all walks of life. Orphaned at a young age, she took care of herself by working as a chorus girl and was exposed to a seedier crowd than an average teenager might have been. The combination of these four planets would represent an actress who was smart (Uranus), sharp (Mars) and highly respected (Capricorn), but also a sensitive (Cancer), visionary (Neptune) artist (Venus).

Barbara Stanwyck had four planets in Cancer and they were all the right ones for this movie: Venus, Neptune, Jupiter and the Sun. Considering the Cancer stellium in the natal charts of both Billy Wilder and James Cain, she was exactly what they needed for the role of Phyllis. Furthermore, her Venus-Neptune conjunction in Cancer was in keeping with Fred MacMurray's same aspect and that of the release date of the film. Her Sun-Jupiter conjunction also resonated with the same aspect in the release chart. As Phyllis, she portrayed the more negative expressions of these aspects. She trumped up the beguiling, seductive elements of Venus-Neptune. The viewer is never certain of her true feelings, especially at the very end of the film when she told Neff that she just couldn't fire the last shot at him. She may have been sincere in these final moments, but Neff didn't buy it. Her Sun-Jupiter conjunction came into play as a greedy, selfish, overconfident liar. Although Ms. Stanwyck was a shy Cancerian, this role stretched her abilities and sealed her reputation as one of the finest actresses in Hollywood history.

She was getting transiting Pluto to her Mercury at the time, signifying a new, darker way of expressing herself verbally. Her banter with Fred in the early scenes of this film is one of the true classic moments in film history. She was quick-witted, fast thinking and sharp tongued. Saturn was transiting her planets in Cancer, adding a hard edge to what was probably a natural shyness and softness. Typical of a Saturn transit, this was hard work for the actress as she confronted her fear of invoking an unfeeling character.

Since the cast, director and novelist were all directly experiencing the arrival of Saturn in Cancer, a turning point occurred for each of them. Cain and Wilder became well known and highly respected. Stanwyck and MacMurray labored intensely, took career risks and each turned out the performance of a lifetime in portraying cold-blooded murderers. Cancer types are masters of psychological projection. When they are not ready to accept their own flaws, impulses and issues, they can impose it upon others and watch them act it out. This comes more naturally to members of this sign than to other signs because of Cancer's willingness to withdraw and become immovable. In the case of *Double Indemnity*, the abundance of Cancer in everyone's charts was used to project a dark tale coming from a dark corner of the life of each main contributor to the film. The theme of projection was especially apparent in the case of Barbara Stanwyck's character.

Phyllis' relationship with Neff instantly began when she appeared wearing only a towel at the top of the staircase in her home. This was a new film occurrence: women didn't appear half naked at the front door in the 1940s. Naturally he would have thought that she's one of "those" women: fast and looking for a good time. He couldn't get his mind off that "honey of an anklet" she was wearing. Neff thought she was a bored wife who wanted an affair, until she mentioned her husband and started to ask him about accident insurance. When he correctly assumed that she wanted to kill her husband, she told him that he was rotten and he left. But it was too late, he had already been taken by the scent of honeysuckle and he had to see her again. Phyllis was obviously the mastermind of the entire plot. Murder was never an idea until Neff appeared at her house, talking about insurance. The wheels of her mind started spinning and she cooked up a scheme to bump off her husband, and get twice the insurance payoff from the double indemnity clause in the policy. She saw Neff's weak, spineless nature and she decided to smoke him like he was just another cigarette. She was able to project all her devious wishes upon him so that he not only committed the crime for her, but protected her as well.

As illustrated by Ms. Stanwyck's chart, a treacherous woman is at the core of the entire film. Without Phyllis' street-smart seduction and use of her feminine wiles, none of these events would have happened. Although this underhanded femme fatale style is now taken for granted as a Hollywood staple, Barbara Stanwyck invented it for the screen. Her portrayal of Phyllis Dietrichson was an evolution for actresses in Hollywood and women in general.

Double Indemnity was nominated for seven Academy Awards, but did not win any. It remains one of the timeless classics of American film.

> **Double Indemnity** Release date: September 6, 1944 Los Angeles, CA
> Barbara Stanwyck: 7/16/1907 Brooklyn, NY;
> Fred MacMurray: 8/30/1908 Kankakee, IL;
> Edward G. Robinson: 12/12/1893 5:00 am Bucarest, Romania 44N28, 26E10
>
> **Director:** Billy Wilder: 6/22/1906 Sucha Beskidzka, Poland 49N43, 19E36
>
> **Writers:** Raymond Chandler:7/23/1888 Chicago, IL
> James M. Cain: 7/1/1892 Annapolis, MD

Sources:

Internet:

The Internet Movie Database: www.imdb.com for birth data and small biographies Ebert, Roger, "Double Indemnity", www.suntimes.com

Hartlaub, Joe, "Raymond Chandler", The Book Report, Inc. www.bookreporter.com

Mills, Michael, "Barbara Stanwyck and Double Indemnity" www.moderntimes.com, 1997

Pegasos: Literature related resources www.kirjasto.sci.fi

Sloniowski, Jeannette, "Double Indemnity," *St. James Encyclopedia of Popular Culture*, www.findarticles.com, Gale Group 2002

Print:

Osborne, Robert. *70 Years of the Oscar: The Official History of the Academy Awards*. New York: Abbeville, 1999.

The Matrix as Birth Process

Jeffrey Kishner, M.A.

The Matrix is a well-made Zen, cyberpunk, action-adventure film, with spell-binding martial arts and special effects. Though all this would be enough to account for the movie's enormous popularity, it has a deeper structure that speaks to the viewer's unconscious. The success of *Star Wars* is attributable partly to special effects and space aliens, but also partly because George Lucas has intentionally tapped into the hero myth that exists in nearly every culture. *The Matrix* resonates with the viewer because it charts the course of the entire birth process.

The Four Stages of Birth

During the 1950s and 1960s, when LSD was still being used medically as a powerful adjunct to psychotherapy, psychiatrist Stanislav Grof studied its effects on a wide range of patients and volunteers. Over years of research, he found that the "nonordinary" states experienced by patients vividly mirrored the four stages of the birth process, on both a literal and a mythic level. Patients often re-experienced their traumatic birth circumstances during these sessions. Grof called these stages Basic Perinatal Matrices (BPMs).[1] (*Perinatal* means "around birth.") These stages correlate not only with biological birth but also with biographical and transpersonal experiences that relate to each stage of the birth process.

BPM 1 occurs before labor begins; the infant is in a blissful, oceanic state of consciousness in the mother's womb. When we curl up into a fetal position and want to be taken care of, this often reflects a yearning to return to the womb. On a mythic level, BPM 1 is associated with Paradise, the Garden of Eden before the fall of humankind.

BPM 2 occurs when contractions begin but the cervix has not yet opened. Intense pressure is being exerted upon the infant, but there is nowhere for the infant to go. Toxins are released into the uterus. BPM 2 is associated with Hell. *BPM 3* occurs when the cervix opens but before crowning. The infant is often exposed to blood, urine, and feces. There is an intense struggle to get out of the mother's body. BPM 3 is Purgatory.

Finally, at *BPM 4*, the infant is born—and separated from the mother—into the world with which we are all familiar. BPM 4 is Heaven.

Richard Tarnas, author of *Prometheus the Awakener* and the best-selling *Passion of the Western Mind*, noted that the archetypes of the four outer planets correlate exactly with the four Basic Perinatal Matrices.[2] (For the sake of brevity and the focus of this chapter, I am simplifying the complex body of correlations uncovered by Grof and Tarnas in their research.) Neptune, the planet of spirituality and ego transcendence, corresponds to BPM 1. As ruler of the sea, the Roman god Neptune is associated with the watery world of the womb. Saturn, the planet of restriction and boundaries, correlates with BPM 2, when the walls are closing in on the infant. Pluto—the planet of death/rebirth mysteries, the Underworld, power, and instincts like sex and aggression—is associated with BPM 3, when the infant is struggling just to survive. Finally, Uranus, the planet of liberation, correlates with BPM 4, when the infant is freed from the womb. Tarnas's research revealed that, during nonordinary states of consciousness, people experienced the precise Basic Perinatal Matrix corresponding to the dominant outer planet transiting at least one of their natal planets. For example, individuals tended to have a BPM 3 experience under transits involving Pluto.

Enter *The Matrix*. The movie begins in what appears to be the late 1990s: Neo (played by Keanu Reeves) is living a double life as a computer programmer and a hacker in a large metropolitan area. As we find out later, Neo's body is actually in a "womb" that harvests his bioelectric energy to fuel Artificial Intelligence (AI), the victor of a war against its human creators in the "now" of the 22nd century. AI has Neo's mind plugged into the "Matrix"—a convincing computer simulation of a time when humans ruled the Earth. Neo is stuck in the realm of Neptune—BPM 1—which corresponds to the Eastern concept of *maya*, the world of illusion. Literally, he is still in the womb. Grof would call this period the "undisturbed intrauterine state."

In the Matrix, Neo suspects that there is something more to the life he is living; he is woken up by his computer, which spontaneously writes: "The Matrix has you…" on the screen. The computer directs Neo to "follow the white rabbit," which leads him to a club. Here, he meets Trinity (Carrie-Anne Moss), a legendary computer hacker who confirms his suspicion that the Matrix exists. She says, "I know why you're here, Neo. I know what you've been doing. I know why you hardly sleep, why you live alone, and why, night after night, you sit at your computer…. It's the question that drives us, Neo. It's the question that brought you here." Neo responds, "What is the Matrix?"

The next morning, he awakens, goes to work late, and is captured by Agent Smith and his colleagues, who are projections of AI inserted into the Matrix to track down those who threaten to expose it. Smith pressures Neo to turn Morpheus, the leader of the resistance against AI, over to them. With the introduction of Trinity and the agents, reality (Saturn) starts impinging on the illusory life that Neo has been living. This is the "disturbance of intrauterine life," according to Grof. Soon, Neo meets Morpheus (Laurence Fishburne), who offers to show Neo what the Matrix really is. Morpheus gives him a red pill and a blue pill. If Neo takes the red pill, he will be shown the truth; however, if he takes the blue pill, he will wake up in the morning and believe whatever he wants to believe. Neo chooses the red pill, which enables Morpheus and his team to pinpoint the location of Neo's physical body. He is violently removed from the womb by a machine that unplugs him from the simulation. The viewer can immediately see that this "womb" experience is not a pleasant one; in fact, it is rather toxic: people in this womb are fed the remains of the human dead!

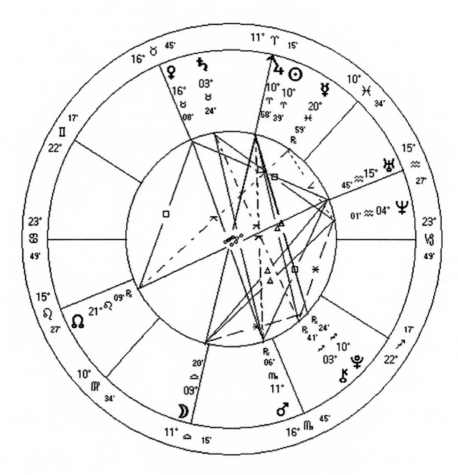

Release for *The Matrix*
March 31, 1999
Los Angeles, CA
12:00 PM

A Chart for *The Matrix*

The release date of a movie correlates with its "birth" into the collective consciousness. The archetypal combinations in the sky correspond to the themes of the film. When *The Matrix* was released at the end of March 1999,[3] Saturn and Neptune were square each other (see Chart). This aspect signifies a conflict between the integration of these two planets. Saturn, which has been traditionally known as a malefic planet, can emphasize the negative or problem-causing potential of any planet it aspects. In this case, Saturn renders the womb (Neptune) toxic. The movie synchronously reflected an archetypal combination that the collective was experiencing during this time.

After Neo is removed from his womb, a hovercraft called the Nebuchadnezzar picks him up. This Neo looks very different from how he appears in the simulation: The "real" Neo is hairless and pale and has several sockets installed throughout his body, notably at the base of his skull; these sockets have been used for harvesting his bioelectric energy and inserting his consciousness into the Matrix. Neo is now thrust into the world of Saturn. In its positive expression, Saturn is the archetype of structure and discipline. The crew of the Nebuchadnezzar rebuilds Neo's atrophied musculature and trains him in kung fu by plugging him into a computer simulation via the socket at the back of his head. Saturn also signifies responsibility and hard-won self-reliance. Morpheus teaches Neo that the rules (Saturn) of the Matrix can be bent; some can even be broken. Neo learns that his only limits are his thoughts. For example, in one computer training simulation, he is unable to jump successfully from the top of one skyscraper to another, because he does not believe that he can do it. Saturn represents fear and limitation, as well as lack of confidence.

Morpheus informs Neo that he is "The One" who will liberate all humans from the Matrix. Cypher (Joe Pantoliano), who also chose the red pill, tells Neo, "Jesus, what a mind job! So, you're here to save the world! What do you say to something like that?" Cypher is expressing the idea that this Saturnian responsibility is a burden on Neo.

Another expression of the Saturn-Neptune square is the struggle between reality (Saturn) and illusion (Neptune). Cypher despises the world of Saturn so much that he makes a deal with Agent Smith: Cypher will be reinserted into the Matrix and forget everything (Neptune) in exchange for giving information leading to the location and capture (Saturn) of Morpheus. One negative expression of Neptune is escapism. For Cypher, the daily grind of his life is so difficult to bear that he prefers permanent delusion.

If any planet in the movie release chart corresponds to Morpheus, it would most likely be Neptune. What archetype better relates to the concept of "morphing" (the transitional change from one image to another, made popular in the *Terminator* movies) than Neptune, the planet of image and illusion? In mythology, Morpheus, the son of Hypnos, is the god of dreams and is associated with sleep; Neptune rules sleep and dreams. This chart's Neptune is in Aquarius, the sign ruled by freedom-loving Uranus: Morpheus "squares off" against the agents (their slow speech, controlled movements, emotional detachment, and positions of authority correspond to Saturn).

Once Neo re-enters the Matrix—this time as a conscious being—BPM 3 begins. Neo has experienced the negative Saturn (pressure from the agents) and the positive Saturn (structure, discipline); now, from the astrological and perinatal perspective, the cervix opens, and Neo is ready for the next stage of the birth process: the world of Pluto.

Forces of Darkness and Light

There are several elements in this part of the movie that correspond to Pluto/BPM 3. Pluto is the archetype of aggression, power, and the mysteries of death and rebirth. According to Liz Greene, Pluto is also associated with fate.[4] Neo's express purpose in entering the Matrix consciously for the first time is to consult the Oracle, a woman who told Morpheus that Neo is The One. She says to Neo, "You're going to have to make a choice…One of you [Morpheus or Neo] is going to die. Which one is up to you." After Cypher betrays Morpheus, and the agents locate the crew of the Nebuchadnezzar, a life-and-death struggle ensues. The humans confront the agents, who are actually extremely powerful "sentient programs" that can bend the rules of the Matrix. Agent Smith captures Morpheus, after the resistance leader attacks him to protect Neo. The agents torture Morpheus in an attempt to extract from his brain the codes to access Zion, the only city harboring humans not mind-controlled by Artificial Intelligence. Tank (one of the few humans who was never "harvested" by AI) suggests to Neo and Trinity that they pull Morpheus's plug to save Zion. Neo, understanding his fate, knows that he can decide whether or not Morpheus dies. He re-enters the Matrix with Trinity to save their leader. The battle is extremely violent, involving machine guns and helicopter fire. (*The Matrix* was criticized for resorting to mainstream violence, but this warfare is archetypally appropriate for BPM 3.)

Morpheus is finally saved. He and Trinity successfully return to the ship, but Neo does not. Agent Smith and Neo fight to the "death" in a subway station.

Neo runs but does not escape. Agent Smith kills him with a round of bullets at close range (the first part of the death/rebirth process). In the Matrix, Neo is bleeding from multiple gunshot wounds. In reality, Neo is in the Nebuchadnezzar and hooked up to the Matrix. The EKG readings show that his heart has stopped beating. Trinity, stunned by Neo's death, tells him that she loves him and knows he is The One, because the Oracle told her that she would fall in love with The One. She kisses him on the lips, he comes back to life, and she urges him to stand up. In the chart of the movie's release, Uranus, the planet of liberation, is square Venus, the female archetype and the planet of love. Through Trinity's love (Venus), she liberates (Uranus) Neo at a time of crisis (square).

Neo is reborn directly into Uranus/BPM 4. Uranus, the planet of breakthrough, awakening, and the flash of insight, manifests as Neo's ability to see beyond the illusory world of the Matrix into the circuitry behind *maya*. The scene where he truly embodies the martial arts master registers with the audience as a spiritual awakening. Neo is now beyond death. He *is* The One. He destroys Agent Smith and, in the movie's final scene, communicates to AI his vow to liberate all human beings (the Bodhisattva Vow) from the Matrix. The Sun in a movie's chart corresponds to the film's protagonist (the Sun also relates to the hero archetype). Hence, the name "Neo" (which means "new") makes sense in light of the chart's Sun sign: Aries, the first sign of the zodiac, which marks the beginning of spring in the Northern Hemisphere. The movie's great box-office and critical success correlates with an exact Sun-Jupiter conjunction trine Pluto, just as Neo's tremendous power relates to the same aspect.

This essay was originally published in Issue # 105 of The Mountain Astrologer

Chart Data and Sources

The Matrix Release date: March 31, 1999.

Sources include:

http://upcomingmovies.com/Matrix.html and
http://www.the-movie-times.com/thrsdir/moviesof99.html

References and Notes

1. Stanislav Grof, *Beyond the Brain: Birth, Death and Transcendence in Psychotherapy* (Albany, NY: State University of New York Press, 1985) 102–127.

2. Richard Tarnas, "Psyche and Cosmos I," a class taught at the California Institute of Integral Studies on February 12, 1997.

3. March 31, 1999 is the date of the general release of *The Matrix* in movie theaters across the United States. The Los Angeles premiere was on March 24, 1999; most of the aspects discussed in this article still hold true for the L.A. premiere. March 31 is used in this article because the film was released into the collective on that date.

4. Liz Greene, *The Astrology of Fate* (York Beach, ME: Samuel Weiser, 1986) 36–51.

Lord of the Rings and the Saturn-Pluto Cycle

Bill Streett, M.A.

Like unconscious ants swarming around a sand hill with abundant food, we pack ourselves into theaters screening movies that best express and resonate with archetypal themes that flavor and suffuse a particular zeitgeist. *The Lord of the Rings*, with its heroic quest; its epic and intensely dramatic battle between light and dark; its exploration of the right use of and attraction to power; and the compelling seriousness of the storytelling all resoundingly amplified the archetypal configuration active globally during its release and mirrored in the opposition of Saturn and Pluto. We packed the theaters that showed *The Lord of the Rings* not only because it was the product of great movie-making, not only because of the book's tremendous popularity, and not only because the film "coincidentally" paralleled the themes of "good versus evil" occurring across the globe, but on the deepest level, we were drawn to the film because of its profound embodiment of an archetypal matrix that was active in the collective psyche.

This brief essay is an examination of the patterns and motifs of the Saturn-Pluto archetypal combination as seen through the themes and experience of viewing *The Lord of the Rings*. When a trilogy of films such as *The Lord of the Rings* so perfectly embodies an archetypal combination such as Saturn-Pluto, it is often an indication that the history, creation, and pivotal figures surrounding the work are also endowed with the mark of Saturn and Pluto in significant angular relationship. *The Lord of the Rings* is no exception. With the movie at the hub of a wheel, we can observe a series of peripheral spokes that connect movie-makers, pivotal periods in history, Tolkien aficionados and predecessors all through Saturn-Pluto archetypal themes and planetary alignments. Hence, the essay will explore key periods in the evolution of *The Lord of the Rings* and the main players in the *LOTR* saga and legend: J.R.R. Tolkien, Ralph Bakshi, Robert Plant, Peter Jackson, and Richard Wagner.

The Lord of the Rings and the Saturn-Pluto film

Dark, heavy, serious, and epic in scope, films that best exemplify the Saturn-Pluto archetypal matrix are often the great, memorable dramas that speak to the supreme conflicts of the human condition. Saturn-Pluto movies exploring collective themes are often powerful, gripping films of an intense and mature subject matter, investigating—unearthing and probing, rather—the great eternal conflicts and tragedies: war, political intrigue and scandal, the corruption and abuse of power, times of crisis, and larger-than-life struggles against impending doom or threats to survival.

On a personal scale, Saturn-Pluto movies penetrate to the heart of the human shadow. Protagonists in these films often endure burdens of guilt, self-judgment, self-doubt and inner torment. These are often confessional films, in which main characters acknowledge shame, humiliation, and display brutally honest self-assessment. On the opposite end of the spectrum, Saturn-Pluto movies often illustrate how external circumstances often force, forge, and sculpt one to live up to one's greatest potentials in the face of almost insurmountable odds. Saturn-Pluto as an archetypal complex is a soul-making configuration that kneads its potential hero through a long journey, a *via longissima*, in which discipline, fortitude, strength, and moral character are forged trial after trial after trial.

These movies are compelling; they often serve to inspire us to our own greatness. We may leave the theater with multiple and somewhat paradoxical feelings. On the one hand, we may be inspired to face our fears with honesty and feel absolutely compelled to improve our situations in life with renewed resolve. However, as these movies speak directly to our superegos, we may also feel heightened self-criticism and shame that we have not matched the true greatness just witnessed on-screen.

Movies created and released during Saturn-Pluto oppositions and conjunctions of the twentieth century include: *Birth of a Nation* (1915; Saturn-Pluto conjunction); *All Quiet on the Western Front* and *M* (1930 and 1932, respectively; Saturn-Pluto opposition); *Hamlet* (1948; Saturn-Pluto conjunction); *A Man For All Seasons* (1965; Saturn-Pluto opposition) and *Das Boot, Reds, Gandhi,* and television's *The Day After* (all films created and released under the Saturn-Pluto conjunction of 1981–1983).

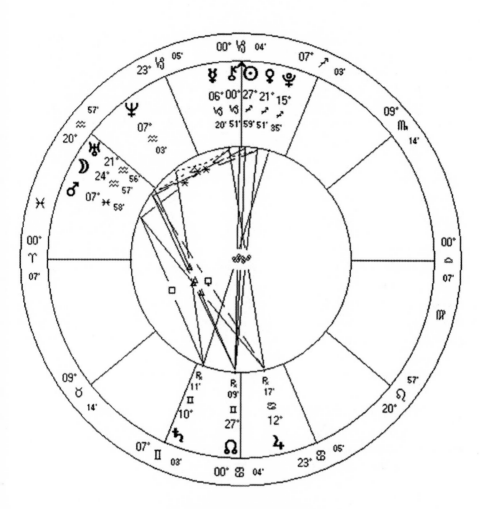

Release for *The Lord of the Rings:*
The Fellowship of the Ring
December 19th, 2001
Los Angeles, CA
12:00 PM

The Lord of the Rings trilogy, produced and released under the 2001–2003 Saturn-Pluto opposition, is the latest set of movies to carry the torch of this profound and significant archetypal combination. Although couched in fantasy, *The Lord of the Rings* is not lightweight fare but a deep and weighty epic tome that speaks to a fundamental theme of humanity: strength, resilience, and perseverance in the face of almost insurmountable evil, temptation, and hardship. Moreover—and what makes the film a prime exemplar of the Saturn-Pluto phenomenon—it is a wonderful exploration of the fundamental and assumed battle between "light versus dark," and "good versus evil" in this world.

As many commentators have alluded, Tolkien's purpose in writing *The Lord of the Rings* was not allegorical or a proselytizing of his own Christian faith; however, he was using the vehicle of myth and story to connote transcendental and perennial truths. One of these transcendental truths that Tolkien believed was that the world polarizes itself into light and shadow in order to realize its own redemption and rebirth, what Tolkien called "eucatastrophe"—an unexpected and joyous outcome resulting from tests of faith and struggle. *The Lord of the Rings* holds little or no ambiguity in its relationship to good and evil: Orcs, Saruman, and the Ringwraiths are wicked to the core as Frodo, Gandalf and the elves of Rivendell are virtuous, good-natured, truthful, and defy temptation.

During periods in which Saturn and Pluto make significant angular relationships to one another, the global situation, it would appear, makes it greatest polarizations, with opposing factions declaring the other corrupt or evil and each camp holding its own claim to truth, morality, and righteousness. Like in the world of *The Rings*, there is little ambiguity between "good" and "evil" during Saturn-Pluto configurations. During the 1914–16 Saturn-Pluto opposition, Europe split itself between a battle of "the Hun" and the "Barbarians" as troops of a unified Germany fought against the Allied forces. Under the 1939–1941 Saturn-Pluto Square, the Final Solution was devised as the "Master Race" intended to annihilate an entire people. As the Cold War peaked under the 1981–1984 Saturn-Pluto conjunction, "The Evil Empire" that was the Soviet Union threatened the solidarity and freedom of the Western world. And currently in our own time, under a Saturn-Pluto opposition, the world once again divides itself into "good and evil," as each side in the multiple global conflicts see themselves as the bearer of all that is good and true with the opposing force as the sum aggregation of all evil.

More than just a brilliant exposition on the themes of Saturn-Pluto configuration, the look, feel, and experiential quality of *The Lord of the Rings* is highly indicative of the archetypal tenor of Saturn and Pluto in combination. There is both an incredibly dark, heavy, and "steely" experiential quality to Saturn and Pluto as there is also a deep and penetrating infernal sense to the combination. This is the archetypal combination of fire and brimstone; grotesque monsters, killing machines, and terminators; "heavy metal"; puritanical authority; steel and concrete; bricks and mortar; dungeons and armor; impenetrable fortresses; sweatshops and slave labor; "do or die" confrontations, battle royale *a la* Armageddon. With Saturn and Pluto, eroticism, seduction, evolutionary power, and life force (Pluto) collide with lead, darkness, density, and gravity (Saturn); this is indeed the heaviest experiential combination in astrology and imagery of this type pervades throughout all of *The Lord of the Rings* trilogy: the satanic mills of Saruman, the mysterious evil of the Dark Riders, the demonic Balrog, the powerful face-off between Gandalf and Saruman, the dense and colorless architecture; the substantial ale steins, battle axes, and steely chainmail.

Perhaps, however, the single greatest expression of Saturn-Pluto in *The Lord of the Rings* is the ring itself. Forged in the bowels of Middle Earth, the ring glows with a mysterious, dark, and gothic eroticism that holds an incredible seductive force through its mere presence. This concentrated power, however, promises two contradictory things: one, the corruption, emptiness, and destruction of those who choose to wield its power, or its opposite fate, ultimate redemption and freedom by those who transcend and destroy its force. In the ring, we see the bipolar, or two-sided, nature of the Saturn-Pluto archetypal combination: the all-consuming destructiveness of a certain type of power and the promise of moral strength, character, and heroism if the temptation to use the power falsely is avoided.

Saturn-Pluto correlations and *The Lord of the Rings*

The Lord of the Rings not only embodies the themes of the recent Saturn-Pluto opposition but the work has had quite a history with Saturn-Pluto alignments. The completion, publication, and sudden rise in popularity of *The Lord of the Rings* all occurred when Saturn and Pluto were in "hard aspect" (a conjunction, square, or opposition) to each other. We might say that the Saturn-Pluto constellation is the invisible field or magnet that constellates the motifs found within this dark fantasy.

The epic writing and revising of *The Lord of the Rings,* which is only surpassed by Frodo's journey in terms of heroic quests, was completed in 1948 after 16 years of meticulous attention given to the tale by Tolkien.[1] However, there was no initial blitzkrieg of enthusiasm for what some would later call the "book of the twentieth century." Publication and popularity would only sprout years after the final completion of the trilogy. After his publishers, Collins, agreed to release *The Lord of the Rings*, the final installment of *The Lord of the Rings* trilogy was published in 1955, under a Saturn square (90 degree angular relationship) Pluto aspect.[2] Hibernating, it would take ten years before the phenomenon of the Tolkien cult caught flame. Tolkien's popularity would not come entirely from ivory tower intellectuals, but the bulk of his avid readership came from the youth of the countercultural explosion of the 1960s. An unauthorized, but affordable, paper back version of the trilogy was released in 1965, and, in that very same year, sales and popularity of the work soared. Once again, Saturn and Pluto correlate with release of this myth, this time in the form of an opposition.[3]

Although lodged in the memories of *The Lord of the Rings* connoisseurs, many casual fans seeing the current film release do not realize that there was a previous attempt at creating a version of Tolkien's classic onscreen. In the late 1970s, gifted animator Ralph Bakshi painstakingly rotoscoped live action into an admirable rendering of the fantasy. The film divided opinion, and the fact that Bakshi was unable to complete the whole story due to financial reasons almost automatically discounted the film from being labeled a masterpiece. However, many images from the film, particularly the rendering of the Dark Riders, remains indelibly stamped upon the imagination of youth who saw the film. Bakshi—the anti-Disney that he is—is the king of underworld animation, and everything in his films—from the setting, themes, and style—is dark and mature. It is no surprise that he had a certain resonance with *The Lord of the Rings* as he was born under a Saturn-Sun-Pluto t-square.

Peter Jackson, the New Zealand director who landed the awesome responsibility of bringing a live action version of *The Rings* to screen, might have seemed an unlikely choice to do justice to the Tolkien opus. Little doubted his ability to render the profane side of *The Lord of the Rings*, as his vivid imagination in his personal films like *Bad Taste* and *Meet the Feebles* displayed an uncanny ability to craft horrid creatures of all shapes and sizes. However, the gravity of the subject matter in *The Lord of the Rings* and the sheer size of the project demanded a director who was cut more from the mold of David Lean or D.W. Griffith rather than John Carpenter or Tod Browning. However, Jackson quelled the doubting voices of *Ring* fandom upon initial release of *Fellowship of the Ring* and received near-unanimous approval ratings from Tolkien groupies. Although not born with a significant Saturn-Pluto aspect, Jackson's progressed* Sun, Mars, and Mercury in Sagittarius formed a tight conjunction with the recent Saturn-Pluto opposition. As the progressed chart is a transcendental reflection of his inner and outer conditions, Jackson not only was in a subjective mood that was congruent with the themes and motifs of the trilogy, but the strength and determination that the archetypes Saturn and Pluto can forge no doubt correlated with the energy needed to helm one of the largest filmings in history.

The Zeppelin Connection

Deciphering the true intentions of Led Zeppelin lyrics ranks with the "Paul is Dead" controversy of the Beatles and the "Dark Side of the Rainbow" synchronicity of Pink Floyd as all-time mysteries of classic rock. Allusions to Tolkien's work are scattered throughout Led Zeppelin's oeuvre. "Over the Hills and Far Away," "Misty Mountain Hop," "Battle of Evermore," and "Ramble On" are songs that not only make direct lyrical references to Tolkien's classic works but could very well be the soundtrack that accompanies Frodo and the fellowship on their long journey. Zeppelin's lead singer, Robert Plant, was an unabashed Tolkien fan, as Tolkien synthesized Plant's love of fantasy, nature, Celtic and Norse myths, and magic into one complete package. Robert Plant was born with a Sun, Saturn, Pluto conjunction in 1948, the year that Tolkien finally finished his fantasy masterpiece. As Plant's personal identity, symbolized by the Sun, was interconnected with the archetypal matrix of Saturn and Pluto, it is fitting that there would be a certain attraction and resonance to the themes, characters, and settings of Tolkien's landscape.

A Tale of Two Rings

Tolkien remained unruffled by assumptions that he had written *The Lord of the Rings* in direct reaction to World War II, but he took greater umbrage at comparisons to Wagner's Ring Cycle. In a letter to his editor, Tolkien wrote of the comparison, "Both rings were round, and there the resemblance ceases."[5] Tolkien's personal dislike aside, the comparisons are unavoidable and have been the subject of many academic essays and research. Although the philosophic motivation for these two epics did differ, the themes, motifs, and experiential feel of these grand epochal narratives are highly resonant. The theme of incredible power concentrated in a ring, the appropriation of Norse mythology, the moral trials of the ring's original possessor, and the joyous, surprising ending after a battle between light and dark forces are all to be found in both narratives.

Equally important, the feel and imagery of Wagner's ring bears resemblance to *The Lord of the Rings*. The orchestrations of Wagner's operas are heavy, dense, and at times bombastic. The onstage singers are burdened with breastplates, horns, and armor. One leaves an opera house drained, exhausted and inspired as the condensed angst and brooding of witnessing the apotheosis of man in his overcoming of teutonic Godhead is quite a burdensome spectacle. Interestingly, Wagner initiated and completed his operatic tetrology in an entire Saturn cycle, conceptualizing the operatic cycle as Saturn conjoined his natal Pluto placement in 1848 and premiering his masterpiece at the Bayreuth Festival in August of 1876 as Saturn returned within orb of Wagner's Pluto birth placement. [6]

Conclusion

Fantasy and myth are not only accurate reflections of our lived experience, but good fantasy and myth can also inform our realities as well. If indeed Tolkien struck gold with a profound metaphysical truth of the "eucatastrophe"—the unexpected twist of rebirth after antagonistic forces battle each other—then we can assume that art and myth are telling us something quite significant about our current global situation. The Saturn-Pluto cycle, as witnessed in our own time—these times of epic battles, deprivation, and forging of character—must not been seen in isolation but be seen in the light of a greater context. It appears that these times of war, economic contraction, national defense and security are part of a continuum of natural processes that are needed for subsequent rejuvenation, rebirth, and renewal. Although this may be as simple as saying that for "every spring there first comes a winter," collectively, it appears, we have become unconscious of this truth, somehow assuming that our global situation has no correlation with and has transcended these very real and very natural processes.

This is not stating that war, conflict, and factitiousness are predetermined and foregone conclusions when Saturn and Pluto make angular relationship to each other. On the contrary, by becoming conscious of the repetition of archetypal cycles we enhance our freedom of choice and create a wider palette to express the spirit of the times. In an astrologically-informed cosmology it may be held true that the collective unconscious, archetypal ground of being, or *anima mundi*—all related concepts alluding to the same thing—may be inflected by certain patterns at certain times, but there is an incredible degree of potential free will surrounding the expression of the energy. It is not surprising, then, that the higher the collective consciousness, the more rarefied the expression. *The Lord of the Rings*—the movie and book—are wonderful outlets for allowing the dark drama, epic heroism, and the allure and seduction of deep power of the Saturn-Pluto combination to shine through all while not succumbing to dilution or sanitization of this powerful archetypal complex.

***Progressions**, or secondary progressions—a technique whereby the planetary positions for each day after birth represent a year after birth. Planetary positions at 45 days after your birth will reflect, partly, your psychological experience and state of affairs at 45 years of age. Generally speaking, progressions are subtler and do not have as much of an impact as transits; their patterns are a little less discernable.

1.   http://www.kulichki.com/tolkien/eng/enghron.html

2.   Ibid

3.   Ibid

4.   For more on the Tolkien and the Led Zeppelin connection see http://www.ledtolkien.com

5.   http://www.isi.org/lectures/read/tolkien.html

6.   Robert Gutman, *Richard Wagner: The Man, the Mind, and His Music* (New York: Harvest, 1990)

The Contributors

Natori Moore, C.A. NCGR, is a counseling astrologer practicing in Encinitas, California. She has been an active member of NCGR San Diego and the San Diego Astrological Society for more than ten years. She has written on astrological topics for *Dell Horoscope* and *The Mountain Astrologer*, and published film criticism in San Diego area publications including *SLAMM Music and Arts Magazine* and *The Light Connection*. She is a past author of a weekly astrology column for *Drama-Logue*, an acting industry casting publication, and has provided astrological services for Women in Film of Los Angeles. Look closely in the dining room scenes before the ship hits the berg—she was also a film extra in James Cameron's *Titanic*. Natori specializes in relationship and family compatibility counseling by telephone via her website, www.soulfoodastrology.com.

Bill Streett, MA has advanced degrees in philosophy and religion and counseling psychology. He is the creator of *Astro-Noetics.com*, a website devoted to in-depth astrological analysis. He has been published through *StarIQ.com* and is a monthly columnist for the popular website *Astrologyforthesoul.com*.

Ray Grasse is associate editor of *The Mountain Astrologer*, and author of *The Waking Dream* (Quest, 1996), and *Signs of the Times* (Hampton Roads, 2002), a study of the emerging Aquarian Age. He obtained a degree in filmmaking from the Art Institute of Chicago. He is a practicing astrologer, and can be reached at jupiter@enteract.com.

Glenn Perry, Ph.D. is a licensed psychotherapist in Marin County, CA. A professional astrologer since 1974, Glenn lectures throughout the world on application of astrology to the fields of counseling and psychotherapy. He has written three books, including *Essays In Psychological Astrology*. Glenn also offers an online mentorship program, which is a personalized course in natal chart interpretation from a depth psychological perspective.

John M. Whalen is an astrologer based in the Washington, D.C. area. He began studying astrology in the early 1970s, and has been active as an astrological consultant for the last 15 years. He has written over a dozen articles for *StarIQ.com*, appeared on National Public Radio's *All Things Considered*, and on the local ABC-TV affiliate WJLA-TV in Washington. He also contributes freelance articles on film and television to *The Washington Post*, *The Washington Times*, and *Filmfax* magazine. In addition, he has been a Washington journalist for the last 30 years. You can reach him by email at john.whalen8@verizon.net.

Jeffrey Kishner, MA has a degree in Integral Counseling Psychology from the California Institute of Integral Studies. He is an astrological counselor and psychotherapist. Jeffrey is webmaster of *Astrologyatthemovies.com*, and has been published in *StarIQ.com*, *The Mountain Astrologer*, and *Dell Horoscope*. He can be emailed at jeffreykishner@yahoo.com.

Deb McBride has been studying astrology for most of her life, in addition to holding degrees in chemistry and mathematics. She began her astrological counseling practice in 1986, and never ceases to be amazed by the workings of the human psyche. Deb is currently the publicity chair for the NYC chapter of the National Council for Geocosmic Research and manages its website. She has published articles in the NCGR's quarterly journal, *The Ingress*, and on the astrological website www.cosmicpath.com in addition to lecturing in the NYC area. When not working on astrology, she studies singing with Katie Agresta.

0-595-32099-6

Printed in the United Kingdom
by Lightning Source UK Ltd.
135379UK00001B/234/A